ROUTLEDGE LIBRARY EDITIONS:
SOCIOLOGY OF EDUCATION

I0130989

Volume 8

A SOCIOLOGY OF
EDUCATION FOR AFRICA

A SOCIOLOGY OF EDUCATION FOR AFRICA

KENNETH BLAKEMORE
AND BRIAN COOKSEY

Routledge
Taylor & Francis Group

LONDON AND NEW YORK

First published in 1980 by George Allen & Unwin Ltd

This edition first published in 2017
by Routledge
2 Park Square, Milton Park, Abingdon, Oxon OX14 4RN

and by Routledge
711 Third Avenue, New York, NY 10017

Routledge is an imprint of the Taylor & Francis Group, an informa business

British Library Cataloguing in Publication Data
A catalogue record for this book is available from the British Library

ISBN: 978-0-415-78834-2 (Set)
ISBN: 978-1-315-20949-4 (Set) (ebk)
ISBN: 978-1-138-22046-1 (Volume 8) (hbk)
ISBN: 978-1-138-22047-8 (Volume 8) (pbk)
ISBN: 978-1-315-41273-3 (Volume 8) (ebk)

Publisher's Note
The publisher has gone to great lengths to ensure the quality of this reprint but points out that some imperfections in the original copies may be apparent.

Disclaimer
The publisher has made every effort to trace copyright holders and would welcome correspondence from those they have been unable to trace.

A Sociology of
Education
for Africa

KENNETH BLAKEMORE, BA, PhD

and

BRIAN COOKSEY, BA, PhD

With a Foreword by
A. BABS FAFUNWA

London
GEORGE ALLEN & UNWIN
Boston   Sydney

First published in 1980

GEORGE ALLEN & UNWIN LTD
40 Museum Street, London WC1A 1LU

© George Allen & Unwin (Publishers) Ltd, 1981

British Library Cataloguing in Publication Data

Blakemore, Kenneth
 A sociology of education for Africa.
 1. Education – Africa
 2. Educational sociology – Africa
 I. Title   II. Cooksey, Brian
301.5′6′096   LA1500   80-41626

 ISBN 0-04-370105-1

Set in 10 on 11 point Times by Inforum Ltd, Portsmouth, and printed in Great Britain by Biddles Ltd, Guildford, Surrey.

Contents

To Peg

Foreword

A comprehensive textbook on sociology of education with particular reference to Africa is long overdue, and Drs K. Blakemore and B. Cooksey have fulfilled this need with the publication of *A Sociology of Education for Africa*.

The book is in three parts:

(1) education and social inequality in Africa;
(2) the sociology of schools;
(3) education and development in Africa.

In the first part of the book the authors examine the relationship between education and social inequality in Africa from the precolonial times to the present. Inequality in one form or another is a universal phenomenon and is therefore not peculiar to Africa, but the authors have made a substantial contribution by relating this concept to the African educational *cum* social and economic scenes.

In the second part of the book the authors discuss the school as a social organisation where students are socialised into disciplined ways of behaviour with the teacher and the curriculum serving as social controls. The chapters on the teacher's role and the place of the curriculum within the school system are bound to generate considerable debate among staff and students; so will the place of the student and the headmaster or principal.

Part Three of the book deals with the relationship between education and development – a very controversial but extremely useful topic in African education. As the authors rightly observe, there may be growth without development and by the same token there may be educational expansion with little or no corresponding employment opportunities for the thousands of school leavers produced by the system. Moreover, change does not always mean a change for the better. There is much that will provide intellectual stimulation for students in this section. For example, the chapter on education and socio-cultural change is a controversial one, and students and other readers will certainly have much to concur with and much to disagree with. If this happens, and it is likely to happen, then the authors will have achieved their objective in writing this book.

The authors have produced a textbook that is both educative and challenging. They raise many issues which will stimulate discussion debate in and outside the classroom. The questions posed at the end of each chapter as well as the glossary will be useful to both the teacher and the taught.

The book will be very valuable to students and teachers both at the teacher training institutions and the departments of education in African universities as well as to those who are interested in education and social change in and outside the African continent.

A. BABS FAFUNWA

Acknowledgements

We wish to acknowledge the invaluable assistance and encouragement of the following, especially for their advice on various parts of the text and their constructive criticisms: David Court, University of Nairobi; Peter Gibbon, Sheffield Polytechnic; Mrs Usha George and Anthony Kokkat of ATC Akwanga, Jos; Jack Maas, World Bank, Washington; Rob Martin, University of Western Ontario; Garth Massey, University of Wyoming, Laramie; Marjorie Mbilinyi, University of Dar es Salaam; and Margaret Peil, Centre of West African Studies, University of Birmingham.

Part One

Education and Social Inequality in Africa

Introduction to Part One

In Part One we examine the relationship between education and social inequality in pre-colonial, colonial and contemporary Africa. The student should read this introduction carefully, as it explains certain key concepts which are used throughout the book. Short definitions of technical terms can be found in the glossary at the end of the book.

Social Inequality

What do we mean by social inequality? We should first distinguish between natural differences and social inequalities between people. Rousseau, a famous eighteenth-century thinker, summed up the distinction as follows:

> I think of mankind as being characterised by two kinds of inequality, one which I call natural or physical because it stems from nature and consists of differences of age, health, physical strength and qualities of the spirit and the soul; the other which we might call moral or political inequality because it is based on convention and agreements made between people. The latter kind of inequality consists of various privileges which some enjoy at the expense of others; for example, being richer, more honoured, more powerful than others, and even getting others to obey your orders. (Rousseau, 1761, p. 6)

What we call social inequality is summed up by Rousseau in the last sentence of the quotation. Thus we do not mean natural differences between individuals when we talk of social inequality. The natural differences listed above (to which we may add sex and, up to a point, certain mental capacities) are primarily biological, and not social, characteristics. People often confuse natural differences and social inequalities or use the first to justify the second. For example, women often occupy an inferior position in society, not because they are naturally inferior to men, but because of social disadvantages attached to being born female. These disadvantages are reflected in school enrolment levels, as we will see in the following chapters.

Another example is that of intellectual differences between individuals. It is sometimes assumed that it is the most intelligent people who are the most successful in life. We can all think of examples of people from poor homes who, because of their above-average intelligence, were very successful in their studies and subsequently in their chosen careers. But it does not follow that the top people in society (the wealthy, the famous, the powerful) are necessarily the most intelligent and that the poorest people are necessarily the least intelligent. In practice intelligence as measured in school is determined by both natural and social factors, and it is difficult to separate these two. But overall social factors are much more important than natural intelligence in determining who goes to school and who occupies which positions in society. We will come back to the question of intelligence in Chapter 3.

There are many social differences between people which do not in themselves constitute social inequalities. For example, in most African countries there are differences between ethnic and regional groups as regards language, customs, family structure, religious practices and so on. These cultural differences should not be thought of in terms of inequality, although (as with natural differences) they are often confused with social inequalities or used to justify them. For example, members of one ethnic group or citizens of one country often think of themselves as being generally superior to all members of other ethnic groups or citizens of other countries. Outsiders are often thought of as uncivilised, backward, stupid, dirty, immoral or irreligious. Sometimes these attitudes towards outsiders reflect real inequalities – for example, inequalities in wealth and power, military and economic inequalities between nations – but cultural differences themselves should not be thought of as social inequalities.

Some sociologists distinguish between three closely related aspects of social inequality, namely *class, status* and *power*. Class inequalities are concerned with economic activities (how one earns a living) and with the ownership and control of property and wealth. Status inequalities are based on the social prestige accorded to individuals or groups, and power is the ability to impose one's will on other people. Closely related to power is the concept of authority, which is the acceptance of the right to give orders and instructions. Thus social inequality can be defined as the unequal distribution of class, status and power within society. We may take a brief look at each of these concepts.

Class
Occupational roles and property ownership and control are the criteria by which we define social classes. Occupations differ widely

as regards their general desirability, and studies in various countries have shown that there is broad agreement on the relative desirability of different kinds of work. The major determinant of desirability is the wage or salary which goes with the job. Other factors include: the nature of the work done (varied work is preferable to boring work); the opportunities for promotion; working conditions (dangerous, dirty and tiring work is undesirable, as are long hours and shift work). Some people would add that a job in which you give orders is preferable to one in which you take orders, but not everybody enjoys the responsibilities that go with power and authority. Another important factor is the general prestige attached to the job. Most, but not all, of this prestige reflects the above-mentioned factors of wage, working conditions and so on. In some societies certain occupations have high or low status for independent reasons. For example, becoming a priest or a nun has high prestige in deeply religious communities. Conversely, trading and moneylending are often looked down on as inferior occupations associated with outcasts or minority groups. In Muslim societies the *malaam* has relatively high status compared with his income, but primary schoolteaching is often thought of as a low status occupation, a point discussed in Part Two.

Sociologists often group together occupations with similar overall levels of desirability in order to establish a hierarchy of classes. The number and name given to these varies with the classification. Some speak of upper, middle and lower classes; others of working, lower middle, upper middle and upper classes; others of blue- and white-collar classes (that is, manual and non-manual workers); yet others distinguish between skilled, semi-skilled and unskilled in the blue-collar class. An added complication is that people do not always consider themselves members of the class in which sociologists have put them, that is, the objective definition of class does not necessarily coincide with the subjective definition. Awareness of belonging to one or other class is termed class-consciousness.

Classes are unequal to the extent that rewards tend to be cumulative, in other words, the occupations with the highest salaries are usually those with the best working conditions, the best chances of promotion or the greatest opportunity for personal initiative. If this were not the case there would probably be less competition between people for available jobs than there is, because the advantages attached to a given job would be cancelled out by the disadvantages.

In Africa the gap between the most and the least desirable occupations is often extreme. For example, a top civil servant may earn twenty to thirty times as much as his office cleaner, and a peasant farmer may earn in a year less than a member of parliament earns in a week. These inequalities tend to intensify competition for jobs and make educational success a matter of vital importance. One of our main concerns in this book is with the role of education in permitting or preventing access to jobs at different levels.

The ownership or non-ownership of property is a very important aspect of economic inequality. By property we mean more than just personal belongings like clothes, radios and household goods. Property includes land, buildings of all kinds, the machinery and factories used to produce wealth and the money and titles (stocks and shares) which represent, or can be turned into, wealth. The economies of the non-communist developed countries have grown through the private accumulation of wealth and property: this is the capital in the word 'capitalism'. It is a feature of these economies that property as defined above is extremely unevenly distributed, that is, a small minority of the population owns the greater part of the wealth. When we talk of class inequalities in this sense, therefore, we are not thinking of occupations with differential rewards but of the ownership and non-ownership of capital. In Africa, many more people own or have access to land than in the capitalist countries of the West, but the ownership of other kinds of property is extremely unequal, even though there is much less of it than in the West. Those with high incomes from their occupation usually acquire property which in turn produces further income.

Education can be seen as a form of property. The skills and qualifications obtained through formal education can be sold on the job market, and the most highly qualified usually get the best jobs. Parents with high incomes from their occupation or property generally invest substantial amounts in the education of their children so as to increase their chances of educational and occupational success. This is one way in which class inequalities tend to be reproduced through time. The nature of the African class structure and the relationship between class and educational achievement are major themes of Chapters 1, 2 and 3.

Status

It is easy to confuse class and status. Status refers to the prestige or 'social honour' attached to any social position. It happens in modern society that the class position of an individual is by far the most important of all the social positions he or she occupies as regards his or her overall status. Generally it is the wealthy, the powerful and those at the top of the occupational ladder who have the highest status, but within these groups there may be considerable differences of status. For example, a big trader may be much wealthier than a top class lawyer or surgeon, but he may well enjoy much less status than either of the latter. Inherited wealth may carry more (or less) status than wealth acquired through personal initiative. As already pointed out, certain occupations have high or low status independent of the income, working conditions and so on attached to them. Civil servants may be held in high esteem in one society, in low esteem in another. The same is true for soldiers, teachers, politicians, priests, prostitutes, beggars or landlords.

There is often disagreement on the status attributed to any particular position. This is related to the growth of what are called subcultures. Any social group may develop its own set of values and behaviour on the basis of common interests or activities. Sociologists have found that such groups as schoolchildren and students, those sharing working and living conditions, prisoners and criminals, sailors and soldiers, musicians and entertainers, sportsmen and so on develop shared definitions of good and bad attitudes, moral values and behaviour, which define the group and distinguish it from other groups or from the larger society. In Chapter 3 and Part Two we will come back to the question of subcultures and their importance in relation to education. For the moment we may note that the status attributed to a particular social position may vary with the social position of the person who is attributing the status. The rich and the powerful may have high status among those immediately below them in society, but little or no status in the eyes of the very poor. Similarly, the job of motor mechanic will carry more prestige for a peasant's son than for the son of a secondary schoolteacher.

As well as occupational roles, people play ritual, religious, political, cultural, recreational and many other types of role, any of which may be a source of positive or negative status. Group membership not directly related to occupational/economic roles is called 'status group' as opposed to class membership. People from different classes may belong to a given status group, for example an urban tribal association may attract membership from all urban classes.

Status groups are defined in terms of life-style and consumption patterns (what members do with their spare time and income) rather than in terms of productive activities. Often those with high class positions also have high positions in the status groups to which they belong. For example, a rich trader may be a leading member of his tribal association, he may take a traditional title which bestows status, and he may use both his class position and status to obtain political office at the local or national level. Conversely, a person with a relatively low status occupation may be a leading member of his local church, ethnic association, trade union or local government. Priests, literates, chiefs, the elderly, men, intellectuals, *malaams*, court officials and others, may enjoy status (at least locally) which is disproportionate to their income or power. We should be careful, however, not to forget that there is generally quite a close correlation between economic position and social status.

Educational achievement is a source of status, both in occupational and in general terms. Occupational status is partially a function of the amount of education associated with different occupational levels. As well as giving access to specialist knowledge and increasing the individual's grasp of the world around him, educational achievement also confers status and improves life chances. In Africa, the most educated people often think of themselves (and are thought of by the less educated) as being the most fit to play leadership roles and to take the initiative in the struggle for social and economic development. The high status of the most educated increases their legitimacy in the eyes of the less educated in playing leadership roles.

Power and Authority

The most extreme form of power is the use, or the threat, of physical violence. Less extreme (and more common) is power based on the threat of sanctions, as when an employer threatens to dismiss an employee. When power becomes institutionalised in roles it is transformed into authority; so that we may define authority as the exercise of legitimate power. Authority is a common feature of all organisations with a distinct hierarchy of command and a more or less well-defined sphere in which orders can be given in the expectation that they will be carried out. Such organisations are commonly called bureaucracies and these have come to play an increasingly important part in modern societies, for good or bad. To exercise authority in a bureaucracy one is supposed to be competent to perform the tasks associated with a given position. Competence is a function of training and experience, and training is more and more a question of formal education. Thus as bureaucracies grow so formal education becomes increasingly important in obtaining positions of authority. This is true in both government bureaucracies (the civil service) and in those found in modern businesses.

Power and authority constitute the political dimension of social inequality. They can be compared with wealth or property to the extent that an individual can enjoy none whatsoever or any amount, ranging from a little to a great deal. As with status, an individual may be powerful or exercise authority in one sphere but not in others. But it is not uncommon to find the same person exercising power or authority in more than one sphere; for example, the wealthy often seek political power, taking advantage of their economic power to do so. Politicians and civil servants also get involved in private business ventures.

At the national level, power and authority are exercised by the politicians and officials who control the state. The state consists of all the machinery of government, including parliament, ministries and their bureaucracies, the police, armed forces and law courts, local authorities and parastatals. The provision of services such as education is an important function of the state machinery and the success or failure of governments to satisfy public demands for such services is a major determinant of the legitimacy of the incumbents of power. Although governments always claim to be acting in the national interest, more often than not their policies and actions serve the interests of some classes, status groups and regions more than others. Education policies and practices are a good example of this, as we try to show in Chapters 3 and 9.

We normally think of power in terms of politics and politicians but it is also exercised in any organisation above a certain size. Thus churches, hospitals, schools, colleges and universities, the military, trade unions, factories, voluntary associations and so on are all structured around relations of power and authority. In Part Two we examine the question of authority within both the school setting and the educational system itself.

Racial and Ethnic Inequalities

In Africa the three aspects of social inequality discussed above – class, status and power – are sometimes found in conjunction with ethnic and racial inequalities. In some African countries one ethnic group dominates all others in the political, social and economic fields. More frequently, dominance in one field does not necessarily imply dominance in all others, and social or tribal conflicts often result from different ethnic groups dominating the social, political and economic spheres. The struggle to extend or limit control within and between these spheres constitutes a major aspect of everyday politics in Africa. Access to education plays a part in this struggle, mainly because, for historical reasons, some ethnic groups are more highly educated than others and therefore tend to dominate the civil service, the education professions and other important areas. Nigeria is an example of a country where educational inequalities have contributed to ethnic and regional conflicts and power struggles.

Ethnic and racial inequality may reflect military conquest, either in the recent or more distant past. The colonial conquest of Africa was the imposition of a foreign racial rule which, to varying degrees, became the basis for social inequalities of class, status and power. In other words, racial and social inequalities were superimposed on one another. The most extreme examples of this superimposition are to be found in the settler colonies of North, East, Central and Southern Africa. The provision of educational facilities for the different races reflected (and in some cases still reflects) these basic inequalities. We explore this point in Chapters 2 and 3.

Social Stratification

The nature and extent of social inequality vary from place to place and change through time. This is as true in Africa as it is anywhere else. Social stratification is a general term used to cover all types of systematic social inequality found in different societies and in different historical periods. In the modern world, class is the basis of stratification systems, but the class structure of the USA is very different from that of the USSR, and that of Nigeria from that of Brazil. Caste and kinship constitute other principles of social stratification. Educational arrangements reflect the system of stratification found in a given society. We begin Chapters 1, 2 and 3, therefore, by outlining the forms of social stratification typical of pre-colonial, colonial and modern Africa.

Chapter 1

Education in Pre-Colonial Africa

Introduction

Human collectivities are never simply homogeneous collections of like beings; even the simplest of them have 'structure' in the sense of a division of labour by sex, age, generation and kinship, and in most communities other distinctions are recognised as well. (Fallers, 1964, p. 65)

The societies of pre-colonial Africa varied greatly in size, complexity and degree of stratification, ranging from the so-called 'acephalous' societies (literally, 'without a head', that is, leaderless) found in many parts of Africa to the great states of West Africa and elsewhere. Social and political life in acephalous societies was based on kinship and descent, and social and political roles were distributed on the basis of age, sex and personal characteristics and achievements. Such societies are often thought of as being highly democratic (decisions were reached after public debate, argument and compromise) and can be said to have been relatively unstratified. This means that social inequalities based on ownership (land, slaves, livestock), occupation or political roles were relatively undeveloped. Low levels of technology and the absence of long-distance trade limited the development of social stratification, which depends on the creation of an agricultural surplus to make possible a more developed division of labour, the growth of specialist trades and skills outside agriculture (blacksmith, weaver, priest, merchant, soldier, functionary, teacher, chief or king) and the development of an exchange sector. These conditions were absent in some parts of Africa in the pre-colonial period.

As stated above, social position in these relatively simple societies was a function of age, sex and personal characteristics. The young were subordinate to the old, a relationship which was often formalised through the system of age grades. Respect for the old is still very widespread in contemporary Africa, even though age can no longer be said to constitute a significant dimension of social inequality.

Women were usually subordinate to men both in social status and in decision-making (politics). Child-rearing, housework and most farming activities fell to the lot of the women, while the men hunted and performed some of the more arduous tasks.

An individual who excelled in physical strength, in warfare, in agricultural production, in public speaking and so on could expect to become a chief or a leading elder. In other words, leadership positions in the community were open to competition; they were achieved rather than ascribed statuses. In the absence of powerful and wealthy classes, differences of status (social honour) were te main dimension of social inequality, but even these were extremely small.

In many discussions about education in pre-colonial Africa it is assumed that all or most African societies were of the above type. For most people the village was the basic social unit and society was relatively undifferentiated in terms of class, status and power. But it is also true that from very early times large states and empires existed in Africa. These rose and fell as a result of war and conquest (sometimes associated with the spread of Islam) and the control of trade routes. They were highly stratified societies with classes of slaves, sedentary farmers and pastoralists, warriors, religious leaders, teachers and bureaucrats, craftsmen, traders and nobles. In such societies inequalities of class, status and power could, to varying degrees, be passed from one generation to the next.

In a few extreme cases it was more or less impossible to move out of the class and status to which one was born. The name 'caste' is given to such rigidly ascriptive societies in which birth determines or ascribes social position. Class and status ascription is accompanied by endogamy (marrying within one's caste) and rules limiting contact between different castes. The best-known example of caste society in Africa is the Hutu-Tutsi of Rwanda in which the Tutsi pastoralists ruled over the Hutu farmers by right of conquest. The two groups were culturally and physically distinct and never intermarried or ate or socialised together.

Elsewhere in Africa certain occupational groups have tended to take on a caste character. According to Peil (1977, pp. 90–1), 'blacksmiths have often been looked on as a caste in the Western Sudan, even in societies which have no other castes. Working in iron is considered polluting and also dangerous (supervised by special gods and providing blacksmiths with special power), so blacksmith families are kept separate from the rest of society.'

In general there was a certain amount of achieved status in the more stratified pre-colonial societies. For example, slaves could sometimes reach high positions in the courts of kings, especially when competition for the throne among members of the royal lineage or family meant that there was a minimum of trust between rival claimants. Over a period of time, slaves could also be assimilated into the families of commoners or nobles through intermarriage. Most slavery in pre-colonial Africa was domestic rather than chattel, although the growth of the Atlantic slave trade probably brought about an increase in the incidence of slave-raiding for purely commercial purposes.

The degree of stratification affects the extent to which subcultures based on class or status group membership develop within a society. In the acephalous societies described above cultural differentiation was minimal: language, life-styles, values, consumption patterns were more or less identical for all. It was possible in the more highly stratified societies, however, for subcultures to develop. For example, states or empires based on conquest might exhibit ethnic, racial, cultural and other cleavages between rulers and subjects. The degree of ascription (that is, the extent to which birth determined social position) affected the degree to which subcultures of class and status could develop.

The degree of stratification also affected the development of education as a *specialist activity* with schools, students and teachers. The nature and amount of education received by an individual was a function of (1) the degree of stratification, (2) the roles he or she was likely to play in adult life and (3) the relative importance of ascription and achievement in the distribution of adult roles. Even in the relatively simple societies, where there was little or no formal education as such, people had to be trained for adult roles, as will be shown in the following pages.

In the modern world most people think of education as what is learned by pupils and students in schools, colleges and universities. In a way this is true, but we must be careful to distinguish between *formal* education in the above sense and learning in a more general sense, including all that young people learn before going to school (*if* they go to school), all they learn outside school, what they learn informally in school (see Part Two) and all that people learn after finishing their formal studies. To a sociologist, education includes both the formal and the informal processes of learning. In modern Africa these two processes are more or less separate, but this was not true in many societies before European and American missionaries began bringing formal education to Africa.

In parts of East and West Africa Koranic education has existed for many hundreds of years, and it still accounts for an important part of educational provision in the Muslim areas of the continent. Secret societies like the Poro and Bundo societies of West Africa also provided a type of formal education, but throughout pre-colonial Africa the most important educational processes were of an informal character and constituted part of the everyday life of the growing child. Although mainly informal, the education of the young was an important communal responsibility and did not take place in a haphazard or casual fashion. In many ways the family and local community are today still the most important educators of the young, for the modern school imported from Europe and America has taken over only a few of the educative functions of family and community. Thus when we talk of pre-colonial or traditional education we should not imagine that these things are of only historical interest. Many of the educational processes discussed below are still found in modern Africa and still constitute an important part of the overall socialisation of the young.

Muslim Education

In parts of Africa, especially in the savanna region of West Africa, Muslim education has existed for a very long time. Through trade and conquest Islam spread slowly across the West African interior from the eleventh century onwards, bringing with it Koranic schools and Islamic scholarship. Persian and Arabic traders brought Islam to the East African coast during the sixteenth century. As with the early mission schools, Koranic education was essentially religious in character and for most students was limited to the memorising of the Koran. Universities were established in Fez (Morocco), Al-Azhar (Egypt) and Timbuktu (Mali) as well as at Jenne, Sokoto and Dinguiraye. In these universities students studied Arabic and mathematics as well as the 'traditional Islamic sciences of Grammar, Law, Exegesis, Theology, Rhetoric and Prosody' (Crowder, 1968, p. 272). Such an education produced an elite who 'read with ease classical Arabic, wrote it fluently and gave witness to a definite culture and science. . . . Works by Negro Muslims on philosophy, law, theology, history and medicine exist all over the Western Suden' (ibid.).

Attendance figures do not exist for the pre-colonial period, but we can obtain some idea of the distribution of Koranic schooling from statistics collected during the colonial period. Thus in 1931 there were an estimated 30,000 to 35,000 Koranic schools with between 200,000 and 360,000 pupils in Northern Nigeria (Hubbard, 1975, p. 153), whereas in 1945 there were an estimated 80,235 pupils attending Koranic schools in French West Africa (Crowder, 1968, p. 373). Figures for Guinea show that in 1910 over a quarter of Muslim children of schoolgoing age were attending Koranic schools (Johnson, 1975, p. 223). Only in the late colonial period did Western schools achieve such high levels of enrolment, and then only in non-Islamised regions.

At all levels Muslim education linked the pupil with the Arabic language and the religion of Islam. The Fulani conquest of Northern Nigeria and elsewhere helped spread Muslim education and religion, just as the colonial conquest helped spread Christian education and religion. For the very few who went past the rote learning of the

Koran stage, Muslim education offered the possibility of upward social mobility to commoners who could aspire to a position of patronage in the court of a Fulani noble. Later Western education played a similar role in relation to the colonial administration. A further similarity between the two religions and conquests is pointed out by Nadel in the case of the Nupe:

> Mohammedan education, by means of which the religion and, indirectly, the whole spiritual background of the ruling classes is diffused throughout the country, [is] one of the 'binding forces' of the Nupe state. . . . Teaching Islam means teaching the holy cause which sent the conquerors down to this country. Praying to Allah means praying to the God of the powerful and sharing with them, if not their power, their beliefs. (Nadel, 1942, p. 142)

Koranic schools thus served as a link between rulers and ruled, with the *malaam* and other religious functionaries serving as the middlemen. Koranic education, again like subsequent mission education in Africa, served as a legitimator of the political power of the rulers. In the following chapter and Chapter 6 we will have more to say about Muslim education in the colonial period.

Indigenous Education: the Poro Society

The Poro society of Liberia, Guinea and Sierra Leone has existed in one form or another for many generations and, together with its sister society (Sande in Liberia, Bundo in Sierra Leone), provides us with a remarkable example of more formal traditional educational practices. In the past, initiation into the Poro secret society involved an extended period of training for adolescent boys, who were taken into the forest for periods of anything up to five years. As well as being initiated into the secret society and learning its rites and rituals, the boys also received various forms of physical, moral and cultural training. These included (1) swimming, running, climbing and wrestling, aimed at preparing the boys for protecting the tribe against outside aggression and for the strenuous manual work which they would have to perform in adult life; (2) learning other male activities such as farming, fishing, hunting and trapping, house- and bridge-building, rowing, carving, tool-making and palm-wine tapping; (3) learning tribal songs, drumming and dancing; and (4) learning the culture and traditions of the tribe and the importance of justice, honesty and respect for elders. The adolescents were also taught to look after themselves and to bear hardships without complaining. On the completion of their training the boys' return to the village was marked with singing and dancing to celebrate their rise to adult status (Forde, 1975, p. 67).

In a similar though less rigorous way the Bundo society prepared adolescent girls for their future roles as wives, mothers and house-keepers.

Government opposition and Western schooling have reduced the educative function of the Poro society but it continues to exist and membership is still keenly sought, particularly in the rural areas.

Informal Traditional Education

In most of pre-colonial Africa there were neither Koranic schools nor Poro societies or their equivalents. How did education take place in these circumstances, and what was taught and learned? Durkheim, a famous French sociologist, defined education as the systematic social-isation of the younger generation by which the latter learn religious and moral beliefs, feelings of nationality and collective opinions of all kinds. In other words, education serves to integrate the individual into the wider community in which he or she is born. Clearly education in this broad sense takes place in every human society and pre-colonial Africa is no exception.

In the introduction to this chapter we pointed out that there was no single kind of pre-colonial society in Africa but a variety of stratifica-tion systems ranging from the acephalous village community to large-scale states and empires. This fact is often ignored in discussions of pre-colonial education, which often give the impression that all Africans lived in villages more or less isolated from the outside world and that the only criteria of stratification were age, sex and kinship. To avoid confusion we will first discuss some of the main aspects of education in relatively unstratified societies. At the end of the chap-ter we will consider educational arrangements in societies with higher levels of stratification.

Parents, older siblings (brothers and sisters), the extended family and the whole village community were responsible for the education of the young. The first teacher the child had was its mother, and this is true in all societies. During its first months the child was more or less totally dependent on its mother for its physical and emotional wel-fare, and under her supervision it learned to crawl and walk and say its first words.

The effects of sexual stratification in village life were obvious in the education of the child from an early age. Boys and girls began to receive separate instruction, the girls staying close to their mothers and other female relatives and the boys moving progressively into male society. In this way the two sexes began to learn the productive and social roles which they would play in adult society. Young girls were kept busy in the household looking after infants, fetching water, sweeping the compound and washing dishes, whereas their brothers were taught to look after the family's animals, chase birds from the crops and hunt. Later on: 'Adolescent boys and girls participated fully in production with increasing independence and responsibility . . . by accomplishing productive tasks . . . the child and adolescent familiarised themselves with adult jobs and were initiated into the different social aspects of their future lives, (Moumouni, 1968, p. 19).

Sexual stratification does not simply mean the division of labour between males and females, however. It also means inequalities between the sexes and these too were taught to growing children. For example, in preparing for marriage, '. . . a girl was told to be agreeable to other wives . . . to work hard on her own, to listen to her husband and obey him, and treat him and his relations with respect . . .' (Castle, 1966, p. 42). The low status of women was reflected in their low participation in public affairs and in the exploitation of their labour power: in many rural communities women continue to work harder than men.

Today many of the skills needed for employment are learned in the context of formal education. In the pre-colonial village, and in many areas still dependent on peasant agriculture, the link between education and work was (and is) a much more direct one: skills were learned by imitating one's elders. The particular skills learned by boys and girls at various points in their lives reflected the sexual division of labour and stratification in the adult community.

The role of the community in the education of the growing child began at an early age. Almost any adult in the village could play mother or father roles in scolding, instructing, advising or rewarding children. The general use of immediate family terms (mother, father, brother, sister) to other villagers reflects the extended family role of the local community in the educational process.

The full integration of the adolescent (especially the male) into the adult community was marked by various initiation rites, often accompanied by circumcision and tests of manhood. Initiation was usually preceded by a relatively short period of formal training similar in intent to that described above in the case of the Poro society.

In many African societies there existed age grade associations to which individuals (especially or exclusively the males) belonged. Rituals, including initiation rites, marked the passage from one age grade to another. According to Nadel the age grade system was important for 'moulding the personality of its members and defining their attitude towards tasks and problems which they are to face in adult life' (Nadel, 1942, p. 400), as well as for teaching co-operation and solidarity. Age grade membership thus served as a preparation for adulthood (known as 'anticipatory socialisation') since it 'introduces social concepts, and practises forms of conduct the effectiveness of which will be proved in adult life' (ibid., p. 392).

In pre-colonial Africa age was not so much related to stratification (although older males generally enjoyed some privileges) as to the division of labour. Certain social and economic roles corresponded to certain ages, which accounts for the educational importance of the age grade system and initiation rites.

Group activities of all kinds, both within age grades and more generally, constitute another important aspect of socialisation. Peer group activities like games and role-playing contribute to both physical and social education and also constitute a form of anticipatory social-isation. In relation to the Kikuyu, Kenyatta tells us:

> The children do most things in imitation of their elders . . Their games are, in fact, nothing more or less than a rehearsal prior to the performance of the activities which are the serious business of all the members of the . . . tribe. The little boys indulge in fighting like big boys. Running and wrestling are very common . . . They play with small wooden spears, and shields made of banana tree bark, bows and arrows, slings and stones . . . The little girls plait baskets of grass and grind corn, like their mothers, and make little pots of the local clay and cook imaginary dishes . . . (Kenyatta, 1959, p. 101)

Thus playing games serves as a preparation for playing adult sex roles.

Education teaches skills (how to farm, how to raise children) which are necessary for the performance of adult roles, but it also teaches the spiritual and moral beliefs and values and the customs and traditions of the group. 'In the evening [the mother] teaches both boys and girls the laws and customs, especially those governing the moral code and general rules of etiquette in the community. The teaching is carried on in the form of folklore and tribal legend' (ibid., p. 103).

Intellectual training may also be combined with the learning of language, culture and history:

> In Yoruba educational theory, two methods of learning were specified: *awoko*, by imitation of older youth and adults; and *ifiye*, by active instruction given by adults. *Ifiye* is often associated with evening gatherings when the father or an older member of the family told stories and posed riddles to the children of the com-pound. This entertainment has a direct educational intent. Children were asked to repeat the previous night's episode as a test of memory and of narrative expressiveness. Competition in solving riddles helped to quicken their natural wit. These sessions thus trained children's verbal dexterity and at the same time introduced them to a wide range of oral literature: myths, folk-tales, local history, proverbs, poems. In the same way as the study of written literature in other cultures, this education gave young people a

heightened awareness of moral values, ethical discernments, and the comic and tragic dimensions of human life. (Callaway, 1975, p. 29)

In non-literate societies reading and writing could obviously not make up part of the growing child's education, but numeracy was taught in a number of ways, including the well-known beanboard game found throughout Africa.

In all these ways – play, demonstration and imitation, age grade membership, initiation, storytelling – the systematic socialisation of the younger generation was assured, and the growing child was progressively incorporated into the community. Education remained a more or less informal process so long as techniques of metalwork, pottery, weaving and other crafts remained relatively simple and agriculture continued to be the principal economic activity of the community.

Education in more Stratified Societies

Societies with specialist occupations and with marked inequalities in the distribution of wealth, status and power tended to have a more differentiated educational system and more formal education than the simple agricultural and pastoral systems described above. Certain specialist occupations were organised on a guild basis and skills were often passed on from father to son. For example, among the Nupe of Nigeria there were guilds (producers' associations) for blacksmiths and miners of iron ore, brass- and silversmiths, glassmakers, weavers, beadmakers, builders, woodworkers, carpenters and butchers. Most of these were hereditary occupations which made up 'a specific social group or class – the class of skilled artisans – which only occasionally enlarged its membership by adopting individuals from other professional or social groups' (Nadel, 1942, p. 286). Moumouni tells us that 'in the case of hereditary occupations, the family hands down to the child the techniques and secrets of the trade, which he in turn will pass on. The important secrets are usually only revealed to the oldest of the male children, or sometimes to the child judged most worthy to receive them, utilise them and keep them in the family' (Moumouni, 1968, p. 27).

Skills were often learned through extended apprenticeships, and it was not rare 'to see young married men still working under the aegis of their elders, continuing to perfect their skills' (ibid.). Apprenticeships sometimes seem to have been unnecessarily long, however, and may have served as a source of cheap labour for the master craftsman.

Some crafts were female monopolies (for example, dyeing, pottery-making) and in these 'specialisation was not based on lineage as in men's crafts for the reason that a girl married and went to live in her husband's compound. There she was expected to fit into the arrangements of her new household and carry out assigned duties, perhaps even becoming adept at a new line of work' (Callaway, 1975, p. 32). In Nupe society weaving at a loom was restricted to upper-class women, who did pass on the skill to their daughters.

Other special kinds of occupation to be found in pre-colonial Africa included soldiers, religious functionaries, administrators and rulers, and educational practices reflected the need to prepare individuals to take on these roles. Thus in the highly stratified Buganda (Uganda) and Ashanti (Ghana):

> administrators . . . could not be educated in the ordinary peasant households. Specialised educational arrangements or institutions were required to train future bureaucrats in the arts and skills of governance which no peasant father could teach. The administrative skills taught in these educational establishments – usually appended to the palaces of kings and chiefs – were not based on writing, and therefore did not have to be taught in special school rooms with desks and tables. (Maas, 1970, p. 179)

Concluding Remarks

Pre-colonial educational arrangements teach us that there was a close relationship between stratification systems and educational practices. Thus education was adapted to local needs. Nowadays a lot is made of the apparent virtues of traditional education by those critical of modern schooling. Some apparently progressive critics decry the pernicious effects of Western education which, they say, has brought about the alienation of the African and the rejection of his culture and traditions. Reactionary critics such as the advocates of Bantu education in South Africa say more or less the same thing. We are not impressed by either of these positions. It is all too easy to romanticise the societies of pre-colonial Africa in condemning colonialism and all its evils. It is also unrealistic to call for a return to pre-colonial traditions and culture, and those who do so often appear to be trying to deny to the younger generation the benefits which they themselves have enjoyed as a result of their own education. In subsequent chapters we will have more to say about attempts to make education more relevant to local needs. Here we may simply note that if education reflects social stratification it is difficult to see how education relevant to one kind of society (for example, an unsophisticated community with few marked inequalities) could also be relevant to another kind such as the complex modern state.

In pre-colonial Africa a full range of educational arrangements was to be found from formal Islamic schooling and craft apprenticeships, through the Poro initiation into adult society, to the informal socialisation of the young, which is a universal feature of human society. Education clearly was not brought to Africa by Europeans: they simply brought their own kind of education with them. The initial importance of European education lies in its relationship with a new form of social stratification, namely, colonialism, and it is this relationship which we examine in the next chapter.

Questions and Discussion Topics: Chapter 1

1 What, in your opinion, were the most important features of pre-colonial education in Africa?
2 What are the main differences between modern education and the traditional education described in this chapter?
3 Think of your own childhood: which of the games and roles you played illustrate the theory that 'play is anticipatory of adult life' (Kenyatta)?
4 What, if anything, has been retained in modern education from traditional education? What, if anything, can teachers learn from traditional education which will be of use in the classroom today?
5 Summarise the goals of traditional education and the ways in which they were attained.
6 Does traditional education still exist in Africa? If so, is it still useful and is it likely to survive the spread of formal schooling?

Chapter 2

Colonial Education in Africa

Introduction

The colonial period in Africa lasted from the late nineteenth to the mid-twentieth century. This period was preceded by centuries of trading contact between Africa, Europe and the Arab world, the most important aspects of which were the East and West African slave trades. Like European influence, Western education predated formal colonialism by centuries: the earliest schools established by Europeans in Africa were associated with the activities of early traders – Portuguese, Dutch, Danish, French and British – dating back to the late fifteenth century. The relatively brief period of formal colonial rule was one of rapid and profound social, including educational, change, and it was during this period that the European presence was most directly felt by the African population. We may briefly consider the nature of colonialism and the ways in which it modified existing systems of stratification.

Colonialism meant different things to different parts of the African continent. We can identify three areas:

(1) *West Africa*

In this general area colonialism was mainly based on trade. Relatively few Europeans came to settle and accordingly little land was appropriated by them. The colonial trade was in primary products such as rubber, coffee, cocoa, groundnuts, palm oil, cotton, and so on, which were for the most part produced by African farmers and exported through the large European-owned trading companies. African farmers either turned voluntarily to cash-crop farming when they saw that there was money to be made from it, or were forced to produce for external markets through threats from the colonial administration or the need to pay taxes.

(2) *Parts of Central Africa, especially French Equatorial Africa and the Congo (Zaire)*

These colonies were dominated by large concessionary companies. The best-known example is the Belgian Congo, which was run as a private empire by King Leopold II of Belgium until 1908. The free hand which these companies were given in trade, which generally meant plunder and the forced collection of such products as rubber and ivory, had terrible consequences for the local population in terms of exploitation and loss of life. Criticism of the concessionary companies and their general inefficiency led to their demise, so that the colonies in this category tended to become non-settler trade-based territories similar to those in West Africa.

(3) *Algeria, parts of East Africa and the whole of Southern Africa*
These areas became the settler colonies in which large numbers of Europeans came to live and, by force and fraud, acquire land from the African population. Taking most of the good land, they forced the male African population to become migrant workers, at first on the white-owned farms and in the gold, diamond and copper mines, later in the growing urban centres. This is still the system practised in South Africa today. Not surprisingly, it was in the settler colonies – especially in Kenya, Rhodesia (now Zimbabwe) and South Africa – that traditional social structures were the most disrupted by the European presence.

With these three types of colonialism in mind we may characterise the colonial social structure as follows:

(a) *Europeans*. In all cases the ruling class was made up of Europeans. In case (1) above, these were the administrators of the colonial service and the agents of the large trading companies; in case (2), the agents of the concessionary companies (until they were replaced by colonial administrators); in case (3), representatives of white agricultural, financial, mining and commercial interests. There were also whites who were not included in the ruling group: medium- or small-scale plantation owners and farmers, shopkeepers, traders, and so on, some of whom were known as 'poor whites' or, in the French-speaking colonies, *'petits blancs'* (small whites).

(b) *Intermediate groups*. In many colonies non-Africans and, for the most part, non-Europeans were to be found as medium-size traders, produce buyers, shopkeepers, transporters and so on. In West Africa these were mostly Lebanese, Greeks, Syrians and Indians; in East Africa and Southern Africa they were mostly Indians. In some colonies, especially those along the West African coast, there were substantial numbers of indigenous traders, some of whom accumulated considerable wealth.

Another intermediate group consisted of half-castes or mulattoes. These were most common in South Africa (Cape Coloureds) and the Portuguese colonies of Angola and Mozambique. Mostly westernised and living in towns, they filled posts as white-collar and manual workers.

A final intermediate group consisted of creoles or resettled slaves. These were Africans who had been rescued from the slave traders or returned from America and settled on the West coast, especially in Sierra Leone (Freetown), Liberia (Monrovia) and Nigeria (Lagos, Abeokuta). For the most part this was a relatively highly educated, Christian and westernised group, socially, culturally and often ethnically separate from the local population. They were to be found particularly among the early professionals (priests, teachers, lawyers, doctors) and in the service of the colonial administration.

(c) *Africans.* A number of new classes began to emerge as a result of colonialism, and the pre-colonial social structure became modified to varying degrees, depending on the type of colonialism experienced in a given area and the type of pre-colonial stratification encountered by the Europeans. We may classify the emerging classes as follows:

(i)   *Manual workers.* Most of the manual labour performed during the early colonial period was forced labour or what is more or less the same thing, labour performed in lieu of payment of taxes. Porterage, road and railway construction and other infrastructural developments depended on forced labour. Gradually wage labour began to replace forced labour, and a more or less permanent workforce began to emerge in the mines of the copperbelt and South Africa, on European farms and plantations, in the ports and public works departments and in the (generally small) transportation, construction and service industries. The slow rate of industrialisation in Africa and, more recently, its capital-intensive nature (many machines, few workers) have meant that the proportion of wage workers in the total labour force has remained extremely small and sometimes even declined.

White-collar workers. The growth of a class of non-manual intermediary workers was a natural result of colonialism, particularly in the non-settler areas where the few Europeans needed to be supplemented by a larger group of moderately educated Africans. Clerks in both government and private service, primary schoolteachers, interpreters, policemen – these were the occupations which accounted for the growth of what has been called the African lower middle class.

A much smaller group of highly educated professional workers also emerged during the colonial period – lawyers, churchmen, doctors and even (at one time) high-level colonial officials. Many of the nationalist leaders and activists of the later colonial period were recruited from among the ranks of these two white-collar groups, and they also provided most of the post-independence political and administrative cadres.

(iii) *Cash-crop farmers.* We have already seen that large numbers of African farmers turned to cash-crop production during the colonial period. The organisation of production took many forms, from the employment of family labour to the hiring of seasonal migrant workers and various sharecropping arrangements, and the scale of operations also varied considerably. Many cash-crop farmers continued to produce food crops, and in more remote and sparsely populated areas subsistence production continued as in precolonial times. Relatively few areas, however, remained unaffected by colonialism and the market relations (money economy) which came with it.

(iv) *Artisans and traders.* There is no agreement among academics concerning the effect of colonialism on local manufactures and handicrafts. It is difficult to generalise, but it is unlikely that all manufactures and handicrafts suffered unduly as a result of colonialism. Local metal smelting often suffered as a result of cheap, mass-produced European tools, and the same is also true for certain kinds of textile manufacture.

The effect of colonialism on internal trade is less disputed: improved transportation and the growth of cash income from agriculture acted as stimuli to local trade. For example, in 1938 there were an estimated 37,000 small produce buyers in the Gold Coast, and 1,500 more substantial coffee brokers selling directly to the European firms. Despite European and other competition there was also a group of substantial traders of both sexes involved in export, wholesale and retail trade (Hopkins, 1973). This pattern was repeated in other trade-based colonies, but was much less in evidence in the two other zones defined above, where European and Indian control of production and distribution severely limited the possibilities of African initiative in these areas.

We may take two final points concerning the effects of colonialism on African societies. In the first place, the impact of colonialism was felt differently within, as well as between, African countries. This meant that the earliest areas which came under the influence of Europeans had a headstart which they have generally maintained as regards the development of economic infrastructure, urban growth, ployment, the spread of cash-crop farming and Christianity and Western education. In some countries these differences in the rate of social change have been added to ethnic and regional differences, leading to the growth of tribalism.

Secondly, pre-colonial stratification systems were more or less radically changed by colonialism. In some areas traditional chiefs suffered a gradual loss of power and authority as the colonial authorities extended their area of control. This was the case in much of Central and Southern Africa as well as in parts of West Africa. Elsewhere Europeans were at pains not to disrupt existing hierarchies of power and authority but tried to work through them to further their own ends, as, for example, with the emirates of Northern Nigeria and Cameroun, and the Buganda kingdom of present-day Uganda. In the long run the effect of colonialism was generally to undermine traditional authority, replacing it with a central political and administrative structure. The tendency in this direction has continued since independence. Colonial administrations often singled out the traditional rulers as targets for their educational policies, with results which will be discussed in due course.

As we have already pointed out, the first schools established by Europeans resulted from coastal trading contacts in the fifteenth century. In these schools the children of local traders and the castle mulattoes (children of mixed blood) could be taught the appropriate European language and basic literacy and numeracy. Such schools were often run by priests, as was the custom in Europe at that time.

The vast majority of schools and colleges opened during the colonial period were run and, for the most part, financed by European and American missionary societies. These were established in the eighteenth and nineteenth centuries with the specific aim of bringing Christianity to the non-Christian world. The list of Catholic and Protestant mission societies opening schools over the length and breadth of Africa both before and during the colonial period is a very long one indeed. The educational activities of these societies were to have a profound effect on the long-term development of many African societies, particularly those which were not already under the influence of Islam. Much of this chapter will be concerned with the activities of the mission societies.

To understand the importance of education in the colonial period we need to answer a number of questions:

(1) Who went to school? Even at the end of the colonial period only a minority of children received any schooling, and they were very unevenly distributed in terms of territories and regions, sex, locality (town and village), ethnic and social background. Also, the schooling received varied greatly in length and quality.

(2) What were the consequences of schooling for those who obtained it and, equally important, the consequences of little or no schooling for those who were less 'fortunate'?

(3) What was the function of education in the colonial context? Whose interests did Western education serve, and how?

These questions are of major importance for the understanding of the social role of education in any society at any period in history, and we will come back to them frequently in this and subsequent chapters. The effects of colonial education are still clearly in evidence in the post-colonial period, and for this reason colonial, particularly mission, education deserves our close attention.

One way in which we may attempt to answer the questions posed above is to consider the many and often complex and contradictory ways in which the actors involved – the missions, the African population, the colonial administration and the private agents of colonialism (traders and settlers) – related to one another. This is a difficult task because none of these groups of actors was homogeneous, and their goals and activities often changed over time and varied from on area to another.

The problem of interpretation also complicates our task, for opinions differ concerning the long-term value of colonial (including missionary) activities in Africa. For example, some see the missionaries as noble altruists, bringing enlightenment, literacy, useful new skills, superior health care and universal values to primitive and ignorant peoples (this is certainly how many missionaries thought of themselves). More in fashion today is the opposite opinion, that is, that the missionaries were, consciously or unconsciously, the agents of an oppressive and exploitative foreign presence, alienating Africans from their traditional culture and beliefs by imposing inappropriate values, school curricula, ambitions and expectations on unwilling and powerless colonial subjects. Which point of view fits the facts of the case most closely? This question is unanswerable, for there are enough facts to support and refute both points of view. The point is, of course, that we are not dealing with a purely factual question, but with a question involving moral or value judgements. In social science we must attempt to suspend such judgements for as long as we can and, by taking as objective a view as possible, we might clarify some of the moral questions involved.

One way to attempt this is to judge the missionary (or any other) enterprise in terms of its long-term results rather than purely in terms of the stated intentions and motives of the missionaries themselves. It is extremely common in social affairs to find that many actions have unplanned consequences which are undesirable from the actors' point of view. This was certainly the case in the colonial period for both public and private educators, for in the long run Western education was a radical force for change, in a direction and to a degree that neither missions nor colonial administrators could possibly have foreseen.

Early Missionary Activities

The mission of the missionaries was to save souls from damnation, to bring Christianity to primitive and pagan peoples throughout the backward regions of the world. The growth of missionary activities during the late eighteenth and nineteenth centuries reflected the expansion of European and American trade and political influence in the world. Similar motives and values justified commercial, political and evangelical expansionism. The technical, industrial and military superiority of the West came to be taken as signs of corresponding moral and spiritual superiority. The ideas of Social Darwinism were used to justify imperial, colonial and missionary activities. According to the Social Darwinists, societies evolved in the same way as animal species, from simple to complex, from lower to higher states. It is easy to see how such ideas could be turned into a racist ideology to justify all kinds of colonial exploitation. Such informed opinions as the following were common in the mid-nineteenth century:

> The assertion that the Negro only requires an opportunity for becoming civilised is disproved by history. . . . Not only has the Negro Race never civilised itself, but it has never accepted civilisation. . . . With the Negro . . . it has been found that the children are precocious: but that no advance in education can be made after they arrive at the age of maturity, they still continue mentally children . . . the reflective faculties hardly appear to be at all developed. . . . From the most remote antiquity the Negro Race seems to have been what it is now. We may be pretty sure that the Negro has been without a progressive history, and that Negroes have been for thousands of years the uncivilised race which they are at the moment. (Dr Hunt of the Anthropological Institute of London (1863), quoted by Ayandele, 1974, pp. 21–2)

Many missionaries were no doubt motivated by the highest spiritual goals, and they were among the few people who protested against the evils and excesses of colonialism, but this does not mean that they were not prone to think in racialist terms or, indeed, to practise some exploitation of their own.

It is no accident, therefore, that most of the early missionaries made little or no attempt to understand African culture or use the local environment for pedagogical purposes. This reflects the European's opinion that there was little of value to be learned from these.

The strategies used by the missions to convey their Christian message changed through time, but they always involved some kind of schooling. This was so that the African would become literate enough to be able to read the scriptures, either in his own local language or in the language of the missionary. In most of the early schools pupils were taught basic literacy and numeracy and considerable amounts of Christian doctrine. In some territories these first schools were called 'catechism schools' and resembled closely the Sunday schools of Europe and America. As we might expect, the schools were run on similar lines to those for working-class children in the home country at the time. For example, in Britain in the early nineteenth century working-class children were generally taught by monitors – usually older children who had reached the top of the school – in schools run by churches or voluntary bodies. One such monitorial system, the Lancastrian system, was used by the Church Missionary Society in Sierra Leone in the early nineteenth century. Racial prejudice, like class prejudice in Britain, influenced the curriculum of these schools:

> Since the prevailing image of the African was of a lazy scoundrel wallowing in heathen superstition, it is not surprising that the early CMS and WMMS [Methodist] workers in Sierra Leone took up the educational forms and content currently in vogue in England for the working class, a group considered to be afflicted by similar weaknesses. This education emphasised the spiritual value of hard work and the tenets of evangelical Christianity. (Berman, 1975, p. 8)

The overemphasis on doctrine in these early schools sometimes came in for criticism. One school inspector attacked 'the scriptural and devotional reading and repetition which at present exclude almost everything else from the Sierra Leone schools'. He suggests that the prevailing overemphasis on religious instruction produces one of two results: either a boy reacts strongly away from it when he leaves school, and 'wastes his precious youth in imitating the amusements and vices of Europeans', or else he develops a 'fanaticism and religious presumption' (Hilliard, 1956, p. 11).

It soon became apparent to many missionaries that the heavy concentration on doctrine in the schools was counterproductive as regards interesting the African population in Christianity. The most fundamentalist missions were very hostile to the idea of catering to non-spiritual needs in the schools: to them the way in which souls were saved was almost as important as salvation itself. But most missions were adaptable enough to realise that they could only hope to gain African adherents by catering for material as well as spiritual needs. T. J. Bowden, an early missionary, put it thus: 'The gospel was never intended to feed and clothe us, or to instruct us in reading, writing . . . and the other things necessary to a correct understanding of the Bible. Yet without food and clothing, and several branches of secular knowledge, the Bible and the Gospel cannot exist in any country' (Ayandele, 1971, p. 24). This realisation of the importance of secular knowledge paved the way for the introduction of both academic and vocational curricula; indeed, the literary curricula which eventually became the norm in both official and mission schools were the most vocational in terms of future job opportunities for school-leavers, as will be shown below.

We may summarise the major characteristics of early mission education thus:

(1) The missions were not always successful in establishing permanent schools because death rates were high among missionaries, they encountered much hostility from local populations and because they did not yet have the protection of colonial administrations. Where they did not meet with actual hostility, indifference was a common African reaction, for the Christian message, with or without schools, raised little enthusiasm among Africans who were otherwise more or less uninfluenced by Europeans. A group of evangelical African fetishists arriving in Europe at the same time, speaking an incomprehensible language, wearing animal skins and advocating polygamy would, we may imagine, have been greeted with a mixture of incredulity, hostility and indifference in a similar way.

(2) The greatest missionary successes were in those few areas, generally on or near the coast, where the local populations were already in more or less permanent contact with European traders or, as in the case of the creole freed slaves of Freetown, Monrovia and elsewhere, already highly westernised. The earliest pupils to attend mission schools were thus atypical minorities: the creoles, the children of a few coastal traders, castle mulattoes and a few slaves sent to school by chiefs who were unwilling to send their own children.

(3) As we have pointed out above, the early schools were generally little more than Sunday schools for the rote learning of catechism, plus a little reading, writing and arithmetic, and often a considerable amount of manual work. This mirrored similar practices in Europe, where education was not yet compulsory and the poor and the lower classes were taught by voluntary organisations, usually with a religious origin.

(4) There was no co-ordination of missionary activities or supervision of standards or curricula, there being no administration to carry out such functions. For the same reason missionary

activities were generally self-financing. These continued to be characteristics of missionary activities after the colonial takeover, with results to be discussed in the following sections.

(5) There was little or no provision of post-primary education, teacher training or technical/vocational education, although these developed relatively early in such areas as southern Sierra Leone and the Gold Coast (Ghana). In most areas the missions had a semi- or total monopoly of what Western education was provided, and this continued to be the case under colonial rule.

The Missions under Colonial Rule

The tenuous foothold of mission education on the African continent was consolidated in the 1880s with the partition of Africa between the French, British, Germans, Belgians, Portuguese and Spanish. In one sense this helped the missionary effort, for the missions were no longer dependent on the goodwill of African host societies or liable to expulsion by them. The colonial authorities tended to look on the missions as taking part in a joint venture, especially when the two were of the same nationality (Berman, 1975). Missionaries could now be protected against hostile peoples and could follow the expansion of colonial power inland from the coast – what the French called '*pacification*' but, more correctly, the defeat of hostile peoples by the force of arms – and establish schools in otherwise unpromising areas.

The white man's religion and education now came, in the eyes of the African population, to be associated with the rifles and taxation of the colonial administration. In other words, resistance to Western education declined as European rule expanded. There was thus a strong element of forced choice in the gradual acceptance of Western education by Africans. Lévi-Strauss (1966, p. 99) sums up the expansion of European culture and its acceptance in the colonies in the following terms:

The acceptance of Western values was less the result of a positive decision than of an absence of choice. Western civilization has sent its soldiers, trading posts, plantations and missionaries to the four corners of the earth. It has profoundly shaken the foundations of traditional modes of life, either by imposing its own mode or by establishing the conditions which lead to the collapse of preexisting modes without replacing them by something else. Subject or fragmented peoples could thus only accept the solutions offered to them or . . . hope to assimilate these solutions sufficiently to be able to fight them on an equal footing. Without such inequalities in power, societies do not give up so easily.

Achebe describes this process of the reluctant acceptance of Western civilisation, including schooling, in his novel *Things Fall Apart*.

Thus missionary activities were an integral part of colonial expansion. Nevertheless, the missions and the authorities did not always manage to avoid conflict. For example, in 1919 the CMS in Kenya protested strongly against colonial labour policy and the increase in poll tax and lobbied actively in London for a change in policy. Conflicts in the other direction were also common, as the colonial authorities were frequently critical of the rate of growth of missionary activities and of the tendency of missions to compete and squabble among themselves (see below).

In general, however, the missions and the colonial authorities benefited from each other's presence. We may ask in what way were missionary activities necessary from the colonial viewpoint? The simple answer is that both private trading companies and the colonial administration needed literate Africans to work for them as clerks, interpreters, and so on, as public and private colonialism expanded. Thus in 1914 Lord Lugard was complaining that in Nigeria

> the commercial interests of the country are no less hampered than the government by the lack of staff, and the merchants say that the greatest boon which at this stage could be conferred upon them is a better supply of reliable natives to occupy posts of responsibility, at present filled by subordinate Europeans, at greater cost and at a sacrifice of continuity. Railway expansion and other progress is retarded. Education has thus become a matter of vital urgency. (Quoted by Fafunwa, 1974, p. 113)

Clearly, one of the main advantages of employing natives was that they were paid less than Europeans for doing the same work!

The missions too needed manpower, for the school monitors and catechists required to expand the missionary effort within the colonial territories were recruited from among the graduates of the mission schools and seminaries. For example, by 1914 the Basel Mission in Cameroun had two African monitors for every European teacher. Elsewhere this proportion was much higher.

For much of the colonial period the European administrations were unwilling or unable to spend much on education: generally much less than 10 per cent of local budgets were allocated to building and staffing schools. The authorities were generally prepared to leave education in the hands of the missions. Only when school provision began to take on a dynamism of its own which threatened to get out of hand by providing, from the official point of view, too much education for too many Africans, did the colonial authorities begin to interfere actively in the educational field, with results which will be examined shortly.

Thus from the 1880s missionary activities expanded along with the military conquest of the continent and the growth of colonial administrations. One factor which stimulated missionary expansion was the growing competition between mission societies for converts. This competition was at its most acute between Catholics and Protestants, as, for example, in Eastern Nigeria, Buganda and the Congo.

> Right from the advent of Christianity in Nigeria, dissension and disunity were rampant among the Christian missions and, to the bewildered African, it was hard to believe that one white Christian mission would discredit another white Christian mission in a desperate attempt to win converts and send glowing reports back to the home mission. . . . The Methodists and the CMS fought for ascendancy in Badagry, Abeokuta, Lagos and Ibadan in the 1840s and 1850s, aided by their home missions. Even today this competition – particularly between the Catholics and the Protestants – has not subsided. (Fafunwa, 1974, p. 84)

In spite of sectarian and doctrinal conflicts, the typical mission school which emerged during this period was less concerned with the teaching of doctrine than had previously been the case. With some notable exceptions, the language of the Europeans was used as the medium of instruction and the schools followed a basic academic curriculum similar to those used in European schools at the time.

A few figures can be quoted to illustrate the impact of Christian missionary activities:

> The Catholic Church in 1951 had in its African missionary services south of the Sahara 7,468 priests, 2,342 brothers and 10,533 sisters, a total number of 20,343, not including the much larger number of Africans who were priests, members of various orders, and catechists. (Herskovits, 1962, p. 188)

Colonialism helped the spread of Christianity in Africa, but it also acted as a spur to the spread of Islam, especially in West Africa, where it became an integral part of the opposition to colonial rule. According to Crowder:

> Both Christianity and Islam were to have a profound effect on African society in the period of colonial occupation. The Christian impact, because it was so closely linked with that of the occupying powers, particularly in the field of education, has often been given greater emphasis than that of Islam, even though Islam made much greater progress than Christianity. By the early fifties 34 percent of the population of West Africa was estimated to be Muslim, that is

some 20,067,000 as against only 4.5 percent Christians. (Crowder, 1968, p. 356)

Christian sources quoted by Herskovits (1962) claimed that in 1951 there were as many Christians of all denominations as Muslims in sub-Saharan Africa. This is probably an overestimate, but we would argue that the number of converts to Christianity is not as good an index of the influence of the missions as the number of converts to Western education. In this sense, the Christian mission impact is probably greater than that of Islam, for Western education has proved to be of greater strategic importance in the recent development of African society than the rather conservative Koranic education discussed in the last chapter. In other words, the secular impact of mission education has been more important than its religious impact. This is a good example of the unintended consequences of missionary activities mentioned in the introduction.

Colonial Education: Policy and Practice

The colonial authorities shared the missionaries' belief in the superiority of European over African civilisation, and this belief is reflected in policy statements justifying colonialism, including its educational aspects. The ideological justification of colonialism is a reflection of the economic and political power exercised by the colonising nations. As Marx said, the ideas of the ruling class are the ruling ideas. During the colonial period few Europeans doubted their right to impose their civilisation on the African population; the French openly claimed to have a civilising mission in Africa, and the British took it upon themselves to carry the white man's burden, that is, the responsibility to lead the backward native to a higher level of civilisation.

The background of the inhuman slave trade and the harsh reality of colonialism (forced labour, taxation, summary justice, land expropriation, *pacification*) were in sharp contrast to the high moral tones in which the colonial powers expressed their aims and motives, showing the highly ideological character of the latter. The meagre educational provision undertaken by the colonial authorities, when compared with their lofty intentions, is another proof of the emptiness of their rhetoric.

As we have already seen, the colonial authorities were generally prepared to allow the missions to carry on their evangelical-educational activities without too much interference, at least during the early part of colonial rule. The French were among the least enthusiastic colonial authorities regarding support of missionary education in Africa, reflecting the long-standing feud in France between church and state. Nevertheless, for nationalistic reasons the French government did not hesitate to make a grant to Catholic missionaries for educational activities in the French Congo (Berman, 1975).

In general, despite the official French opposition to missionary activities in Africa 'it cannot be denied that the missions established themselves and progressed thanks to the support of the colonial regime' (Suret-Canale, 1964, p. 455). But enrolment rates were generally much higher in British than in French territories, partly because missionary activities began earlier in the former, partly because most of the French territories in West Africa were highly Islamised.

In certain parts of Africa rivalry between the colonial powers stimulated metropolitan support for missionary activities. 'When the French saw that mission schools were helping England to entrench itself in Africa, the French government asked the aid of their own Catholic church to secure national interests' (Rodney, 1972, p. 282). Similarly:

> After 1878, foreign Protestant missions developed their activities throughout Angola. Responding at least as much to the political as to the religious challenge, Portugal began to expand its own support of Catholic missions. . . . Even after the beginning of the anti-Catholic First Republic in 1910, the government provided financial support . . . and used the missions as a political extension to occupy a void that the government itself was unable to fill. (Samuels, 1970, pp. 126–7)

Thus the first kind of official support for missionary activities came direct from the home government and was related to the establishment of political control in areas where the colonial powers were competing for influence. Only at a later date did the local colonial administrations begin to subsidise the missions on an appreciable scale.

British colonial administrations prohibited the expansion of missionary activities into Muslim areas, mainly in order to avoid conflict with the traditional rulers of these areas. The French pursued a more aggressive policy against Islam which resulted in much bloodshed and the closing of many Koranic schools. Often Muslim areas were areas of relatively little colonial activity, so that it was more or less unnecessary from the point of view of the authorities and private traders to produce Western-educated middlemen in any quantity. Where colonial activities were at a maximum, namely, in the towns and ports, in the mining, plantation and cash-cropping areas, missionary activities were at a maximum also.

French and British administrative and educational policies in West Africa have often been contrasted. The French administrative policy was based on direct rule of the African population by colonial officials and their education policy was one of assimilation, that is, of bringing Africans up to European standards of civilisation by providing them with a purely French education. The British, on the other hand, are characterised as practising indirect rule, whereby the traditional social hierarchy was maintained and respected and integrated into the colonial administrative system. The corresponding educational policy was one of adaptation, that is, of providing an education which would integrate the individual into his own rather than into European society.

In practice, however, both the French and the British were obliged to adapt their administrative and educational policies to the realities of the colonial situation: the French were never as assimilationist and the British never as adaptionist as they claimed to be. For example, the French did not create an educated elite of Africans during the colonial period on any significant scale. The first *lycée* (grammar school) was not established in French West Africa until 1928, and the first university (Dakar) opened in 1957. By contrast, secondary schools were established in Nigeria, Gold Coast and Sierra Leone well before 1900, and the first graduates of Fourah Bay College (Sierra Leone) received their degrees in 1878. Similarly, anglophone Africans were attending British universities well before their francophone counterparts started going to French universities on any significant scale.

One assimilationist policy introduced by both French and British was to build schools for the sons of chiefs in order to produce educated traditional leaders and facilitate administration. A French West African decree of 1924 even went so far as to make attendance at these schools compulsory for the sons of chiefs and notables. These policies were largely unsuccessful and reflected a rather naïve assumption on the part of the colonial authorities concerning the traditional system for the transfer of power. Chiefs frequently refused to send their sons to school or sent other children in their place. We will come back to the question of the reaction of traditional rulers to Western education in the next section.

Overall, the French exercised a greater degree of control over education than the British, establishing a network of village, regional and urban schools, designed to produce the manpower required by the colonial system. For example, in 1931 of a total of forty official schools in the Ivory Coast twenty-seven were *écoles rurales*, with a curriculum based on manual labour and vocational training. The figure for Senegal was sixty-one out of a total of eighty. According to Crowder: 'As a generalisation it is fair to say that the French absorbed a carefully controlled elite into their colonial system, while the British frustrated an elite over whose growth they had no control since the educational system was only indirectly administered by it' (Crowder, 1968, p. 383). In French colonies the highest educational level open to Africans was the *école primaire supérieure*, a middle school, training school monitors and routine-grade civil servants. The elite coming out of these schools was a relatively modest one.

In Belgian and Portuguese colonies almost no post-primary school facilities existed for Africans until the post-independence period. In British settler colonies educational provision at all levels was far inferior to that in the non-settler colonies. For example, in British West Africa 'some post-primary education existed from the mid-nineteenth century, reflecting the early development of mission education before the beginning of formal colonial rule. But the British authorities were also hostile to the over-rapid expansion of academic education. For example, Lord Lugard commented that missionary expansion in southern Nigeria 'seems to have produced discontent, impatience of any control and an unjust assumption of self-importance in the individual' (Abernethy, 1969, p. 85).

As the colonial period progressed the various European administrations became more and more involved in education, both as builders of schools in their own right and as supervisors and subsidisers of mission schools. The main impetus behind this increasing involvement was not the desire to expand educational facilities for Africans, as might be expected from a reading of policy statements, but rather the opposite, namely, the desire to restrict the expansion of schooling, particularly of academic secondary schooling, which was deemed to be inappropriate to African needs.

Although the colonial authorities in the non-settler colonies needed considerable numbers of Africans with a basic Western education, they were concerned that the supply of such Africans should not outstrip the demand for their services. There are signs that in some places such an oversupply did exist, particularly in areas of early mission expansion such as the southern Gold Coast where, according to Foster (1965, p. 67) 'there were already indications by 1850 that the supply of literates was already exceeding the demand for their services'. Clearly the unemployed school-leaver problem is nothing new!

Part of the problem was a result of the introduction of racial segregation in the administration of the colonies, which increasingly blocked the promotion prospects of the most educated Africans.

We can see the elite suffering from a real setback in the colonial era. Thus in 1875, in Lagos, the head of police, the head of posts and telegraphs, head of customs, and the registrar of the Supreme Court were all Nigerians. At the same time, an African bishop headed the Anglican Mission on the Niger. Yet later, in the period of colonial rule, all Africans of their competence were relegated to subordinate positions in Nigeria. In Sierra Leone, where the Creole elite had supplied many senior government officials, including an Acting Chief Justice, an Acting Colonial Secretary and even a Secretary for Native Affairs, it was disinherited after 1900, with the final establishment of the British Protectorate over the hinter-land. (Crowder, 1968, p. 9)

The frustrations to the educated African as a result of this segregation can be judged by this quotation from the autobiography of Nigeria's first president:

> The civil services of British West Africa were controlled then [1930s] by a European elite which rigidly closed the doors of opportunity for the employment of indigenous West African uni-versity graduates, some of whom were engaged only under the most humiliating conditions of service and at parsimonious salaries, on the basis of racial discrimination and segregation. Therefore, the main reason for refusing me suitable and respect-able employment in this sector of the public service of my own country . . . was not because I did not have a suitable qualification or because I was not a desirable character, but because of the colour bar. (Azikiwe, 1970, p. 172)

This kind of discrimination has continued in the settler areas of Zim-babwe and South Africa until today. Arbitrarily imposed educational and occupational restrictions were a serious source of frustration to the most highly educated Africans and an important factor in the growth of nationalist movements in the twentieth century.

One way in which the colonial authorities attempted to control mission education was by granting subsidies known as 'grants in aid' to those schools who followed an official curriculum sanctioned by inspection and a final examination. This policy was based on the assumption that existing curricula were too academic and bore too close a resemblance to those used in European and American schools, resulting in the alienation of pupils from their traditional milieu and encouraging them to seek white-collar jobs on graduation. The ques-tion of curriculum reform during the colonial period is dealt with in detail in Chapter 6. Here we may note that the type of curriculum reform advocated depended on the type of colony. In Kenya, where whites dominated farming and Asians filled all clerical posts, it was decided that Africans should learn manual skills:

> Just as handwork has been found useful in the training of mentally defective children so the most useful training which the African can receive in his present condition is continual contact with material processes. The discipline imposed by the exactness required in joinery, carpentry, building, smithing, etc., develops the process of thought. (1926 Kenyan Department of Education Annual Report; quoted by Anderson, 1970, p. 40)

On the other hand, in West Africa, where colonialism meant cash-crop production by Africans and not settlers, it was decided that the African needed agricultural education above all else. As the Advisory Committee on Education in the Colonies put it: 'The basis of African life is, and is likely to remain, agriculture. If this is so, one of the primary tasks of African education must be to assist in the growth of rural communities securely established on the land' (Foster, 1965, p. 160).

It is difficult to avoid the conclusion that the local needs which education was meant to serve were in fact local *colonial* rather than local African needs. At all events, in the colonial context, the African was thought of as destined to play a subordinate role to his white master, and a manual or agricultural education was considered the most appropriate for his inferior status.

In practice, the reform of education from academic to adapted curricula never took place, with the exception of the Portuguese colonies and South Africa, where government control of schooling was stricter than elsewhere. The reasons for the failure of adapted education are discussed in Chapter 6. The main reason concerns the African reaction to Western education, to which we may now turn.

The African Reaction

So far little has been said about the African reaction to Western education. In the long run, it was this reaction which determined the success or failure of Western education as an institution capable of setting down roots in the African soil and proliferating over the years. Africans were never simply the passive recipients of schooling: even though the colonial system imposed severe restraints on their freedom of action they were nevertheless active participants in the educational process, sometimes even building and staffing their own schools. Strictly speaking, there were many African reactions, differing over time and space, so we must look at the question both in historical terms and in specific social contexts.

It has already been pointed out that the initial reaction to mission education was, outside the areas of well-established contact with Europeans, generally hostile or indifferent. Education (and Christianity) had no relevance to traditional society and systems of stratification. More important, the missionaries were powerless to impose their worldview on their target populations if the latter were not prepared to listen. The establishment of Western education and ideas depended on the totality of colonial power and influence which came with military conquest, the implantation of the colonial administration, the growth of trade and a monetary economy and, most important of all, with occupational opportunities requiring Western education. All these forces were instrumental in destabilising traditional African society, albeit to a very variable degree in different parts of the continent. Most vulnerable were the relatively unstratified societies of certain coastal areas, which were the earliest to feel the full force of colonial expansion. Least vulnerable were the relatively highly stratified societies, for example the emirates of Northern Nigeria, which were much less affected by colonialism, at least in the short run.

It should be stressed that those who took advantage of Western education were far fewer than those who were taken advantage of by colonialism. Colonialism can be seen as a mechanism for incorporating the peoples of the conquered territories into a wider international network of economic and political relations. The colonial powers were interested above all in gaining access to Africa's mineral wealth and in developing cash-crop agriculture in tropical products (cocoa, coffee, rubber, palm oil, groundnuts, cotton and so on). Education was unnecessary for the vast majority of Africans, whose land and labour were put to use, often in the most brutal ways, in order to further the ends of the colonial powers. The forced labour which was used to build the roads and railways, the migrant labourers working in mines and on farms, the labourers in the docks, public works departments and so on – none of these groups needed to be educated in order to be incorporated into the colonial system.

By comparison, the clerks, interpreters and school monitors employed by the trading companies, administration and missions, constituted a relatively small group, but one of immense strategic importance. From the point of view of income, status and work conditions it was in most cases clearly preferable to be a member of this small white-collar group than of the much larger group of non-educated manual workers. If education offered some hope of escaping from arduous agricultural work or from the demands of the colonial rulers and their local agents, the chiefs, then it is not surprising that the demand for schooling increased as the colonial regime became more and more entrenched. In the 1940s Fortes described the situation in Ashanti, an area which had not accepted Western education at all easily, as follows:

> The demand for schools is sweeping the country. [This] represents an effort to adapt Ashanti social organisation to the pressures of European civilization. The combination of high and steadily increasing income, security for life and power and prestige . . . forms the ideal to which every schoolboy aspires. Failing a 'white collar' job, any job in the European sector is more desirable than one in the African sector. . . . There has been an increasing demand for clerical service and commerce and for other workers of a skilled and semi-skilled type in mining, in transport and so on. This demand has stimulated competition to enter schools. (Quoted by Foster, 1965, p. 132)

In many other parts of Africa the Ashanti sequence was followed; initial indifference or hostility towards Western education eventually being replaced by enthusiastic acceptance. For example, the Governor of French West Africa declared in 1930 that

> everywhere natives in their multitudes are clamouring to be educated. Here, a chief wants a school of his own, so he builds it; or, again, some village or other may offer to bear the cost of fitting out a school; at certain places in the Ivory Coast the villagers pay the teachers out of their own pockets. (Quoted by Crowder, 1968, p. 385)

This positive acceptance of education reflected its growing importance in relation to opportunities in the wider society in terms of economic advantage, status achievement and occupational mobility. Although these opportunities were more or less limited by discriminatory recruitment policies on the part of the authorities, the missions and private colonialists, they were nevertheless attractive enough in the context of colonial exploitation. Opportunities were most limited in the areas of white settlement, where the African's involvement in the colonial economy was mostly restricted to semi- or unskilled manual labour on white farms or in mines and factories. In West Africa there were relatively more opportunities for Africans to find white-collar employment since there were many fewer Europeans or Asians to compete with. This was somewhat more true in British than in French territories as the practice of indirect rule was more widespread in the former. Also, there were more *petits blancs* in the French colonies, many of whom occupied posts which Africans performed in British colonies, for example train driver and shop assistant.

Except in the depression of the 1930s employment opportunities in the administration, the missions and trading companies steadily increased with the development of colonial rule, but by the end of the colonial period the number of Africans employed in white-collar occupations was still only a small proportion of the working population.

Thus colonialism created a rather small but highly 'visible' group of Africans who reached a modest white-collar status on the basis of their educational achievement. In some areas an even smaller group existed which has been called the African middle class or educated elite, a group which in terms of educational level, life-style and (sometimes) income most closely resembled the elite of white colonial administrators. Some West African creoles and coastal traders come into this category. They were among the first to benefit from secondary and higher education, and sometimes showed an extreme level of identification with European culture, as this description of Cape Coast society (in the Gold Coast) at the end of the nineteenth century demonstrates:

> Everyday life in Cape Coast took on the colour of the Victorian era. The school Assembly Hall would echo one evening to the resolutions of the local branch of the Society for the Prevention of Cruelty to Animals; the next it would be filled with an enthusiastic audience treated to a magic lantern lecture on the Stately Homes of England, followed by 'selections on a patent organ which combines the whole effect of a brass band in itself'. ... Beeton's *Complete Etiquette for English Gentlemen* sold at the bookshop. English clothing and English names were postulates of the Christian life. (Smith, quoted by Foster, 1965, p. 43)

Not all middle-class Africans were as detribalised as those described above, of course. The most organised and vocal critics of colonialism were to be found in the African middle class of doctors, teachers and lawyers (where these existed) and among the less well-educated group mentioned above.

Closely related to the emergence of white-collar employment was another tendency inherent in colonial society, namely, the decline of the traditional community as the central focus of everyday life. Again, this decline is relative and highly variable over time and space. In some parts of Africa traditional rulers still exercise considerable power. Elsewhere traditional chiefs and rulers continue to exist but exercise no real power, or have been eliminated completely. It is generally the case that colonialism and its after-effects have tended to disrupt traditional society and reduce the power of traditional chiefs and rulers. We may briefly examine the educational dimension of this process.

Traditional leaders frequently opposed Western education because they perceived it as a threat to their authority. They were often more reluctant to send their children to school than were their subjects. This meant that, according to Foster,

> the position of traditional elites [in the Gold Coast] was progressively weakened by their inability to perceive the necessity for European education. For, once European political control became effective, there was always the possibility that the locus of power would shift from the chiefs in favour of alternative groups who had earlier recognised the potential significance of schooling. (Foster, 1965, pp. 63–4)

We have already pointed out that not all chiefs reacted in the same way to attempts by missionaries and colonial authorities to introduce education. Those who accepted education at an early date stood a better chance of surviving than the apparently stubborn traditionalists who opposed it. For example, the Obas (traditional leaders) of Yorubaland (in Nigeria) profited from education from an early date.

As a consequence they consolidated their powers at the expense of their traditional group of advisors. The function of selecting and replacing the Obas passed from this group to the colonial regime, which carried on its administration by using the Obas as intermediaries. It is probable that the colonial administration would have effectively bypassed the Obas had they not been literate, by using local clerks, officials and councils as their intermediaries. This is what happened elsewhere during the twentieth century as the colonial administrations 'consolidated their power and took on more and new functions which deprived chiefs of much of their wealth, influence and prestige' (de Graft-Johnson, 1966, p. 168).

In Buganda both Protestant and Catholic missions used education to ingratiate themselves with traditional chiefs. In pre-colonial Buganda both commoners' and local chiefs' sons could aspire to political office by becoming pages at the court of the *Kabaka* (king) and in the households of other great chiefs. 'Once missionaries entered Buganda and established schools based on achievement criteria, status achievement quickly became associated with schools; schooling and mobility soon became synonymous' (Berman, 1975, p. 26). Fallers quotes the Anglican education secretary thus: 'Knowing that in the ordinary course of events such boys (the sons of chiefs) were destined to become future leaders of the country, we cast about for some means of getting them.' The answer was to provide an elite secondary education based on the English private boarding school. 'The chiefs were delighted with the idea and readily promised to build the boarding houses and to pay for the support of their children' (Fallers, 1964, pp. 183–4). As only the wealthier parents could afford to pay the fees, the new educated elite tended to be more narrowly recruited from the traditional chiefs than the old elite had been. Consequently, 'there is a very significant hereditary element in the present-day elite' (ibid.). Subsequently, the *Kabaka* was deposed and the Buganda elite lost its autonomy (1967).

In the above example and in many others Western education played an important role in modifying traditional political structures. It is difficult to generalise about this role, because both the way in which Western education arrived on the scene in a given area (backed up by the colonial regime, offered by competing missionary groups and competing regimes) and the way in which traditional leaders reacted to it (adoption, adaption, refusal) varied enormously. However, it seems safe to say that in the long run African rulers as a whole had little chance of surviving in their pre-colonial positions, irrespective of their reaction to Western education. Their perceptions of the importance of education or their freedom of action in adapting to it mattered less than their general position in colonial society in determining their gradual decline.

Increasingly the most educated came to replace the chiefs as *the* elite. Both their educational and occupational achievements gave them status in the eyes of the local population according to the emergent hierarchy of values, namely, that which stemmed from the European presence. The rise of occupational opportunities based on educational achievement and the decline of traditional authority were opposite sides of the same coin. Expressing this in sociological terms we may say that the traditional status hierarchy based on the ascriptive criteria of age, sex and birth (lineage) was gradually replaced by a new hierarchy based on the achievement criterion of Western education. Where achievement criteria already existed in pre-colonial society, the adoption of Western education was, other things being equal, a relatively smooth process. We can illustrate this point by citing the contrasting examples of Ibo society (relatively low level of stratification) and Buganda (highly stratified).

The growth of achievement criteria meant an increasing popular demand for schooling, particularly academic schooling, the growing pressure on the missions and colonial authorities for expanded post-primary facilities. These pressures increased towards the end of the colonial period, and it is to this period that we now turn.

Education at the End of the Colonial Period

By the end of the Second World War it was becoming increasingly clear that the days of colonialism were numbered and that the demands for the independence of colonial territories could not be refused indefinitely. By the early 1950s many African countries had some degree of internal autonomy or representation in the European metropolis, and most of them gained their independence around 1960.

The realisation that colonialism was coming to an end had important consequences for educational policy and practice. It now became necessary for colonial authorities to think seriously about who was to fill the power vacuum created by their eventual departure. As part of the strategy of decolonisation priority was sometimes given to the formation of an administrative elite to take over the civil service. In countries like Ghana, Nigeria, Sierra Leone and Senegal such an elite was already forming, for growing numbers of local people had been receiving secondary and higher education from the end of the nineteenth century onwards. In the settler colonies this elite had not been allowed to form, and the colonial powers were less willing to give way to local and international pressures to decolonise. Thus little or nothing was done to train local cadres for eventual independence, sometimes with catastrophic results.

We have already seen that the colonial authorities tended to intervene more and more in educational affairs as colonialism developed, and this intervention grew rapidly after 1945 for the reasons just mentioned. A boom in the world market for tropical products after the war provided most of the funds needed by the authorities for their programmes of expansion, as well as providing money for school fees and school construction by Africans. Mission activities also continued to expand, reflecting the growth in demand for education in both urban and rural areas. For example, in Nigeria the authorities spent nearly £223,000 on education in 1941, over £485,000 in 1944 and £615,660 in 1945, more than half of which was allocated to voluntary agencies. These figures represent an absolute increase in the proportion of revenue spent on education by the colonial government. Nevertheless, in 1947 voluntary agencies still controlled 96 per cent of the primary schools, 93 per cent of teacher training colleges and 85 per cent of the secondary schools in Nigeria (Weiler, 1964).

One of the ways in which the colonial authorities pursued their policy of elite formation was through the construction of a small number of high status secondary schools closely resembling British public schools (which are in fact private schools) or the French *lycées*. These schools were designed to attract the most able children (or those from the wealthiest families), provide boarding facilities which should develop a sense of common identity among the pupils, and enter them for metropolitan examinations.

The policy paid off; a large number of political leaders and top civil servants eventually emerged from these schools. For example:

> An examination of the list of graduates of the William Ponty school [Dakar] shows that on or just before independence the following graduates were at the head of French-speaking West African governments: Modibo Keita, President of the Republic of Mali; Mamadou Dia, Prime Minister of Senegal; Hubert Maga, President of Dahomey; Ouezzin Coulibaly, Prime Minister of Upper Volta . . . ; Felix Houphouet-Boigny, President of Ivory Coast; Djibo Bakary, Prime Minister of Niger . . . ; only Guinea and Mauritania did not have a President or Prime Minister educated at this school. Similarly for Northern Nigeria the Katsina College, now Government College, Zaria, has a school roll that included the Premier, the Minister of Finance, the Minister of Education, the Federal Prime Minister and three Federal Ministers, the leader of the opposition in the North, the Speaker of the Northern House and the Governor of the Northern Region before the January 1966 military coup. (Crowder, 1968, pp. 383–4)

A second way in which elite formation took place was through the provision of grants for university study abroad. For example, in 1953 there were 148 Camerounians studying in France with government scholarships, 444 in 1962 and in the same year about twice as many again with no official support. The growth of African universities will be discussed in the following chapter.

The French authorities could now talk of assimilationist education with more conviction than before, but they undertook the expansion of post-primary education too late for many top-level civil servants to have been trained by the time of independence. Thus, although between 1947 and 1957 enrolment in primary schools doubled in Senegal, increased fourfold in Guinea and sixfold in the Ivory Coast, the three countries combined were only producing about 150 students with the *baccalauréat* by the mid-1950s, and many of these were Europeans. Consequently, many of the former colonial administrators retained their posts after independence, and many modestly qualified civil servants were rapidly promoted to more senior posts. The expansion of the public sector and the continued close relationship between France and most of her ex-colonies have meant that Europeans still hold many top posts in the civil service, especially in countries like Senegal, the Ivory Coast and Gabon.

The most highly educated Africans were not only the greatest beneficiaries of independence, they also helped bring it about. Many colonialists had foreseen the disruptive potential of the spread of education, and their fears proved to be justified. One of the major challenges to colonial power came from the educated: the highly educated who aspired to the top posts but whose aspirations were frustrated by the virtual white monopoly at this level, and the less educated 'dissatisfied younger elements recently arrived in the urban areas' (Apter, 1963, p. 270). These latter constituted one group of nationalist militants, as Apter points out in the case of the Convention People's Party (CPP) (Ghana).

In politics it was not essential to be educated to be successful but the growing prestige attached to the diploma sometimes made it a useful asset, as, for example, in the cases of Senghor, Nyerere, Nkrumah and Azikiwe. In some cases, however, the most highly educated Africans were seen by the less educated as 'too westernised, detribalised, snobbish, individualist and arrogant' (ibid.). Individual elite members did, of course, play major roles in the nationalist movements both before and after the Second World War, but in general they were moderates rather than radicals, reformists rather than revolutionaries.

Although the anti-colonial activities of the highly and not so highly educated Africans were important in bringing about independence, it should not be thought that they were the only or the most important force involved. Trade unionists, traders, farmers, women, youth movements and other groups were all involved in anti-colonial activities, and the actual process of decolonisation in Africa was closely bound up with anti-colonial struggles in other parts of the world, for example in India and Vietnam.

Since independence, competition for jobs in the civil service and major private companies has intensified, and the pressure for the expansion of secondary and higher education has increased proportionally. The high salaries, job security and prestige of civil service employment and the relative lack of comparable openings in the rest of the economy have guaranteed the popularity of academic as opposed to vocational (technical, manual or agricultural) schools and curricula.

Results of Colonial Education

In this chapter we have looked briefly at the manner in which Western education came to Africa and the motives and activities of the missions, the colonial administrations and the African population. It is no exaggeration to say that the educational systems inherited by African nations at independence have had and continue to have a profound impact on the nature and direction of social change.

The pattern of educational provision which developed during the colonial period was a very uneven one, reflecting the uneven impact of colonialism itself both within and between territories. For example, the enrolment of children of schoolgoing age in 1951 was 18 per cent in Senegal, 15 per cent in Dahomey, 6 per cent in the Ivory Coast and 2 per cent in Upper Volta. The missions themselves must bear part of the responsibility for the uneven distribution of education. In Kenya, for example, 'fierce and unscrupulous competition between the Catholics and Protestants developed in the more populated areas . . . often leaving the less attractive areas relatively uninfluenced' (Anderson, 1970, p. 15). In Nigeria the missions were eager to open schools in the Northern Region but were restrained by the administration. The uneven impact of colonialism and colonial education meant that certain regions and ethnic groups have had an educational headstart over others, and this has been translated into uneven access to positions of power and authority, for example among civil servants, professionals and others who work in the modern sector of the economy – that is, in the modern bureaucracies and business firms which dominate the organisation and control of the economy.

Almost all the 134 degrees awarded by Fourah Bay between 1878 . . . and 1949 went to Creoles, an important factor in the perpetuation of their economic and political dominance. Outside Freetown missionaries concentrated their efforts on the pagan Mende people rather than working among the Islamised tribes to the north. In 1938 eighty per cent of the missionary schools were among the Mende; not surprisingly this group dominated the police, civil service and liberal professions of the Protectorate (the area outside

Freetown), just as the Creoles dominated the Freetown area. (Berman, 1975, pp. 40–1)

Government policies to reduce inequalities of access have generally had little effect, mainly because other interregional and ethnic inequalities (income, cash-crop farming, urbanisation) have continued, and often become more marked. This point is discussed at length in the following chapter, and its political implications are dealt with in Chapter 9.

For similar reasons to those mentioned above, educational inequalities developed between urban and rural areas. For example, primary enrolment in Ghanaian urban areas was 55 per cent in 1960 compared with only 35 per cent in rural areas (Foster, 1965, p. 157). Elsewhere inequalities are much greater than this.

Girls have not benefited as much as boys from the establishment of Western schooling. Colonial administrations and missions were more concerned with the education of males than of females for the simple reason that it was male labour that they required. From the African point of view it was seen as quite normal for pre-colonial sexual inequalities to be perpetuated in the new stratification system introduced by colonialism. This is perhaps the only example of a definite continuity between the old and the new forms of stratification.

The stratification system which colonialism established was based on the Western capitalist model rather than on traditional forms of inequality. Thus local structures of power and authority have given way to those based on control of the state, and new class and status hierarchies have emerged, based on modern sector employment and educational achievement. As the new system of stratification did not grow naturally and gradually out of the old system but was imposed from outside, it is not surprising that the present incumbents of high positions have often been recruited from among the mass of the people rather than (where they existed) from traditional leaders. Even among the traditionally highly stratified Baganda there are a 'large number of men who apparently have risen from relatively humble origins. . . . Contemporary Buganda would appear to be a relatively open society' (Fallers, 1964, p. 199).

Colonial stratification was based on race. With the exception of South Africa and Zimbabwe this racial element has been removed, but the political, social and economic inequalities which developed with colonialism have remained since independence. The relatively open educational system corresponds to a period when Africans have achieved independence and have begun to consolidate their power. In contemporary Africa a relatively open educational system coexists with extremely high and growing levels of social inequality. It is this contradiction which we will attempt to explain in the next chapter.

Questions and Discussion Topics: Chapter 2

1 What arguments would you use to prove that the missionary school was in the long run *either* beneficial *or* harmful to the African population? (Take care to define the population you are talking about.)

2 In what ways did educational provision in the colonial period differ from educational provision today? (You should read the following chapter before answering.)

3 How did the growth of education in the colonial period affect the distribution of educational opportunities, (a) within a given territory and (b) between territories?

4 Discuss the way in which African attitudes towards education changed during the nineteenth and twentieth centuries in an area known to you.

5 'The only thing the British left out of their model was themselves' (Abernethy, 1969, p. 90). How would you relate this statement to the failure of curriculum reform during the colonial period? (See the section on colonial influence in Chapter 6 for help with your answer.)

6 *Project*. You probably do not remember the colonial period but your parents and other older relatives do. From information which you gather from informal discussions with them, attempt to reconstruct the growth of mission and official schooling in your area during the colonial period. You may supplement their oral reports with written evidence, should this exist.

Chapter 3

Education and Social Inequality in Modern Africa

Introduction

In Chapter 2 we outlined the kinds of social stratification which developed in Africa during the colonial period and their educational consequences. Independence brought some modifications to the colonial social structure but much of that structure still remains. The principal change brought about by independence was, of course, that Europeans were replaced by Africans within the political and administrative apparatus of the state. In much of West Africa this process was accomplished relatively smoothly, partly because there existed a considerable pool of educated manpower, at least in the British colonies, which made it easier to Africanise the administration at a rapid rate. We have seen that colonial education policies after the Second World War were adapted to the need to train these administrative cadres. In the French-speaking territories this process had not gone very far by 1960, so that large numbers of French personnel stayed on after independence. Even today these countries are still heavily dependent on French cadres, which is one aspect of neo-colonialism. Ties between France and her ex-colonies have remained strong, but the term neo-colonialism can be applied to most African countries, reflecting their continued dependence on the Western world for technology, investment, aid, markets, manufactured goods and personnel.

The transition to independence was not so smooth elsewhere. The French in Algeria, the Belgians, Portuguese and British in Central, East and Southern Africa were much more reluctant to yield their colonial possessions (South Africa lost its colonial status in 1909), which led to protracted violence and the eventual independence of all but Zimbabwe, which declared unilateral independence (as Rhodesia) under white minority rule in 1965. Low levels of schooling and the unpreparedness of the settler colonies for independence helped make the transition to majority rule problematic in these territories. In the Congo (Zaire), for example, there were virtually no university graduates to take over the higher levels of the administration on independence. The expansion of central administrations since independence and the need for ever larger numbers of technical, medical, educational and so on personnel have meant continued shortages of adequately trained manpower, frequent dependence on expatriate cadres and the rapid growth of the educated elite. We will be looking at the educational consequences of this in the coming pages.

Many writers have argued that the new administrations have not altered in any radical way the colonial structures which they inherited, with the result that a black elite has simply replaced a white elite, taking over the powers and privileges of the latter and even expanding them:

> Government employees . . . take up to eighty per cent of the national budget to provide services often of more benefit to themselves than to the population. . . . Free secondary schooling benefits their children most, as they are likely to do well on entrance examinations to the best schools; they have easy access to agricultural extension advice . . . ; they can organise contracts for their trading wives and jobs for their duller children; they get subsidised housing and car allowances and secure pensions, yet they pay relatively low taxes. In return, they are often slow to respond to public demands and concerned largely with furthering their own interests and the status quo; the state as established at independence suits their purposes very well. (Peil, 1977, p. 100)

'Inherited' would be a better word than 'established'. The relationship between educational achievement and elite membership will be examined in this chapter.

Despite attempts by some governments to reduce or eradicate social and economic inequalities between classes, regions and ethnic groups, such inequalities still remain and are sometimes greater than they were during the colonial period. Economic growth is often concentrated around a single town or area; villages often fall behind the towns in terms of income and access to social services like education, housing, health and water supply. By international standards most African countries are very poor, but their poverty is not shared equally by all citizens. Great wealth and great poverty exist side by side, and the gap between rich and poor is as wide as anywhere else in the world. Inequalities of wealth and power are reflected in educational inequalities although there is by no means a one-to-one relationship. In general, however, high levels of social inequality are accompanied by high levels of inequality within the education system. This is a major premise of the sociology of education and the principal theme of this chapter.

Educational Inequality Defined

There are a number of kinds of educational inequality:

(1) Not all children have the same chance of going to school. This we call unequal *access* to schooling.

(2) There are wide differences in *performance* between children. Some drop out before completing primary school, others have to repeat classes, the majority of candidates fail the secondary entrance examinations.

(3) Within the education system there are different streams which can be followed leading to a variety of qualifications and possible occupations. These streams may be officially equal but are generally considered to be unequal. For example, in Africa, technical education is generally considered to be inferior to academic education.

(4) Schools and colleges which are theoretically equal (following the same syllabus and leading to the same qualifications) vary widely in *status*, *quality* and the *market value of the qualification obtained*. Thus private schools may be of a higher or lower quality than government schools, places in high-status schools will be more difficult to obtain than places in low-status schools, and the qualifications earned from the best-known schools, colleges and universities may be more marketable than the same qualifications earned elsewhere.

When looking at the question of educational inequality these various dimensions of schooling must all be borne in mind. Systematic relationships exist between the four groups of variables listed above, and we will be looking at some of the most important of these in the following pages.

The question of what causes the inequalities listed above is the main concern of this chapter. Such factors as class background, race, sex, ethnicity, culture, religion, region, birthplace and intelligence will all be considered, as well as some of the interrelationships between these factors. We must also attempt to explain the ways in which these factors influence educational inequalities. The three main ways in which this happens are through:

(1) *Material factors*. For example, the availability of funds from parents and other family members will affect such things as the quality of school attended, the number of children in a family who get sent to school, the likelihood of attending private secondary school, the number of books which a pupil possesses and the employment of a private tutor. Material considerations also affect the amount of housework or productive labour which a child performs.

(2) *Motivations and aspirations*. Not all parents and students are equally highly motivated as regards schooling. This may or may not reflect material factors.

(3) *Cultural factors*. Irrespective of parents' financial means and educational aspirations for their children, the culture of home and community affect educational chances. For example, parents' command of the language of schooling may have an effect on school performance.

We should not take it for granted that, for example, social background affects school enrolment and performance but look into the possible *intervening* factors (above) which explain the relationships between these two.

Figure 3.1 summarises some of the major variables mentioned above and may be useful to the reader in ordering the relationships between the groups of variables involved in the processes of educational selection. The factors listed under the four headings should not be thought of as acting independently of one another; in practice there are complex interactions between the different factors, and we will be pointing out many of these in subsequent sections.

Any basic cause of educational inequalities (I in the figure) will be expressed in terms of one or more of the factors under II. I and II combine to bring about enrolment and performance variations (III) within the various types and levels of education (IV). In the following pages we will be looking at the major dependent variables (III and IV) in terms of the independent and intervening variables (I and II).

Other major themes of this chapter are the relationship between educational and occupational achievement, the effects of educational expansion on educational opportunities and inequalities, and the relationship between changes in the educational and the social structures. Some observers argue that a distinct class structure is emerging in Africa with the result that access to and performance in education is increasingly a reflection of class background. Others argue that, by Western standards, education continues to be relatively accessible to all, reflecting a rather open stratification system (excluding South Africa) in which long-distance social mobility is still a regular occurrence. To conclude the chapter we will examine the possibility of education playing an independent role in shaping the stratification system.

Access to Schooling

In the industrially advanced countries virtually everyone goes to primary and secondary school, and over recent years there have been considerable increases in post-secondary enrolment levels. In the USA about one in two young adults receives some kind of higher education. By contrast, no African country has yet achieved one hundred per cent primary enrolment, although serious efforts are being made in this direction, for example in Nigeria and Tanzania. In many countries rapid population growth, lack of resources, parental resistance or poverty and high dropout rates make universal primary education an extremely distant prospect indeed. In the African context, therefore, it is essential to distinguish between those who have access to schooling and those who do not.

On its own, a primary education is now almost useless for obtaining paid employment of any kind, but it is important as a first step up the educational ladder. In other words, the availability of primary education is an important precondition for further educational and occupational success.

As we have pointed out in Chapter 2, the uneven impact of colonialism both between and within territories resulted in the uneven distribution of schooling. Despite a general growth of enrolment since independence these inequalities are often still considerable. We may consider the major dimensions of unequal access in turn.

Ethnic and Regional Inequalities

There are wide variations in the availability of schooling between regions and between ethnic groups. There is nothing special about regions and ethnic groups *per se* to account for these variations; rather they redlect social and economic factors such as occupational structure and income which themselves vary between regions and ethnic groups. These variations reflect differential penetration by colonialism as measured by the level of urbanisation, cash-crop production, the growth of trade and the exchange economy, employment opportunities and so on. Such factors affected and continue to affect the level of provision of schooling by missions and government (and businessmen) and the level of demand for schooling among local populations. They also affect the ability of parents to pay school fees for their children and to build and run schools on their own initiative.

The demand for and supply of primary schooling tend to be low in areas and among ethnic groups with any of the following characteristics: low population density; predominance of subsistence farming, pastoralism or migrant labour; poor communications; absence of non-farming activ ties. For example, only about 5 per cent of school-age children are enrolled in primary school in the North Eastern Province of Kenya, an arid area inhabited mostly by a low-density population of pastoralists. In West Africa the northern regions of the coastal countries and most of the countries of the sahel also tend to exhibit the characteristics listed above. It is unlikely that the people living in these and similar areas will be able to overcome the social and economic

I

Dimension of Inequality

Class background
Ethnicity
Region
Culture
Religion
Urban/rural
birthplace
Sex
Race
Ability

Independent variables ⟶

II

Mode of Operation

Material factors
Motivations and
aspirations
Cultural
environment

Intervening variables ⟶

III

Enrolment and Performance Variations

Percentage of age-group going to school
Dropout rate
Repeating rate
Starting age
Examination performance
Passage to next educational level

within:

IV

Educational Type and Level

Pre-primary, primary, middle, secondary,
teacher training, higher
Academic, vocational, technical
Short/long course
High/low quality
Grammar/modern
Public/private

Dependent variables

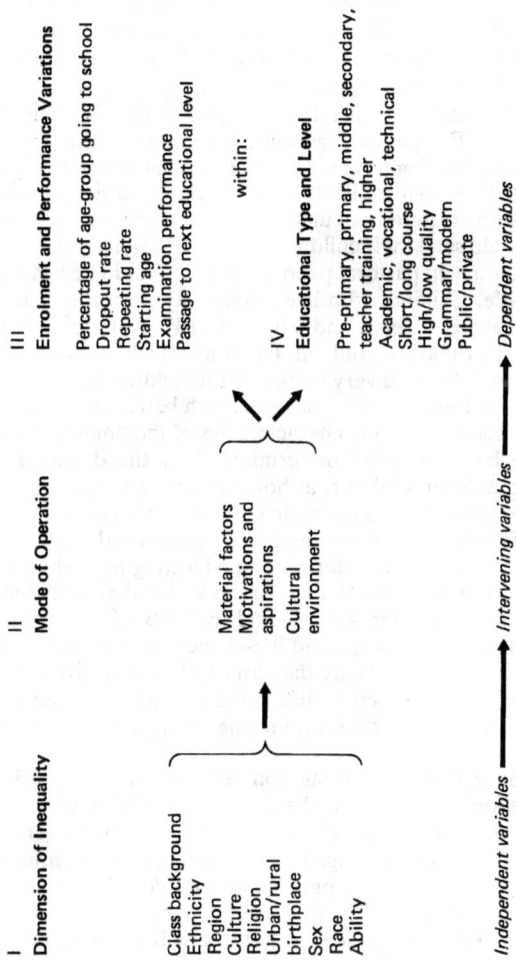

Figure 3.1   *Variables involved in the analysis of educational inequalities*

disadvantages which they face, and equally unlikely that they will be able to catch up their more prosperous and fortunate neigbours. Such poor countries and areas are likely to continue to serve as sources of unskilled and uneducated migrant labour (seasonal or permanent) for the more prosperous countries and areas.

Ethnic prejudices and conflicts reflect unequal access to resources, including education. For political reasons, governments often try to overcome ethnic/regional enrolment inequalities, but generally without much success (see Chapter 9). It is extremely expensive to build and staff schools for scattered populations and to convince poor parents that they should send their children to school. It is difficult to see how schooling could help pastoral peoples or how it could be adapted to their way of life. Children who live a long way from the nearest school are prone to absenteeism and fatigue. C. Elliott (1975, p. 230) quotes a study of primary schools in Tanzania which 'showed that attendance at school declined very markedly for children more than a mile from school and that absenteeism was much better explained by distance than by socio-economic characteristics of the home'. School attendance may be interrupted or terminated by the demands of parents for their children's labour, at home or in the fields.

All these problems show how misleading it is to talk of tribal attitudes towards education. We should try to go beyond such statements as 'those people are not interested in educating their children' and find out why, if others consider education such a desirable thing, this should be the case. Often we will find that lack of interest is a reflection of economic conditions and life-chances which themselves affect values and attitudes. Usually the latter reflect objective conditions (productive activities open to different ethnic groups, their participation in modern sector activities, income levels) rather than the other way round.

In some poor agricultural areas soil exhaustion, overgrazing, drought, population increases and the economic exploitation of the inhabitants by governments and private interests have led to a general decline in living standards and stagnant or declining levels of primary enrolment. As long as socio-economic conditions do not improve in these poor areas, parents are likely to continue to be unwilling or unable to send their children to school. Studies by Blakemore (1975) and Hinchcliffe (1970) have documented declining enrolment levels in some areas of Ghana and Nigeria as parents become discouraged by the lack of returns relative to their sacrifice in sending their children to school. Government exhortations to parents to enrol their children are unlikely to be successful in such circumstances. The political aspects of enrolment inequalities are examined in Chapter 9.

Religious and cultural variations are often related to regional and ethnic factors, so that access to primary education often varies with religion and culture. But, as with region and ethnicity, it does not seem that culture and religion play an important part in determining school enrolment. It is often maintained that Muslim parents are reluctant to send their children to non-Koranic schools for fear that they will be converted to Christianity and reject traditional values. The association between Western education and Christianity stems, of course, from the activities of missionary bodies, so that the gradual replacement of Christian mission education by secular government-provided schooling has removed the religious misgivings of many Muslim parents. Also, the low level of schooling in predominantly Muslim areas such as Northern Nigeria reflects the policies of the colonial governments rather than the hostility of Muslim parents.

There is evidence that Muslims are not unreceptive to Western education but respond like almost any other group when the benefits of schooling are demonstrated and schooling made available. For example, when universal primary education (UPE) was first attempted in the old Western Region of Nigeria overall enrolment in the region increased by 78 per cent between 1954 and 1955, but in Abeokuta, Ibadan and Oyo, the three divisions with the highest Muslim population, the increase was 110 per cent (Abernethy, 1969). Attitudes towards the education of girls may be more important than religious values *per se* in accounting for low enrolment rates among Muslims, but it does not seem that Muslim parents are more hostile to girls' education than any other group (see below). Overall historical factors associated with religion and culture explain enrolment variations better than more or less imaginary resistance to modern schooling.

Urban/Rural Inequalities

There is an important overlap between the factors described above and urban/rural inequalities of access to schooling. This reflects the fact that there is generally a higher degree of urbanisation in areas of intensive colonial activity (administration, commerce, industry) than in other areas. The ports established along the West African coast are a case in point. Nevertheless, the urban/rural dimension of access to schooling is an important independent cause of educational inequalities. With some exceptions, urban primary enrolment levels are generally higher than those in surrounding rural areas. (At a national level, of course, rural enrolment levels in the advanced regions may be higher than the urban levels in the backward areas.) Many children migrate to urban areas for their primary schooling. Cooksey (1978) found that one-third of Class 6 pupils in Yaounde (Cameroun) had migrated from villages. The search for improved educational opportunities is a major cause of rural–urban migration.

Population density is an important factor explaining urban/rural enrolment inequalities: it is easier to build and staff schools to cater for a concentrated urban population than a scattered rural one. In some cash-crop areas with a long tradition of colonial mission contacts every village has its school(s), but elsewhere this is by no means the case. Having to run ten miles to school and back may be good for training future long-distance running champions, but not so good for academic performance. Inequalities between enrolment levels in different rural areas are, therefore, as important as urban/rural inequalities themselves.

Up to a point, urban/rural enrolment inequalities reflect economic inequalities between town and village. On average, farming parents are poorer and use their children's labour more than urban parents. Some would argue that this is because rural areas are exploited by towns. Much of the value of cash crops, it is argued, is syphoned off by marketing boards and traders, co-operatives and import-export companies which are based in the towns (as well as multinational companies based abroad). Part of this value is spent or invested in the towns and thus does not benefit the farmer. In Ghana the enormous amounts of money accumulated from cocoa sales during the late colonial period were used to finance the development programme after independence, and this consisted largely of industrial rather than agricultural projects. Many governments are heavily dependent on their marketing boards to balance their budgets, and a large proportion of government spending consists of civil servants' salaries.

But only a relatively small number of people benefit directly from the exploitation of peasant farmers, so it is not accurate to think of all urban residents as taking advantage of all farmers. Many urban workers are as poor as or poorer than farmers from surrounding villages, and the educational effects of this will become clear in due course.

Also, it is not accurate to think of farmers, even in one locality, as constituting an homogeneous group. Large-scale cash-crop farmers employing labourers, sharecroppers working on someone else's land and subsistence farmers in remote and impoverished areas are all farmers. Some wealthy urban residents are also farmers in the sense that they invest their savings in cash-crop agriculture. Big farmers may form an influential group capable of protecting their interests by securing inflated prices for their products by lobbying the government. They may also benefit disproportionately from government loans and credit schemes and from extension services. In these cases the farmer may exploit the consumers, most of whom are resident in urban areas. But the former case – where small farmers are taken advantage of by public and private interests in the urban areas – is much more common. In our discussion of educational inequalities it is important to bear in mind economic differences both within and between urban and rural populations.

As in the case of ethnic and regional enrolment variations we must conclude that urban/rural variations reflect social and economic forces, especially occupation and income. The operation of these forces is hidden by average figures for enrolment levels in different regions and urban and rural areas. Migration patterns also complicate the picture. For example, it was clear from our Yaounde sample that wealthier farmers were prepared to send their children over long distances to attend urban primary schools. Twice as many Class 6 pupils were from large as from small farming backgrounds. Having close relatives in town with whom one can stay and who can help with school fees, and so on, is clearly an advantage. In Yaounde, over three-quarters of farmers' children were living with their aunts and uncles or older brothers and sisters, compared with only a quarter of the whole sample.

When we come to study secondary enrolment variations the importance of differentiations among farmers will become more evident.

Sex

Throughout the world females are the victims of educational inequalities. This is not an isolated phenomenon but directly reflects the monopoly or semi-monopoly which men enjoy in the higher levels of the economy and the polity. It is common in Africa for sons to receive education before daughters and for the latter to catch up only as schooling becomes universal for boys. Even then, considerable inequalities of enrolment are common at the post-primary level.

Up to a point, the underenrolment of girls reflects previously mentioned determinants of school access. For example, it is in the rural areas that the largest gaps between male and female enrolment levels are to be found. This sometimes reflects the sexual division of labour in the village. Overall, young girls' labour is more essential than young boys', both in domestic chores (cooking, baby-minding, water-carrying) and (sometimes) in agriculture. Also, if education is looked on as an investment, it makes more sense to invest in the education of boys who, in the long run, have the best occupational openings. In his study of village polytechnic leavers in Kenya, Court (1974, p. 93) found that 'of those who were receiving no money for work at the time of the investigation, the majority were girls, and almost all are engaged in virtually full-time farm work'.

It is sometimes said that Muslim parents are particularly reluctant, for cultural and religious reasons, to send their daughters to school. There is no proof, however, that Muslim parents are any more reluctant than other parents in areas of general low enrolment to send their daughters to school. In a study of Hausa parents in northern Nigeria, Hake (1970) found that over half of those interviewed were in favour of education for their daughters, even though more than two-thirds of the sample said that the attitude of girls towards their parents changes for the worse after primary education. Findings by Blakemore (1975) and Dubbeldam (1970) also show that Muslim parents are as concerned with the education of their daughters as any other parents, if not more so. In Mwanza Region in Tanzania, for example, 46 per cent of Muslim children attending primary school (Standards I to IV) were girls, compared with only 35 per cent of Protestant and Catholic children (Dubbeldam, 1970, p. 41). Thus, although Islam does not favour the emancipation of women, it does not seem to add to the already considerable handicaps from which girls suffer, particularly in rural areas with low overall levels of enrolment.

As primary enrolment levels expand so girls tend to catch up with boys. In the case of southern Nigeria Abernethy (1969, p. 238) tells us that

> UPE [universal primary education] gave a fillip to the education of young girls, who had traditionally been regarded by Nigerian parents as less suited for academic pursuits than boys. In the West, female enrollment in Primary One rose by 374 percent from 1954 to 1955 as compared with a 184 percent rise among the males; for the primary course as a whole girls accounted for twenty-five percent of total enrollment in 1954 and thirty-four percent the following year. That proportion rose steadily . . . after the introduction of UPE, reaching forty-one percent by 1965. That an educated girl could command a higher brideprice than an illiterate one probably influenced the decision of many parents to let their daughters attend school. Whether the trend towards sexual equality in education would continue in view of massive unemployment among school leavers, however, remains an open question.

In our Yaounde sample there were more girls than boys attending Class 6 and sitting the secondary school entrance examination. Overall, however, in most parts of Africa sexual equality is far from being achieved, as we will see in relation to secondary and higher enrolment.

Class Background

In many ways, the first two sets of factors mentioned above could be discussed under the heading of class influences on enrolment, since regions and ethnic groups and urban and rural areas have different class compositions. For example, professional and administrative cadres are found almost exclusively in urban areas, cash-crop farming and migrant labour areas tend to be distinct and certain ethnic groups are often specialised in such activities as trade, pastoralism, white-collar work, and so on. Thus there exist complex overlaps between class, region, ethnicity and urban/rural residence.

Parental income, occupation and education are extremely important determinants of school enrolment at all levels. It will be remembered that we previously defined class in terms of both occupation and property ownership. Property is concentrated in the hands of rich farmers, big traders and businessmen and top professionals, politicians and civil servants. This classification cuts across urban/rural, ethnic and regional boundaries, but in practice there tend to be concentrations of wealth in some regions and in urban areas. From the point of view of educational opportunities, income from property has the same significance as income from employment: it permits parents to assure their children's schooling, buy their school uniforms and books, provide them with adequate housing and food and private tuition when necessary, and to dispense with the labour of their children. High-quality private education, from nursery level upwards, is used disproportionately by the children of the better-off classes. The best quality post-primary education is usually paid for out of government revenue, so that wealthy parents, whose children are more likely than others to make use of secondary and higher education, benefit more than other parents from state subsidies.

Poorer parents can often only afford to educate some of their children, even when education is free. They may decide to send their sons rather than heir daughters to school, or the youngest and oldest children rather than those in between. Unfortunately we know very little about how the decision is made to send a child to school, which child to send from any one family and whether or not to keep a particular child at school. The charging of school fees is a definite handicap to the education of the children of poor parents. Abernethy (1969, p. 356) shows that the reintroduction of fees in the old Eastern Region of Nigeria led to widespread popular protest and a fall of one-third in enrolment levels between Class 4 and Class 5. In Ghana, overall enrolments in primary school fell by 100,000 the year fees were reintroduced (Peil, 1977, p. 195). Thus, where fees are charged at primary school, parental income will be a major determinant of attendance rates.

There is considerable evidence that pupils in regions of low-average enrolment levels tend to be from above-average class backgrounds. This means that in localities where not all children go to school it will be the children of the better-off parents (richer farmers, for example) who will be overrepresented in the schools (Dubbeldam, 1970). In predominantly rural areas, children whose parents have above-average levels of education and who practise non-agricultural occupations tend to be overrepresented in primary school. This is especially true among girls (Mbilinyi, 1973).

There is evidence that the community itself has a somewhat independent effect on enrolment rates. This means that in a community with a high level of primary enrolment even the children of the poorer and lower occupational groups will attend school through the demonstration effect of other children, whereas they would be unlikely to do so if enrolment levels were low. Thus children of a given (low) socio-economic background will be more or less likely to attend school according to the average for the local community.

Thus income levels are not the only determinants of educational inequalities at the primary school. In fact, parental education is a better predictor of educational achievement than either income or occupation. Parental occupation cannot be reduced to these two factors, even though there is a large degree of overlap.

We will have much more to say about the effects of occupational differences between parents on enrolment and performance variations among their children. The occupational classification we use distinguishes between farmers of different kinds and urban occupations, and within the latter we distinguish between different groups of manual, white-collar and commercial occupations. In part, occupation (usually of father) is used as a substitute for income, but it also reflects important non-economic factors such as parental ability to effect educational success through encouragement, the use of English or French in the home, provision of supplementary reading materials, and so on. These cultural factors are of great importance in relation to educational opportunities.

Race
Race is of particular importance in relation to educational inequalities in Southern Africa and Zimbabwe. In these parts of Africa educational provision follows a strict racial pattern, with white children being favoured at the expense of other groups, namely Asians, coloureds (mixed race) and Africans. According to official statistics, in 1969 the South African government spent 282 rand on the education of each white child compared with 81 rand on an Indian, 73 rand on a coloured and only 17 rand on an African child (Troup, 1976, p. 31). The practice of apartheid, which keeps the mass of the African population economically exploited, politically subordinate and socially marginal, is directly reflected in educational practice. The following quotation sums up the Zimbabwe-Rhodesia situation:

> Education is segregated, with separate schools for each racial group. . . . There are two separate education departments, one for Africans and one for Asians, Coloureds and Whites. . . . Whereas education is compulsory for white children and the fees relatively low, it is not enforced for Africans, whose parents in any case may find the fees prohibitive. In 1976, over half of Zimbabwe's black population of 6·6 million were under the age of 15, yet only 846,260

of them were in primary school. More than half of all black children admitted to school drop out before completing their primary education, and only a tiny fraction, around 0·5 percent, reach the sixth form. The regime spends over ten times as much on the education of a European child as on an African. . . . African schools are overcrowded and the teachers are far less qualified than their white counterparts. (International Defence and Aid Fund for Southern Africa, 1978, p. 22)

To the extent that racial inequalities are also economic inequalities, there is a large overlap between race and class. But race cannot be reduced to class; it has an important independent effect on life-chances and educational opportunities.

Performance in Primary School

Access to primary schooling is the main determinant of overall educational chances. Once a child enters primary school it is performance which determines his or her progress. In performance we include dropout and repeat rates as well as examination results.

Where access to primary schooling is low, dropout rates tend to be high, and vice versa. High dropout rates are thus an important determinant of enrolment levels. We may take an example from Cameroun, where north/south enrolment inequalities are high. In the Northern Province only 22 per cent of 6- to 14-year-olds attended primary school in 1967, and the dropout rate between Forms 1 and 2 was no less than 65 per cent. By contrast, in the Centre-South Province the enrolment level was 86 per cent and only 6 per cent dropped out between Forms 1 and 2 (Labrousse, 1970).

In areas where education is well established and has become a normal part of a child's life and the community's culture, dropping out during primary school is an infrequent occurrence, though repeating classes may be quite common. Dropout rates tend to be highest among girls, in rural areas and in areas of recent educational expansion. Similar reasons explain low enrolment and high dropout rates: poverty, language and cultural gaps beteen the home and the school, alternative demands on pupils' time. High dropout rates also reflect certain school characteristics such as poor teaching and supervision, lack of chalk and textbooks, substandard schoolbuildings and overcrowded classes. These factors are generally associated with recent and rapid educational expansion (UPE programmes, for example) and schooling in more remote/rural areas. Unfortunately we have no detailed study of how children drop out of school and the importance of the various causes of wastage. High dropout and repeating rates have been cited as causes of the high cost and inefficiency of primary

been cited as causes of the high cost and inefficiency of primary
education in Africa. From our perspective, they constitute important
educational inequalities and obstacles to the goal of universal education.

The major hurdle for those fortunate enough to finish primary
school is, of course, the secondary school entrance examination. Failure in this examination (and most pupils fail) generally means the end
of formal schooling and a drastic limitation of life-chances. When
enrolment levels are low and dropout rates high only the most intelligent children or those from above-average socio-economic backgrounds manage to reach the end of primary school, and such children
stand a good chance of progressing to secondary education. In areas of
high enrolment, however, children of different levels of ability and
from the whole range of social backgrounds reach the end of primary
schooling, and many of these will fail to obtain secondary school places
through the competitive examination. In this case, ability and class
background are reflected in examination marks rather than in dropout
rates.

In his Ugandan study, Heyneman (1976) found that primary school
leaving examination pass rates were higher in rural than in urban areas,
and higher in areas with low population-density and poor communications than in areas with high population-density and good communications. Children from underrepresented ethnic groups outperformed
their more favoured neighbours. Intelligence, sex and the teachers'
level of English were the factors most closely related to variations in
performance, not social background or birthplace. These findings do
not, of course, contradict our remarks concerning the importance of
social factors in determining educational inequalities, nor do they
prove that educational opportunities are more widespread in Uganda
than elsewhere. Heyneman has no information on class background,
but it is nevertheless fairly clear that it is mainly the able children who
manage to survive the primary course in areas of low overall enrolment, and children from often atypicallt high social backgrounds who
go to school in these areas in the first place.

Our own study of Yaounde primary-leavers demonstrates that
where enrolment levels are high and dropout levels low, family background will have a very marked effect on examination performance
(see Table 3.1).

Children from professional and higher administrative backgrounds
outperform all others, those from large commercial and business backgrounds outperform those from petty trader families and the children
of skilled workers do better than those of semi- and unskilled workers.
The latter are noticeably unsuccessful in the exam, even though many
of them were born or brought up in town. The children of small farmers
outperform those of large farmers, which indicates that only the most
able children from small farming backgrounds sit the exam.

Table 3.1 Secondary Entrance Examination Pass Rates by Occupational Background for Yaounde Class 6 Pupils (Percentages)

Fathers' occupation		Pass Rate (%)
Elite		34
Other white-collar		18
Large trader		28
Small trader		19
Skilled manual worker		16
Semi-skilled manual worker		12
Unskilled manual worker		0
Large farmer		15
Small farmer		22
	Average	21
	N	1345

Source: Cooksey (1978, p. 126).

Parental occupation and education were the two major determinants of secondary school access in our urban sample, followed by sex. There were more girls than boys among those taking the exam, but overall the boys outperformed the girls. But sex was closely related to social background: girls from farming backgrounds performed very badly, whereas girls from elite and large trading families had higher pass rates than all the boys. In this case the disadvantage of being a girl was outweighed by the advantage of coming from a privileged background. Factors such as birthplace and ethnicity had very little independent effect on performance.

One final important factor affecting performance is the rate of repeating Class 6. The pass rate of repeaters was over twice that of non-repeaters (34 as opposed to 16 per cent), and repeating helped candidates from the intermediate and lower occupational groups more than the more privileged children. Heyneman also found that repeating Class 6 once helped performance, and Somerset (1974, p. 177) found that 12 per cent of non-repeaters obtained places in government secondary schools compared with no less than 50 per cent of repeaters. Neither author links repeat rates with occupational background, however.

The implications of the above description are quite clear: if all those who started primary school finished the course family background would be decisive in determining the pattern of secondary school entrance, through its effect on examination performance. As enrolment levels still vary widely within any given country, differential access to schooling and differential dropout rates still play an important part in relation to educational opportunities.

Educational Growth and Equality of Opportunity

What difference does educational expansion make to overall educational inequalities? It is often assumed that the expansion of schooling leads to greater equality of opportunity among children of schoolgoing age. It seems reasonable that as education becomes more widely available the effect will be to reduce overall inequalities between regions, social classes, urban and rural areas, and so on. This in turn may lead to greater equality of occupational opportunities. There are a number of objections to this line of reasoning.

First, as long as educational facilities expand more rapidly than job openings for school-leavers (as is usually the case) the net effect of expansion will be to devalue qualifications received from schooling. This is clearly what has happened in both the developed and underdeveloped countries. University graduates in the USA, Britain and India are forced to accept semi-routine white-collar work and many PhD holders are either unemployed or working in jobs which once would have been considered too lowly for those with such lofty qualifications. In Africa, the university graduate is still almost sure to find satisfactory employment, but this is much less true at lower levels. Primary expansion leads to the devaluation of the primary leaving certificate, so that without secondary education a young boy or girl stands little chance of finding paid employment. Thus the growth of schooling has the effect of raising the level at which selection takes place (from primary to secondary), but does not eliminate selection. Consequently, children from wealthy, urban or literate backgrounds will continue to have better educational opportunities than children from poorer, rural and illiterate backgrounds. The growth of primary schooling *per se* is unlikely to help many of the disadvantaged children, although it will have the important effect of incorporating them, at least temporarily, into the education system. While primary schooling is expanding in the backward areas, secondary schooling is expanding in the advanced areas. Parents and pupils in the advanced areas are hardly likely to stop to wait for the rest to catch up with them.

Secondly, there is little evidence to support the argument that enrolment inequalities are bound to decrease with time. If the educationally advanced areas have more or less reached UPE, and if enrolment ratios continue to rise in the educationally backward areas, then by definition educational inequalities at the primary level are bound to fall. But there is no inevitability about this process. Both the national resources to provide schooling and levels of parental demand for it may be inadequate to eliminate inequalities. Relatively wealthy countries like Nigeria seem to have the resources to provide UPE, but many poorer countries do not. Schools can always be constructed cheaply, using local materials and labour, but teachers have to be paid, and their salaries constitute a relatively heavier burden on national resources than is the case in wealthier countries. High dropout and repeat rates increase the cost per pupil of education in the backward areas. Thus poverty on the national level makes it unlikely that the poorer African countries will be able to eliminate inequalities of access to primary education in the foreseeable future.

There are also problems on the demand side, for poor parents may neither desire nor be able to afford education for their children. We have already indicated why this should be the case. In the final analysis, educational inequalities reflect economic and social inequalities between classes, regions, ethnic groups, and so on, and these are extremely difficult to eliminate. There is plenty of evidence that in Africa economic inequalities increase over time rather than decrease; in which case it is difficult to see how overall educational inequalities could fail to do the same.

Lastly, we may mention population growth as a factor inhibiting the spread of educational opportunities. Compared with the developed countries Africa has a very young population, and the 15-year-olds and under often constitute the majority. Rapid population growth puts an increasing burden on the productive members of society, that is, those who produce the wealth to support the others. Full-time education consumes resources and reduces the amount of productive activity among the population. Thus population growth and educational expansion together constitute an increasing burden on society. In many African countries enrolment ratios (the percentage of the school-age population attending school) are actually falling, even though the total number of children going to school continues to rise. If the population of 5-year-olds in a country rises by 2·5 per cent per year (not high by African standards), then every year the government will have to provide 2·5 per cent more school places just in order to keep the enrolment ratio from falling. Official statistics of absolute enrolment levels should be read bearing population growth in mind. (Official statistics are often highly inflated and should not be taken too literally). Percentage increases in regional enrolment levels can also be confusing, for large percentage increases in enrolment may be paltry in absolute terms, and vice versa.

From the above discussion we may conclude that the reduction of educational inequalities through the expansion of primary schooling is highly problematic (evidence from secondary and higher education will be looked at in due course). This is because of high population growth, the devaluation of diplomas, unequal access to post-primary education and the continuation of mass poverty and unequal growth.

Enrolment and Performance at Secondary School

When we look at secondary school students in Africa we should not forget that we are dealing with a very small proportion of the total secondary schoolgoing age-group. When we add together the number of children who never go to school, the number who fail to complete primary school and the number who, through examination failure and/or lack of funds, fail to obtain secondary school places we inevitably account for the overwhelming majority of children in any African country. Why should we ignore the majority, the failures, and study only the fortunate few, as Clignet and Foster (1966) have called secondary students (and, even more fortunate, the handful who go to university)?

We personally feel that not enough attention is paid to those young people who are to be found outside the formal education system. There are too few studies of informal training and apprenticeships compared with the number of studies of secondary school and university students. It is, of course, much easier to count and question full-time students than those outside the education system. It is also easier to deal with secondary and university students than with primary pupils: there are fewer of them, they are more concentrated in urban areas and they can more easily understand and fill in questionnaires in a foreign language. These factors explain research biases, but do not justify them.

Students at the secondary and university levels are important, of course. All or most of a nation's medium- and high-level manpower passes through secondary school and higher education. This group also exercises much of the political power within the nation and adopts cultural, normative and consumption patterns which have important consequences for society in general and its development. In other words, the educated minority have an importance much greater than their numbers.

Recruitment Patterns
As secondary students are found in more manageable numbers than primary pupils, it is easier to get a reasonable idea of overall patterns of selectivity within a nation in terms of the main types of inequality we have been dealing with so far. As well as looking at the students we must also consider the types and quality of schooling available to them. For the point of view of general employment opportunities and life-chances, which school you attend is a matter of great importance.

From our previous discussion it will be fairly obvious that secondary students are atypical of the population in general. By population we may mean the population of children in the relevant age-group, the population of adults (parents) or the whole population of the country in question, including its regional and ethnic composition. If we state, for example, that farmers' children are underrepresented in secondary school we mean that there are proportionally fewer farmers' children in the secondary school population than there are farmers in the adult population. We may quantify this by using a *selectivity index*. Taking the above example, this is the proportion of farmers' children among secondary school students divided by the proportion of farmers in the total population. If the former is 50 per cent and the latter 75 per cent then the selectivity index is (50÷75=0·66). A selectivity index of less than 1·0 indicates underrepresentation and an index of more than 1·0 indicates overrepresentation. This index is of some use as a rough guide to patterns of selection.

Studies of secondary enrolment patterns often concentrate on the question of which social classes are over- and underrepresented in the schools. Within the urban context, whose children are the most successful? How do urban and rural classes compare? As these questions take us to the centre of the urban/rural and the class dimensions of inequality, we may conveniently begin our discussion here. The major secondary school studies are now somewhat dated, but are quite adequate for present purposes. We will discuss trends over time in a subsequent section.

Invariably, studies of secondary school enrolment have shown that there is a 'very definite association between parental occupational characteristics and access to secondary schools' (Foster, 1963, p. 158). The children of higher professional and administrative cadres are more highly represented in the school system than any other group, and the children of farmers are among the most underrepresented. This is what we would expect on the basis of our discussion of the factors affecting primary enrolment and performance inequalities. By way of illustration we may look at Foster's sample of Ghanaian fifth-formers attending state academic secondary schools (see Table 3.2 overleaf). Abernethy (1969, p. 245) found a very similar pattern in southern Nigeria.

The most underrepresented group were the children of semi- and unskilled workers, which was also what we found in Yaounde. The children of traders and businessmen were overrepresented, but less so than the children of professional and administrative workers. The latter were, proportionally speaking, eleven times more numerous than the children of farmers and fishermen. The occupational breakdown is not very exact, however, and fails to show the whole picture. For example, the first occupational group includes all civil servants from the permanent secretary down to the most humble clerk, and the farmers' group includes large- and small-scale cash-crop farmers, sharecroppers and subsistence farmers. It is also useful to divide the business group into large and petty traders. Hurd and Johnson's sample of Ghanaian sixth-formers (1967) breaks down the professional and white-collar group in Table 3.3.

Table 3.2   Parental Occupation of Academic Secondary School Students and Occupational Characteristics of the Ghanaian Male Population (Percentages)

Occupational group	Percentage of male labour force	Students' parental occupation	Selectivity index
Professional, higher technical, administrative and clerical	6·9	40·3	5·7
Private traders and businessmen	3·8	10·3	2·7
Skilled workers and artisans	11·8	12·1	1·0
Semi- and unskilled workers	13·4	1·5	0·1
Farmers and fishermen	62·8	32·5	0·5
Others, no answer, don't know	1·3	3·3	0·5
Total	100·0	100·0	

Source: Adapted from Foster (1963, p. 159).

If we only consider the first four categories in Table 3.3 (administrative to lower professional) we find that 3·7 per cent of the male population provided 45·9 per cent of the sixth-formers, and that the remainder of the population (96·3 per cent) provided the remaining 54·1 per cent, giving selectivity indexes of 12·4 and 0·56 respectively. Thus, sixth-formers with fathers in the top white-collar grades are extremely overrepresented compared with other students.

Hurd and Johnson also break down the farmer category into cocoa farmers and others. In their sample fully 69 per cent of farmers' children were from cocoa farming backgrounds (selectivity index of 4·7), and the remaining farmers' children were highly underrepresented (index of 0·17). In Ghana, cocoa farmers are concentrated in the southern and central regions of the country, so that the selectivity pattern for farmers' children shown above reflects distinct regional inequalities in types of farming activity and income. It has been calculated that the top 5 per cent of Ghanaian farmers earned one-third of total farming income in 1971, whereas the bottom 38 per cent earned only 7 per cent (Ewusi, 1971, p. 75).

These tables tell us that both urban and rural stratification patterns are extremely important determinants of enrolment inequalities in secondary school. Parental education, which is closely related to occupation, is also strongly related to enrolment variations. For example,

**Table 3.3   Sixth-Form Representation within the Ghanaian Profes-
sional and White-Collar Group (Percentages)**

Fathers' occupational subgroup	Male working population 1960	Fathers of sixth-formers 1964	Selectivity index
Administrative, executive, managerial	0·3	15·9	53·0
Higher professional	0·5	11·1	22·2
Supervisory	0·6	9·3	15·5
Lower professional	2·3	9·6	4·2
White-collar, non-clerical	0·5	3·2	6·4
White-collar, clerical	2·7	5·9	2·2
Subtotal:	6·9	55·0	8·0
Other occupational groups	93·1	45·0	0·5
Total:	100·0	100·0	

Source: Hurd and Johnson (1967, p. 72).
* Figures in this column were reached by dividing those in first column into those in second.

cocoa farmers in Hurd and Johnson's survey had a literacy rate of 55 per cent compared with only 21 per cent of Ghanaian males over 25 years old (1960 census figures). Other studies (Peil, 1976; Wallace, 1974; Clignet and Foster, 1966) have underlined the importance of parental (including mothers') education in relation to children's schooling. According to Wallace (1974, p. 35), 'when the mother had no education it was the father's educational status that had most influenced the chances of the child but when the mother had had some formal education then her influence was the most important'. Foster (1965, p. 243) established selectivity indexes of 0·4 for fifth-formers whose fathers had received no formal schooling, compared with 8·4 (secondary school) and 17·7 (university).

We may briefly discuss the other major determinants of variations in secondary enrolment levels.

Sex
We have already established that girls in general suffer from educational disadvantages but that these vary with social background. It is not surprising, therefore, to find that girls attending secondary schools are from substantially higher socio-economic backgrounds than boys. Superior performance in the entrance examination and a greater willingness and ability on the part of parents to pay school fees for girls' education explain the higher social selectivity of girls entering secondary school compared with those leaving primary. Foster (1963, p. 241) showed that one-third of male fifth-formers were from professional and clerical backgrounds compared with two-thirds of females,

whereas 37 per cent of the boys were from farming backgrounds and only 12 per cent of the girls. This again demonstrates the combined social and urban/rural nature of the unequal schooling of the two sexes. Girls, of course, account for decreasing proportions of primary, secondary and university students.

Urban/Rural Factors

We have already discussed the main urban/rural dimension of inequality in relation to the class background of students. Here we are concerned with the question of whether urban/rural factors have any effect on secondary schooling independent of the socio-economic factor. Clignet and Foster (1966) found that in the Ivory Coast the selectivity index for secondary students was the same for those born in villages and small towns as for farmers' children (0·8), and in Ghana it was almost identical (0·5 compared with 0·6). At the other extreme, Ghanaian students coming from towns with a population of 50,000 or above were three times more likely than their Ivory Coast equivalents to be attending secondary school (selectivity indexes of 2·5 and 0·8 respectively). The reasons for this are unclear and complicated and need not detain us here. Birthplace is not a particularly satisfactory index of the effect of locality on enrolment inequalities. As already indicated, many children who are born in villages migrate to town before or during their primary schooling. Also, many of the children of large farmers are effectively permanent urban residents (see Hurd and Johnson, op. cit.). Where a child grows up is probably more important than where he or she is born, from the point of view of educational opportunities.

Ethnic/Regional Factors

Like urban/rural factors, ethnic/regional selectivity is largely a reflection of socio-economic variations between ethnic groups and between regions. According to Foster (1965, p. 240), 'although there is some ethnic selectivity into Ghanaian secondary schools, other social characteristics are of greater apparent importance in determining enrolment'. In general, ethnic/regional enrolment inequalities can be directly explained in terms of the level of urbanisation, parental literacy and occupation and the diffusion of a cash-crop economy. There are exceptions to this rule, however. For example, parts of Volta Region in Ghana are well represented in secondary schools, but the region has no town with a population of over 18,000 inhabitants and is not an important region for the production of cash crops. In this instance, the Bremen missionaries seem to have had an effect greater than (and independent of) the colonial penetration itself. Similar instances in the Ivory Coast lead Clignet and Foster (1966, p. 68) to conclude that 'special investigations of the process of educational diffusion need to be made among the peoples of the Ivory Coast'.

Secondary school students tend to come from similar occupational backgrounds irrespective of ethnic origin. If some ethnic groups are overrepresented, therefore, it is because they have a higher proportion of white-collar professional workers and a lower proportion of small farmers than the underrepresented ethnic groups. It follows that as long as the occupational profiles of different ethnic groups vary, so will their secondary enrolment levels. The same argument holds true for regional inequalities.

Ethnic/regional enrolment inequalities are greater in Ghanaian secondary schools than in the Ivory Coast, even though there were approximately ten times as many Ghanaian students at the time of the surveys. This underlines our previous conclusion that educational expansion is no guarantee of reduced enrolment inequalities; indeed, the reverse may be the case.

An important factor affecting the level of ethnic/regional selectivity patterns is the way in which recruitment into secondary schools is determined. In some countries pupils compete for government secondary school places through a national examination and the top performers are given all the available places. In other countries, although the examination is national, pupils compete for places in specific schools, which means that each school will in effect recruit pupils from a local catchment area. Where demand for secondary school places increases pass marks are adjusted upwards, and vice versa. In the Centre-South Province of Cameroun, for example, pass marks varied from 50 per cent in the best urban schools to under 25 per cent in the newer schools situated in small towns (figures for 1975). This system means that many students will obtain secondary school places who would not have done so on the basis of a national competition. This favours disadvantaged areas, ethnic groups and classes to the extent that secondary school places are more evenly distributed than high performers in the entrance examination. Secondary dropouts and examination failure may somewhat redress the balance, however, as may the highly uneven distribution of private secondary education. We will discuss the political aspect of this reverse discrimination in Chapter 9.

Religion

Religion is related to the ethnic/regional dimension of selection. Almost by definition, Christians are overrepresented in secondary schools compared with Muslims, because Christian mission schools were mostly established in areas where tribal religions, rather than Islam, were dominant. About a seventh of students in Clignet and Foster's Ivory Coast sample were Muslims, compared with two-thirds Catholic and one-tenth Protestant. Interestingly, there were proportionally more Muslims among the girl students than among the boys, perhaps reflecting above-average socio-economic status among Muslim parents (Clignet and Foster, 1966, p. 59). This finding is consistent with that of Dubbeldam (1970) quoted above. In general, religious affiliation does not have much independent effect on secondary enrolment levels.

Race

In South Africa racial and economic inequalities determine who gets how much secondary education. Proportionally speaking, South African whites have eighty-four times the chance of blacks of matriculating from secondary school, and less than 2 per cent of African pupils starting primary school in 1962 had reached the fifth form of secondary school by 1974 (Troup, 1976, p. 66). High dropout rates in primary school are the main cause of this, not failure in the secondary entrance examination. Given their subordinate position in economy and society, the best that most South African blacks can hope for is some primary/vocational education. Consequently, although primary enrolment levels are not low by African standards, post-primary education levels are extremely low bearing in mind white levels of enrolment and the available government revenue for the provision of welfare services of all kinds.

Quality of Schooling, Recruitment Patterns and Performance Variations

Having outlined the main characteristics of secondary school students we may now turn to some of the other important aspects of educational inequality listed under III and IV in Figure 3.1. We may begin with the question of who attends schools of different status and quality within the academic secondary system. Foster shows that schools of different status vary somewhat in social composition. Status is a function of the size, age, number of examination candidates and passes and the qualifications of the teaching staff in the various schools. The oldest government schools have the highest status and the newer private schools the lowest. Students' perceptions of the school hierarchy were very similar to the objective order based on the above criteria. Clearly, from the point of view of educational and occupational life-chances, the school one attends is of great importance. Achimota and Mfantsipim are the highest-status boys' schools in Ghana, and half of their fifth-form students were from white-collar backgrounds, compared with only 18 per cent from farming and fishing families. By contrast, in the low-status schools the corresponding figures were 35 and 36 per cent respectively (Foster, 1963, p. 164). Overall, however, there is little difference in the social composition of all high- and all low-status schools. In the Ivory Coast 'the offspring of fathers with high occupational status tend to be more numerous in the long academic and technical streams and in the higher cycle of studies. Conversely, the short academic and agricultural streams draw a higher proportion of their students from farming families, although the differences here are not great' (Clignet and Foster, 1966, pp. 82–3). The authors also found that there was little difference between the social composition of students in public as opposed to private (fee-paying) schools. Bibby and Miller (1968) found a rather different picture in Accra private schools compared with Achimota. They found that in private schools only 9 per cent of fifth-form boys were from higher professional and managerial backgrounds (57 per cent in Achimota), whereas no less than 42 per cent of private students were from farming families (14 per cent in Achimota). Twelve per cent of students in Achimota had illiterate fathers compared with 39 per cent in private schools. In Accra, at least, high-status parents do not seem to need private schools even for their less able sons.

In our Yaounde study we found that only a quarter of elite children from the sample entering secondary schools having failed the common entrance examination went to technical/vocational rather than academic schools, and even fewer children from other white-collar backgrounds. In contrast, between 43 and 56 per cent of children from semi-, unskilled and farming backgrounds preferred technical to academic education. There were no differences between fees which could explain these variations.

Thus there is some evidence that socio-economic background affects the kind and quality of secondary education received. From our previous discussion, however, we should not be surprised to find substantial numbers of children from low socio-economic backgrounds in the highest-quality schools. To overcome background disadvantages such children have to be highly motivated and of above-average ability. When highly intelligent children are identified, poor parents and other family members often make extra sacrifices to maximise the children's chances of educational success. Such children are not only likely to be successful in entering the highest-status schools but are also likely to have an above-average chance of academic success. Conversely, privileged children who manage to obtain secondary places because of their background rather than their intelligence might be expected to have difficulty in surviving in the secondary system.

Bibby (1973) shows that Ghanaian children attending fee-paying primary schools had a 63 per cent success rate in the common entrance examination compared with a national average of 15 per cent. The private schools have the best teachers and are extremely efficient in training pupils for the examination. In this situation it is not difficult to understand Bibby's finding that only 12 per cent of children from white-collar backgrounds passed four or more O levels, compared to

15 per cent of manual workers' children and 25 per cent of the children of farmers. Bibby and Peil (1974, p. 408) found that 'once in a particular secondary school the influence of family background is, if anything, the opposite of that conventionally assumed – elite children do less well than expected, the sons of illiterates do best'.

At the secondary school level there are both high- and low-quality private schools. In countries such as Kenya what were white-only boarding schools before independence have now become exclusive schools for the elite, who alone can pay the high fees. This is true from the nursery level upwards, and in Kenya a system of feeder schools exists which channels the progress of elite children from one level to the next. Less intelligent elite children are often overrepresented in the poorer quality secondary schools where their (and other students') chances of academic success are extremely low. In Bibby and Peil's study (1974), over four-fifths of O level candidates in private schools failed in all papers, compared with nearly six passes per candidate in Achimota school. If people continue to invest scarce resources in low-quality private education it is in the hope that their son or daughter will be one of the lucky ones, despite the heavy odds against this.

Able children from poor families tend to do well in secondary school and less able children from elite families, less well. But this does little to redress the educational balance in favour of the disadvantaged social classes, as our discussion of fifth- and sixth-form selectivity indicates. Also, intelligence as measured in examinations cannot be separated from the totality of social background and educational experiences, a point which we will return to later.

Educational and Occupational Aspirations

What affects the level of education and the kinds of occupation to which students aspire? In the West, the development of a distinct class structure has led to the emergence of definite class-based subcultures. The latter are important in the present context because they affect attitudes towards the education system, have a direct influence on the chances of educational success and, up to a point, determine attitudes towards the occupational structure. In working-class subcultures people often have a low opinion of students and formal education and may think that 'education is not for the likes of us'. To the extent that working-class children are less competitive in the education system, these attitudes may reflect objective circumstances. To the extent that subcultural values persist over time, they may become independent causes of educational inequalities by discouraging working-class children from aspiring to education and occupations of a certain level.

In Africa it has been claimed that class-based subcultures either do not exist or are much less pronounced than in the West. This is one reason why, so the argument goes, substantial numbers of secondary students are from rural areas and families with low levels of literacy and modern values. We will return to this general point later; here we are concerned with the effect of occupational background on aspirations.

Clignet and Foster maintain that the common experience of secondary education is the main determinant of occupational expectations and ambitions, not social background. In other words, children from ordinary social backgrounds who are successful in secondary schooling have occupational goals and expectations similar to those of more privileged children. Their study showed, however, that social background affected attitudes towards teaching as a profession (preferred by those from more humble backgrounds) and elite positions and medicine (preferred by those from higher-status families) (1966, p. 144).

Peil (1968) showed that attitudes towards education and choice of occupation vary between areas (of Ghana) according to the size of the locality, its educational history, educational and occupational structure and the attainments of parents and siblings. In another study Peil (1972) shows variations in parental attitudes towards children's education among different groups of factory workers. Fifteen per cent of unskilled workers and 34 per cent of foremen wanted their sons to become professional workers. The figure was 9 per cent for those with no education and 50 per cent for those who had attended secondary school. Desire for education for children also varied with age and education received. Bibby and Miller (1969) found that there were important variations in occupational choice among Ghanaian fifth-formers which reflected social background. For example, over half the pupils whose parents both had post-primary education desired occupations in medicine, law and the civil service, compared with a quarter of the students with uneducated parents. On the other hand, agriculture and teaching appealed to similar proportions of pupils in the two groups, although the children of manual labourers were seven times more likely to choose these occupations than children from elite backgrounds.

As we might expect, there is a strong relationship between the type and quality of school attended and educational/occupational aspirations. Somerset (1974, p. 78) found that the amount of further education desired by Kenyan fourth-formers depended on the type of secondary school attended: high-quality and status national schools, intermediate local and low-quality Harambee schools. Over three-quarters of Harambee students were content to stop at O level compared with less than a third of those in high-status schools. Conversely, 59 per cent of the latter group wanted to go to university compared with less than 20 per cent of Harambee students. Clignet and Foster (1966, p. 138) show a similar pattern for Ivory Coast students in different streams (agricultural, technical, academic) and cycles (low to high).

We may conclude that there is evidence that both parental background and the type of secondary school attended affect aspirations. The effects of subcultural factors are more likely to be in evidence at the lower educational levels, and they may also affect the decision to attend school in the first place. The further a student progresses up the educational ladder the more likely it is that his or her job expectations will reflect those of his or her educational level rather than socio-economic background. Generally girls are less ambitious than boys, despite their higher class background. Thus, as with performance and school attended, the effect of social background factors on aspirations becomes less and less in evidence as we move up the educational ladder. But even at the university level there is evidence that social background still affects the type of course undertaken and occupational aspirations. Thus, although it is undoubtedly true that class-based subcultures are much less in evidence in Africa than in the West, there are signs that such subcultures are already having some effect on educational and occupational choice.

Students generally have quite realistic attitudes towards the kinds of job they are likely to obtain. These attitudes are more closely related to the objective conditions of the job market than to social background. So few students reach the sixth form or university that those who do are already experiencing anticipatory socialisation into elite or sub-elite roles. Many of the elite are first generation, so it is not thought abnormal for long-distance social mobility to take place between generations. We would not expect this state of affairs to continue much longer, however.

University Enrolment

To complete the picture of educational inequalities we may look at the pattern of recruitment into African universities. Less than one-half of 1 per cent of any cohort manage to obtain university places in most African countries, but this minute group is important in that it contains a large proportion of the future elite of high-level government and professional cadres. Where these students come from (which regions and ethnic groups) and their socio-economic background (parental occupation, income and education) are extremely important from the point of view of the perpetuation of social inequalities and the way in which they change over time.

Ethnic/Regional Inequalities
We may look at some Nigerian data to illustrate the ethnic/regional dimension of inequality. During the early days of higher education in

Nigeria the overwhelming majority of students were drawn from the southern part of the country. The opening of Nsukka (1960) and Ahmadu Bhello University (ABU) (1962) led to a modification of recruitment patterns which has continued with the subsequent opening of a further ten universities throughout the country (see Table 3.4).

Table 3.4 Percentage of Ibadan Students Coming from the Main Regions of Nigeria (1948–66)

Regions	1948–52	1953–7	1958–62	1963–6	All years
Lagos, West and Mid-West	50	53	53	65	55
East	47	42	36	33	39
North	3	5	11	2	6
Total	100	100	100	100	100
N	499	813	1001	702	3015

Source: van den Berghe and Nuttney (1969, p. 360).

The opening of more and more universities has made recruitment an increasingly regional phenomenon. Thus, in 1974, 84 per cent of ABU students were from the northern states, and relatively few northern students found their way to universities in other regions. This was somewhat less true for southern students attending ABU and, currently, other northern universities. For example, fewer than 10 per cent of students in the University of Jos, Plateau State (central Nigeria) were from the northern states in the 1978–9 academic year.

In absolute terms, the gap between north and south in university enrolment levels is increasing. According to Beckett and O'Connell (1977, p. 27), 'more than half of the northern students attending southern universities came from Kwara State, the most southerly of the northern states, and were mostly Yoruba. . . . The far northern states were scarcely represented outside ABU.' Official figures from the joint admissions and matriculation board show that the northern states are improving their relative position over time. Thus students from the ten northern states made up 17 per cent of total university enrolments in 1970 and 24 per cent in 1974. Twenty-nine per cent of new enrolments in the 1978–9 academic year were from these states (*Daily Times*, 9 March 79, p. 7). In spite of this relative improvement the absolute gap between north and south has increased, reflecting the rapid expansion of enrolment in recent years.

In ethnic terms the above figures mean that 'the Yoruba ethnic group, representing approximately seventeen percent of the total Nigerian population, provides approximately fifty percent of all the university students in the country. . . . Yoruba and Ibo students together probably account for more than two-thirds of Nigeria's student population, yet their share of the country's total population is not much more than thirty percent' (ibid. p. 29). Thus, despite the positive discrimination which is practised in Nigerian university recruitment, the gap between north and south is still enormous. Educational inequalities between north and south constitute one of the most divisive elements in Nigerian society, and similar divisions exist in many other African countries. Governments' awareness of this fact and their general inability to do anything about it are dealt with in Chapter 9.

Social Background Inequalities
We have already established that the children of farmers and manual workers are underrepresented in the educational system and those of professional and white-collar workers overrepresented. Not surprisingly, these patterns continue at the higher level. A comparison of West African universities shows that between one-third and a half of students are from farming backgrounds compared with between a quarter and a third from white-collar backgrounds. Unfortunately it is impossible to make closer comparisons or to identify distinct trends in recruitment patterns since occupational classifications vary from one study to another. Also, large variations in the student composition within a given university over short periods of time suggest that some samples are less representative than others. Bearing these points in mind we may take a closer look at the study of Nigerian universities quoted above (see Table 3.5).

Table 3.5 Fathers' Occupation and Student Enrolment in Three Nigerian Universities, 1973 (Percentages)

Fathers' occupation	ABU	Ibadan	Nsukka
Farmer	51·6	49·2	30·1
Civil servant	6·1	12·3	13·1
Professions	2·9	4·6	5·2
Teacher	6·1	5·1	7·3
Trader/businessman	14·1	14·4	19·3
Artisan, labourer	4·0	3·6	3·7
Other	15·2	10·8	21·4
Total	100·0	100·0	100·0

Source: Beckett and O'Connell (1977, p. 30).

Large (though variable) proportions of students in all three universities were from farming backgrounds, and the same was true in the universities of Lagos and Ife. Moreover, a high proportion of students declared themselves to be from families with relatively low incomes. Between 40 and 50 per cent of students in the three samples declared that their fathers earned N400 per annum or less. In a combined 1970–1 sample the same authors found that no less than 62 per cent of Ibadan students from farming backgrounds declared their fathers' income to be under N100 per annum. This does not mean that, overall, Nigerian students do not come from families with above-average incomes: half or more of the students in the 1973 samples had fathers with an annual income of N400 or more, which is approximately five times the national average. Although considerable proportions of students were from illiterate backgrounds (up to half the fathers and nearly three-quarters of the mothers), Beckett and O'Connell consider that 'these parents are less typical of the relevant general population in terms of education than in terms of occupation and income' (ibid. p. 33). In other words, pupils are more likely to come from relatively well-educated than from relatively wealthy or high-occupation groups. This is particularly true in the north: only 37 per cent of ABU students' fathers were illiterate, compared with over 90 per cent of the northern population in 1952. The figure of 90 per cent is not very helpful as a comparison, however, because it includes the general population of women, children over 7 years of age and males who are not fathers as well as those who are; it does not tell us much about levels of literacy among northern fathers at present. There are, of course, many variations within the northern population regarding literacy rates, income and so on, and therefore parental education is more likely to be similar to overall patterns within restricted parts of the north rather than in the north as a whole. Nevertheless, it seems that parental education constitutes an important determinant of educational success independent of occupation and income.

The authors conclude that 'tendencies towards greater class selectivity have been offset all over Nigeria by the rapid growth of the universities' enrolments, meaning that the system as a whole has actually become more open in recruitment from among the poorer, rural areas' (ibid.). It should be noted, however, that the well-established Nigerian elite often send their children abroad for secondary and higher education, although we do not know whether this fact would alter the figures quoted above to any great extent (we doubt it very much). Also, students in certain faculties come from significantly higher social backgrounds than others. This will have an important effect on future occupational patterns: doctors, for example, are likely to come from higher social backgrounds than teachers. Table 3.6 shows the occupational breakdown of the different faculties in the University of Yaounde.

Overall, equal proportions of students are from white-collar and farming backgrounds, with national selectivity indexes of approxi-

Table 3.6   Occupational Background of Students in the University of Yaounde in 1972 (Percentages)

Fathers' occupation	Arts	Science	Higher TTC*	Faculty Agri- culture	Medicine	Poly- technic	All
White- collar	30	40	30	5	48	28	34
Trader	5	8	17	5	9	13	8
Manual	5	5	15	0	3	4	6
Farmer	40	29	28	77	27	46	34
Other	20	18	10	13	13	9	18
All	100	100	100	100	100	100	100
N	821	922	458	56	191	54	2529

* Teacher Training College.
Source: University of Yaounde (1972).

mately 13·0 and 0·4 respectively. Farmers' children account for relatively high proportions of students in low-status faculties (agriculture and polytechnic), but relatively low proportions in the higher-status Higher Teacher Training College and Medical Faculty. This table confirms our previous finding that social origins are important in determining post-primary academic orientations.

Female representation in Nigerian universities is extremely low, varying from 12 per cent in ABU to 17 per cent in Nsukka. Figures from Ibadan show that the proportion of female students rose from less than 5 per cent in the 1950s to over 20 per cent in 1966. But by 1973 this figure had fallen to 17 per cent. As we would expect from our previous discussion, girl students are from distinctly higher social backgrounds than males. In ABU, for example, 'the women were less than half as likely to have fathers who were farmers and five times as likely to have fathers who were civil servants' (ibid, p. 35).

Because of the difficulty, mentioned above, of comparing different enrolment studies no definite trend has so far been identified in the pattern of social selectivity in African universities. Studies by Peil (1965), van den Berghe and Nuttney (1969) and Finlay, Ballard and Koplin (1968) show a tendency for recruitment from farming backgrounds to increase over time, a trend which is disputed by Bibby (1973), Currie (1974) and a comparison of enrolment patterns in some more and less developed countries and areas (southern Nigeria and Ghana versus northern Nigeria and the Ivory Coast). Invariably, however, the children of professional workers, higher civil servants and those with high educational levels and incomes are extremely over-represented in the universities, and the children of clerical workers, traders and businessmen, somewhat less. The relatively large number of farmers' children in the university population reflects the fact that farmers make up the overwhelming majority of the adult population. Low levels of selectivity among farmers' children (especially small cash-crop and subsistence farmers' children) are, therefore, not incompatible with quite high overall representation in university populations.

It is interesting to note the very low representation of the children of manual workers in both secondary and university education. Hurd and Johnson's conclusion on Ghanaian secondary students is of general relevance here:

> There emerge within the modern sector differences of life chances greater than those that distinguish the modern sector from the traditional. In other words, the rigidity of the emerging class system is such that achievement through higher education is more difficult for the child of a labourer than for the child of a subsistence farmer. (1967, p. 72)

The statement is much less true for the children of subsistence farmers than for the children of cash-crop farmers, who may well be overrepresented in the post-primary system. By other Third World standards (Asia and Latin America) a remarkably high proportion of university students are from relatively poor, illiterate and farming backgrounds. In the Nigerian case it seems that the tendency for elite children to be highly overrepresented at the university level has been offset by the expansion of higher education (with the help of oil revenues) which has facilitated access to increasing numbers of able children from disadvantaged backgrounds.

African Education: Open or Closed?

Having surveyed the major dimensions of educational inequality in Africa we may pause briefly to ask whether we should think of African educational systems as being relatively open or relatively closed. If by 'open' we mean that relatively large proportions of places at the higher levels of the educational pyramid are filled by children from poor, rural and illiterate backgrounds, then it is clear that African education (excluding South Africa) is relatively open. If, however, we take 'open' to mean that children from all backgrounds have similar chances of educational success, then it is equally clear that African education is not at all open. Thus, stressing the absolute rather than the relative figure gives an image of openness, and stressing the relative figure gives an opposite picture. Which picture is the more meaningful?

From different points of view both absolute and relative aspects of the question are important. Let us first consider absolute enrolment levels. From the sociological point of view it is extremely important that significant numbers of higher secondary and university students come from underprivileged backgrounds. First, the possibility of long-distance social mobility through educational success is likely to have a strong effect on the ambitions of new generations of under-privileged children. This is likely to weaken the tendency towards the growth of class-based attitudes towards education. Second, upward mobility through education is likely to strengthen the legitimacy of the education system in the eyes of those who pass (or fail to pass) through it. As long as some underprivileged children are successful, lack of success can be put down to lack of ability or laziness. In this way the inequalities which we have been considering in this chapter are over-looked and success and failure are explained in purely subjective and individual terms. Continued mobility also serves to justify the politi-cians' claim that they are concerned to guarantee equality of educa-tional opportunity to all citizens, even when there is little or no evi-dence to support this claim. Thirdly, continued educational and occu-pational mobility for some poor children limits the process of class formation at the top of the occupational hierarchy. One of the major characteristics of classes is that they tend to reproduce themselves through time; that is, individuals tend to stay in the class into which they are born. Feelings of common interest and group solidarity, class-consciousness and the growth of class subcultures follow from this process of reproduction. To the extent that contemporary elite groups in Africa still contain significant numbers of first-generation sons of peasants, a ruling class cannot yet be said to exist in the strict sense. These kinds of considerations are based on absolute access patterns.

The relative aspect of educational success and failure for different groups of children is also important. Selectivity patterns are highly variable between the more and less privileged students. This means that any elite child has a much greater chance of succeeding in school than any child from a manual or peasant background. Wealthy, edu-cated and higher-occupation parents constitute only a small propor-tion of all parents, so that their children do not monopolise the secon-dary and university systems. In the recent past, secondary and univer-sity enrolments and elite opportunities have all expanded rapidly. This means a constant growth in the number of educated and wealthy parents, that is, those who are the most favourably placed for assuring the educational success of their children. It is highly unlikely that elite positions will continue to expand at a rapid enough rate to absorb all the products of the top levels of the educational system. This will mean increasing competition for elite positions, the devaluation of higher qualifications and the likelihood of non-educational criteria being used for elite recruitment, such as favouritism towards family and friends.

In such a situation it is the least competitive students who are likely to be eliminated at an ever-increasing rate. In other words, the present growth of the elite is the main factor limiting the likelihood that in future those struggling to achieve elite status through the education system will be able to do so. Thus the proportion of elite members who are first generation is likely to fall off rapidly. This is the importance of relative recruitment patterns. We conclude that education in Africa is absolutely open and relatively closed, and we think that its absolute openness is a temporary phenomenon.

Many authors have come to similar conclusions. According to Peil (1977, p. 192), 'the direction of change seems to be shifting from increasing openness to some closure and increased advantage for children of elite families'. Lloyd says:

> It is becoming increasingly apparent that the well-educated are today able to ensure, by their wealth and their ability to understand and manipulate the school system, that their own children receive as good or a better education than themselves and that they will constitute the educated elite of the coming generation. Conversely, the urban worker has the least chance of any social category that his son will enter secondary school. An open society is rapidly closing. (1974, p. 3)

We would not single out the children of the urban worker in particular in this context but rather the children (and daughters more than sons) of semi- and unskilled workers, small cash-crop and subsistence farmers and the most petty traders and artisans. Dore (1976, p. 79) concludes similarly that 'it may well be that the enormous educational advantages which accrue to the children of university-educated parents will lead to sharply entrenched class divisions very rapidly'. On its own, however, the education system cannot bring this about. It is important to identify the intervening variables which come into play to establish these 'enormous educational advantages'.

First, the most educated parents are those in the best jobs and with some of the highest incomes. This provides them with the material resources to assure the education of all or most of their children. It includes the ability to pay fees for nursery education and high-quality schooling where this is not free. Negatively, it allows them to dispense with the labour of their children at all times, a luxury not available to poorer parents. In this context we include household labour (looking after young children, cooking, fetching firewood, cleaning the house, washing clothes and all other chores performed by servants in the better-off households), and other productive activities such as farmwork and petty commercial activities in the urban areas. These activities may effectively keep poorer children out of school all the time or at least reduce their attendance rate and (especially among the girls) amount of time available for homework and recreation. In our survey of Yaounde primary pupils boys from elite and large trading backgrounds did the least housework and girls from large farming, small trading and unskilled manual backgrounds did the most.

Secondly, the general cultural environment of the home is likely to vary according to parental education and this will tend to help the elite child at school. For example, it is common for elite parents to use (and to use correctly) the official language of the school at home and to teach it to their children at an early age. In our Yaounde sample twice as many common entrance candidates from elite homes as candidates in general, said that French was their first language, and elite children who said this had a 45 per cent pass rate compared with only 25 per cent among elite children who said they spoke no French at home. Speaking French (or English) in the home is no doubt associated with numerous other factors which affect educational performance, such as the ability of parents to explain schoolwork to their children, encouraging them to read by buying them educational books, rewarding and punishing them according to their school performance and making sure that they do their homework. Invariably the cultural values transmitted by the school are those of the educated minority rather than those of the mass of the population. In Part Two we will be looking more closely into this question. Studies in the West have clearly demonstrated the importance of the cultural environment of the home on school performance. Some writers argue that this subcultural factor plays little or no role in the African context, given that classes (and therefore class subcultures) are still in the formative stage. However, a study by Lloyd (1966) shows that distinct differences exist between modern elite and traditional Yoruba families regarding socialisation practices and strategies for the education of children. Although the traditional parents generally thought that education was a good thing, they tended to leave the question of educational success or failure to the will of Allah. They thought that an intelligent child would succeed automatically at school without any active help on their part. Elite parents, on the other hand, actively intervened in their children's education in order to maximise the chances of educational success.

In the industrialised countries, including those of Eastern Europe, cultural and subcultural factors play an extremely important role in determining who goes to which kind of school and obtains higher education. Even very able children from working-class subcultures often underachieve in the education system. This phenomenon cannot be explained in purely material terms. In Africa, material factors are of overwhelming importance in determining educational achievement.

While subcultural differences do not yet constitute an insurmountable obstacle to the clever child from a poor family, it is likely that subcultural factors are increasing in importance. Little research has been done in this area, however.

A Word on Intelligence

Material and cultural differences between classes help determine school enrolment and performance variations. Does intelligence also vary between classes? This hypothesis could be advanced on one of two grounds. First, as many members of the elite are first generation they might well be of above-average intelligence to have achieved elite status. This intelligence may be inherited by their children, which would go towards explaining the superior educational performance of the latter. Secondly, elite children are better fed, taller and healthier than the rest of the population. There is definitely a relationship between diet and physical and intellectual growth. Children who suffer from malnutrition may well suffer from retarded mental development as a result.

Of these two hypotheses we tend to take the second one more seriously than the first. Levels of absolute poverty are rising in many parts of Africa and unbalanced, inadequate diets are a part of everyday life for far too many children. Stunted intellectual growth may well be an extra cause of low academic performance, although as yet there is little conclusive proof of this in the African context. Certainly the urban elite are protected from the periodic shortages of basic foodstuffs which many peasants and poor urban dwellers suffer from. These shortages are caused by a combination of natural (pests, drought, flooding) and social causes (overexploitation of the peasantry, forced production of cash-crops as opposed to food crops). Rapid population growth and soil exhaustion/erosion from overcropping and overgrazing increase the likelihood of periodic famine. Provisionally, then, we may add stunted growth to our list of class-related causes of educational inequalities.

So far we have talked of intelligence as if it was a single entity rather than a complex combination of different faculties. Some people are better at manipulating numbers and figures than others, other people are more at home with language (spoken or written), yet others have a highly developed sense of shapes or are more imaginative and creative than the average. Yet schooling develops only certain dimensions of intelligence. Most secondary school entrance examinations contain a high degree of language (vocabulary, grammar), memory and arithmetic tests. We have quoted some evidence which suggests that elite children can be trained to perform well in this kind of examination irrespective of their inherent ability in these particular intellectual processes. It was pointed out above that language testing is as much a test of parents as of pupils. These facts may help explain the poor relationship between common entrance results and performance in secondary schools.

Thus moderately able children from privileged backgrounds may overachieve in the education system, and intelligent children from underprivileged backgrounds may fail to make the most of their talents through environmental and educational disadvantages. For how long can the less able elite child survive in the education system? Secondary education is extremely competitive and selective, and it seems unlikely that all privileged children – including the least able – will manage to complete the secondary course and go on to university. We should not, however, underestimate the importance of diet, material and cultural factors in guaranteeing the above-average performance of elite children. The greater the material and cultural gap between the classes, the more will the privileged dominate the education system.

It is difficult to separate inherent intelligence from the effects of the environment, including schooling itself. The well-known IQ tests on which secondary entrance examinations are based have been developed to measure inherent abilities, but in practice they tend to measure these *plus* the effects of social and cultural background and education on these abilities. Inherent intelligence cannot be studied or measured in isolation from these determinant environmental forces.

Meritocracy

Closely related to the concept of IQ is the ideology of meritocracy which has developed in the West, especially in the USA. In this ideology it is asserted that social position should be determined by inherent ability plus hard work. Thus free, universal education should be provided to allow clever children from disadvantaged backgrounds the maximum opportunity of achieving high educational and occupational success. Such ideas serve to hide the close relationship between social and educational inequalities which we have been at pains to document in this chapter. If we ignore inequalities of class, status and power it is possible to see the education system as a sifting mechanism which separates the able from the less able on the basis of objective criteria and allocates people to jobs appropriate to their abilities. The whole point is, of course, that we cannot ignore background inequalities and their effect on intelligence, access to school and school performance. Competitive schooling is a handicap race rather than one in which the runners start off with equal chances.

The realisation that free education did not equalise social opportunities in the USA led to the introduction of compensatory education for underprivileged groups (particularly blacks and Spanish Americans). The widespread failure of such programmes has led more recently to the introduction of positive discrimination favouring females, blacks and Spanish Americans in universities and jobs. This policy is more or less an acceptance of the impossibility of using education to compensate for racial, sexual and class inequalities and their manifestation in academic performance.

In Africa, long-distance social mobility, though statistically rare, is a frequent enough phenomenon to make the meritocratic myth plausible. Governments make great efforts to assure the fairness of the educational system by introducing strong checks on examination cheating and by devising computer-corrected tests which eliminate the subjective element involved in the individual correction of essays. By demonstrating the fairness and objectivity of the educational system and examinations and by making schooling more widely available, the onus of success and failure is placed on the individual child. Success is now taken to demonstrate intelligence and hard work, failure to demonstrate dullness and laziness, and social causes of performance variations are ignored or accorded only minor importance. As long as parents and pupils accept the myth of equal educational opportunity and selection by merit social inequalities will be legitimated or ignored.

Schooling and Occupational Mobility

The link between formal education and access to jobs is extremely close in the modern age, and this is as true in Africa as anywhere else. It is also true that in Africa 'many are called but few are chosen', that is, for the vast majority of young people the level of education which they manage to obtain and the subsequent employment fall below their hopes and ambitions (though less noticeably below their expectations).

We have already referred to the phenomenon of diploma devaluation which results from rapid expansion of education without an equivalent expansion of job openings. Occupational mobility between generations is limited to the extent that new job openings are themselves limited. Many school-leavers are obliged to take jobs which once would have been considered too lowly, or are unable to find any employment at all. Clignet (1976, p. 67) found that in Cameroun 'no less than sixty-nine percent of the younger individuals with a post-primary education are currently engaged in manual work compared with fifteen percent of the older'.

The problem of unemployed school-leavers is a growing one all over Africa, and one which is often commented on. It should not be thought that educational expansion causes unemployment, however, or that school-leavers are only prepared to take white-collar jobs. One cannot blame the education system for low levels of job expansion or for rising rates of unemployment throughout Africa. The causes of this problem should rather be looked for in the poverty of the rural economy and the capital-intensive nature of investment in the modern sector. This means that the latter may expand considerably without creating many work openings. In the industrialised countries unemployment rates are beginning to rise for similar reasons.

When population growth is added to the above factors it should be clear that the statistical likelihood of a peasant's son or daughter finding a modern sector job is extremely low and probably falling rather rapidly. This is especially true among primary-leavers and middle and pre-sixth-form secondary graduates. The continued expansion of the education system creates jobs for the graduates of teacher training colleges. For the moment, a sixth-form education and a university degree still more or less guarantee good job prospects and elite or semi-elite status in the long run. The expansion of the civil service and the private sector continues to create openings for those with A levels or above. Competition for these openings is intense, given the relatively high salaries, promotion possibilities, fringe benefits and status which are at stake, especially in the private sector. Knight (1967) found that in Uganda an extra year's education meant an increase in income of 18 per cent, much higher than in any developed country, where highly skilled manual workers often earn more than university graduates (or lecturers). The contrast between success – educational qualifications leading to well-paid jobs – and failure – low educational achievement leading to unemployment, apprenticeships or unskilled work in the informal sector, return to agriculture – is stark indeed.

The difficulty of obtaining secondary school places and the lack of adequate job openings for the moderately qualified discourage many poorer parents and pupils, those who are the least competitive. Low returns on investment in education (and the returns will be lower the more you descend the occupational ladder) may lead to a drop in enrolments along certain groups of pupils, as already pointed out. More competitive pupils are likely to compete even harder and try to remain in school for longer periods in order to obtain suitable employment. This clearly favours the children from the more educated, better-off occupational groups. Given that much secondary and all higher education in Africa is provided by the state, the overrepresentation of children from privileged backgrounds at these levels constitutes an important subsidy from the rest of the population to the elite. According to Foster (1976, p. 43), 'far from facilitating social equity and assisting poorer groups, present arrangements merely perpetuate inequality and reinforce the occupational status of groups that are already among the "haves" '.

Here we may note the increasing likelihood that non-educational criteria will be used in determining who obtains employment. Given increasing competition for jobs among school-leavers and graduates, favouritism based on ethnic, family and class criteria may become increasingly prevalent (Price, 1973; Okedara, 1971). In sociological terms, ascriptive criteria in job placement may come to supplement achievement criteria. Both criteria favour the privileged at the expense of the underprivileged.

Sex and race constitute two other major obstacles to occupational achievement which can be called 'ascriptive'. Generally, very few females are employed in the modern sector of the economy. According to Little (1973, p. 33), females make up only 15 per cent of the employed population in Kenya and South Africa and only about 3 per cent in Ghana, Sierra Leone and Liberia. He concludes that 'the modern sector is in every [African] country virtually a male preserve'.

In a similar way race excludes most blacks from the middle and higher occupational levels in South Africa. According to the South African Department of Labour Manpower Survey (April 1973), there were no African engineers, chemists, architects or quantity surveyors. There were sixty-nine African medical doctors (of a total of over 9,000), two dentists and fifty-five pharmacists and druggists (total of over 4,000; quoted by Troup, 1976, p. 68). These figures reflect the almost total exclusion of South African blacks from higher secondary and university education. In 1974, out of nearly 112,000 university students onl 7,845 were Africans (ibid.). Low educational achievement is the direct cause of the underrepresentation of blacks, females and children of the lower classes in the modern/urban, high-status and high-income occupations. Both educational and occupational inequalities are ultimately caused by, and are a condition for the reproduction of, structural inequalities in the distribution of class, status and power.

Summary and Conclusions

Educational inequalities in contemporary Africa should be analysed within the framework of general social, political and economic inequalities. In this chapter we have concentrated on the question of class inequalities and the ways in which they both cause educational inequalities and then reflect these inequalities. Educational success is the main condition for occupational success in modern Africa, and the benefits of an individual's occupational success are likely to be reflected in his children's school performance. Thus the openness of the educational system is limited by the consequences of educational success. In an unequal world there can be no guarantee of equal educational opportunities for everybody irrespective of racial, ethnic and class origins.

We have shown that the majority of farmers are exploited by urban-based political, administrative and commercial interests, and lose much of the value of what they produce in the process. Only the richer peasants and capitalist farmers are in a position to protect themselves and, in turn, to exploit the labour of other (often migrant) workers. Small peasants, pastoralists, landless rural and migrant labourers make up the bottom strata of rural society, with the most limited life-chances for themselves and their children. Inequalities of occupation, income power and status in the rural areas are reflected in educational inequalities.

Similar inequalities exist in the urban areas, where occupational differentiation is also strongly reflected in educational inequalities. The children of semi- and unskilled workers and the most petty artisans and traders have virtually no chance of upward mobility through educational achievement; they acquire productive skills through informal means and apprenticeships (King, 1977). The children of skilled workers and routine-level clerical and other white-collar workers and medium-level traders are somewhat better placed, but lag significantly behind the children of higher civil servants, professional cadres and big traders and businessmen. Thus there are privileged minorities in both urban and rural areas, so that class inequalities and their educational consequences (variations in access and performance) cut across the urban/rural division. The concentration of schools in urban areas, the higher quality of the urban teaching force, greater supervision and so on favour urban inhabitants in general. Rural–urban migration helps to counter this disadvantage for some village children.

Unequal educational provision constitutes one of the major ethnic and regional dimensions of inequality in modern Africa. Ethnic rivalries and hostility reflect competition over access to state benefits such as employment opportunities, new schools and hospitals, roads and other services. There are often overlaps between ethnicity and control of such things as the civil service, trade, cash-crop farming, the military, higher education and other vital areas of the economy and polity. It is rare for a single ethnic group to dominate in all these spheres, however, and there are examples of successful challenges being mounted against dominant ethnic groups. We have given reasons for the likely continuation of social and educational inequalities between regions and ethnic groups.

In the case of racial domination in Southern Africa, the overlap between the dimensions of stratification and race and their reflection in unequal education are much clearer than in the ethnic case outlined above. Conflicts over educational provision and quality are inevitably articulated as racial conflicts in South Africa.

The loosest connection between stratification, education and other factors is that relating to sexual inequalities. This is because, up to a point, women suffer from social and educational disadvantages in all societies, classes, ethnic and regional groups. But our previous discussion has shown a number of overlaps between sex and class inequalities. Girls from elite backgrounds have better educational opportunities than boys from all non-elite backgrounds, girls from underrepresented regional and ethnic groups and from farming/rural backgrounds have extremely low educational opportunities. In other words, sex inequalities in education overlap considerably with class considerations. To the extent that elite growth is limited and attitudes of male superiority not limited to any one class, it is likely that processes of class formation will not, in the short run, have much effect on the underrepresentation of girls in schools, colleges and jobs. The improvement of women's social position depends on their ability to organise themselves in defence of their group interests. At the moment there is not much of this in Africa, and most women continue to accept the myth that men are innately superior.

Educational systems serve contradictory purposes in modern Africa. On the one hand they permit a small number of children from modest backgrounds to achieve varying degrees of upward social mobility. On the other hand they help to perpetuate and deepen general social inequalities between the privileged and underprivileged classes. Education is at the same time both a force for social change and a guarantee for the reproduction of existing inequalities. The major stimulus to educational growth since colonial times has been the hope that success at school will lead to a job in the minuscule modern sector, even though the chances of this happening are, statistically speaking, extremely low. At the moment the African class structure is still relatively ill defined and fluid, and many of those entering manual and white-collar occupations are not from manual or white-collar families. The struggle for the control of the state has not yet resulted in the establishment of a distinct ruling class with its own subculture and group identity, tending to reproduce itself through time on the basis of its wealth, solidarity and education. Whether such a class will emerge in the near future is a question beyond the scope of the present discussion, but the role of formal education in such a process is beyond doubt.

The social mobility function of education is likely, in our view, to decline rapidly and the class reproduction function to increase in importance. It seems to be in the nature of things that most parents try to pass on their advantages to their children. We believe that higher education is likely to become more or less monopolised by the elite. Foster calls this phenomenon 'elite closure', but we prefer to see it as part of the process of class formation itself. There is nothing inevitable about this process, but it is possible that in the future educational achievement will (1) condition the formation of a distinct class structure and (2) be used by the rich and powerful to assure the reproduction of that structure.

One of the main tasks of the sociology of education is to analyse the ambiguous and contradictory role of educational systems in Africa. Social equality is an elusive and rare commodity, and the claim that education can bring it about is a myth. At present, education in Africa is helping to deepen already extremely high levels of social inequality. In the long run, elitist and competitive education cannot serve the interests of the mass of the population, but it may be a long time before they come to realise this.

Questions and Discussion Topics: Chapter 3

1 Consider your own educational history. Which of the factors affecting enrolment and performance listed in Figure 3.1 at the beginning of this chapter (p. 55) have been significant in determining your educational career so far? Perform the same exercise for a close relative or a friend.
2 Do you consider your home area to be relatively advanced or backward educationally? Justify the criteria you use and back up your answer with enrolment statistics.
3 How does education (a) help and (b) hinder upward social mobility?
4 Discuss the relationship between educational expansion and equality of educational opportunity. (Chapter 9 may help you here.)
5 How does the cultural environment of a child affect his or her educational chances?
6 *Project*. Obtain some recent Ministry of Education enrolment statistics for your state or area. Analyse them from the point of view of (a) urban/rural, (b) sexual and (c) regional/ethnic inequalities. Do these three seem to be related in any way?
7 'Class background determines educational opportunities.' Discuss.

Part Two

The Sociology of Schools, Teaching and the Curriculum

Introduction to Part Two

In Part Two we will cover the sociology of schools and classrooms (Chapter 4), studies of the teacher's role in school and in society generally (Chapter 5), and the sociology of the curriculum (Chapter 6).

There has always been some sociological interest in school organisation, the curriculum and the practice of teaching, but in recent years particular attention has been drawn to these topics. This is mainly because it has been realised that social mobility studies and analyses of the role of education in social selection (see Part One) only tell us part of the story about educational success and failure. To understand fully why students reach different levels of attainment, we must also consider the knowledge they have to acquire, the difficulty of the tasks they are set by teachers, the kind of examinations they are expected to pass and the quality and organisation of the schools in which they study. All these factors would be described as parts of the general content of education; sociologists now consider that it is as important to study content as it is to estimate the effects of home background or social origin upon school attainment.

We also hope that discussion of sociological studies of teaching, school organisation and the curriculum will throw light on teachers' and students' everyday experiences of education. Reading a sociological interpretation of social control and the use of language in the classroom (see Chapter 4) may be of some help to practising teachers, for example, while debates about what should be inclued in school curricula (see Chapter 6) may challenge some established ideas about how knowledge should be relayed to students. In short, analysis of the content of education not only implies macro issues (for example, the relation between curricula and the culture of a society), but also micro issues such as face-to-face interaction between teacher and student, or the way in which a formal syllabus is actually interpreted and taught in the classroom.

Part Two will build on the information and ideas contained in Part One, so some background knowledge of education in the colonial period and of education and social selection will be assumed. Naturally, Part Two will also introduce some new key concepts and these will now be discussed briefly.

With regard to Chapter 4, perhaps the most important idea to grasp is that the school is not just an ordinary place where students and teachers happen to meet. The school is a social organisation which transmits social messages to students. In school, students are socialised into standard ways of behaving: they learn that timekeeping is regarded as very important, and that they are treated as one of a group rather than as individuals, and that they should respect teachers' authority. Thus, by the way they are organised, schools give hidden or implicit messages to students. For example, by dividing the school day into a number of periods, students are taught to divide their thinking and working into separate blocks – history for forty minutes, geography for forty minutes, and so on – rather than being given opportunities to integrate knowledge. As another example, respect for the teacher's authority also communicates the hidden message that society should be seen as a hierarchy and that orders from above should not be questioned (although in reality they often are). We call these hidden messages which are communicated by the school organisation the 'hidden curriculum' of schooling. In Chapters 4 and 6 this term is explained more fully than it is here, but we also mention in passing that the hidden curriculum can sometimes undermine the formal curriculum. For example, attempts to establish a formal curriculum of technical education may be undermined by students who perceive, according to the hidden curriculum, that education is for acquiring academic knowledge and qualifications rather than proficiency in technical subjects. Consequently they may pay lip-service to the aims of the formal technical curriculum, but their real ambitions may lie elsewhere.

Having introduced the idea that the school is not just a neutral ground upon which education takes place, but that it is a distinctive kind of organisation which socialises students in particular ways, it is also important to remember that teachers themselves are affected and influenced by the school. In Chapter 4 we introduce the conceptof bureaucracy and examine it to see to what extent teachers are being controlled by bureaucratic forms of organisation. The role of the headteacher is particularly important in this respect because he or she can be seen as a mediator or go-between who has to carry out instructions from bureaucratic offices above (the educational administration) and has some power over the teachers in the school. As we shall show, however, the individual teacher – particularly at the secondary school or higher education level – is not always at the bottom of a bureaucratic pyramid of authority. Teachers have some limited professional freedoms, and in Chapter 5 we will examine the ways in which they have been trying to extend their freedoms and power in Nigeria.

Most of the teacher's power lies within rather than outside the classroom, however, and in Chapter 4 (second section) we examine the ways in which this power is exercised. The teacher's control of the classroom should not be taken for granted as something which is achieved easily. As we shall attempt to show, every teacher has to establish and occasionally renew his or her authority. Students always test a teacher to find out whether he or she really knows the subject being taught, whether the teacher is really interested in their work and progress and whether the teacher is willing to discipline them. If teachers successfully establish their authority and knowledge they earn a legitimacy to exercise power in the classroom. An unsatisfactory teacher, on the other hand, will usually find that his or her legitimacy is challenged, and that the students will try to control the classroom. We should therefore view the classroom as something of an arena or battleground between teacher and students, particularly during the first meetings of a class and its teacher. Later, any conflict or bargaining for control between teacher and students may lessen or become institutionalised.

In establishing their authority teachers are aided a great deal by the hidden curriculum of the school, with its messages of control, discipline and respect for authority – unless, of course, the school is so disorganised that students become cynical about teachers' authority and do not respect it. Teachers are also helped in their task of controlling students by the formal curriculum. Most students are highly motivated to attain knowledge and pass examinations. They are willing to subscribe to the teacher's authority as long as the teacher helps them with their learning and structures the teaching according to the syllabus. In this way, therefore, school curricula indirectly act as mechanisms of social control. Teachers are able to enforce order in the classroom by saying: 'Be quiet and continue with your work because we have a lot to learn before the examination at the end of the year!'

As we will try to show in Chapter 6, school curricula are also instruments of social control because they represent only that knowledge which is approved by the dominant groups in society. During colonial times, for example, the authorities tried to prevent the spread of academic types of curricula because Europeans favoured only a limited technical kind of instruction for Africans. School knowledge is strongly influenced by the ideology – beliefs which support vested interests – of ruling groups. In the USA, for example, school civics textbooks would not be allowed to explore the principles of communism – except, perhaps, in a very negative way – and in Africa, as in many other parts of the world, some kinds of knowledge (for example, political education) are not considered suitable for inclusion in school curricula.

In addition to leaving out vital and important areas of human knowledge, some believe that school curricula also distort the knowledge they do contain. Young (1971) and others suggest that school knowledge tends to create artificial barriers between information and ideas which are really connected, mainly because the curriculum is divided sharply into different subjects and disciplines. They argue that the school timetable and all the subjects contained in it are really mystifications of reality. Students accept these artificial subject boundaries because they wish to pass examinations, but according to Young they do not learn about the world as it really is, or about the connections between the various subjects studied. Young's view of school curricula has been heavily criticised, and it is now suggested that subject boundaries are necessary if students are to make sense of the knowledge they are given. It is also pointed out that different subjects like mathematics and history have characteristics which are inherently different from one another, and that schools can do little else but reflect these essential differences.

It is not necessary to master the intricacies of this debate about the nature of school knowledge as long as one fundamental question is remembered: are the ideas and the information taught in school basic truths, or are they not basic truths but distortions, much affected by the way school curricula are designed?

Chapter 4

The Sociology of the School

Introduction

Schools can be thought of as societies within a society. They have effects on students which are additional to more general influences from the education system, such as the curriculum. In this chapter we will look at how schools are organised, how school cultures develop and how teachers and students interact in classrooms.

Schools and Society

Schools are not a recent invention. As mentioned in Part One, schools of various sorts have existed in Africa for centuries. Two well-known examples are Koranic schools and traditional initiation schools.

The existence of schools tells us that a society has become or is becoming complex. As societies develop they begin to create all kinds of specialised roles and occupations which require long periods of training. Education can no longer be left in the hands of the family or kin group if such societies are to maintain their development.

The link between development and the building of schools is well illustrated by the early empires or Sudanic states of West African history such as Kanem, Mali and Songhai. The ruling groups of these states embraced Islam. Schools and universities were built. The traditional function of higher Koranic schools was to spread Islamic culture and ideas, as well as literacy in Arabic. Gradually Islam spread from the rulers and better-off merchants to the ordinary people in many parts of West Africa. The growing complexity of West African societies, the development of trade and the production of agricultural surpluses all supported the existence of schools and teachers.

African societies have not only developed their own tradition of Koranic schools but have also received and adapted the European type of school. This was much affected in its organisation and style of discipline by the Industrial Revolution in Europe. During the last century, when illiteracy was common in Europe, the ruling classes opposed the idea of mass schooling. They feared the rapid spread of literacy and revolutionary ideas and protest among the working population. But gradually some of the better-off – particularly the liberal middle classes – realised that schooling was essential for the continued growth of industry.

There was a demand for literate workers and for employees who would conform to the new disciplines of industrial and clerical work. The social training of European elementary schools in the last century reflected human qualities which every employer wanted to see in a docile labour force: punctuality and cleanliness, a willingness to work hard at routine tasks and obedience to authority.

The nineteenth-century school of European society therefore imparted social training as well as instruction in school subjects. All kinds of school, whether in Europe or Africa, do this. A special term, 'the hidden curriculum', refers to the social training and social messages which schools transmit to students.

The Western school, including elementary and secondary types, was introduced by missionaries and colonial governments to Africa. The existing indigenous forms of school were almost certainly as strictly disciplined as the types of school introduced by Europeans. But the Western school contains different social messages, as well as imparting new types of knowledge (Shipman, 1975, p. 112). The school day is organised according to a fixed timetable, and in larger schools there are frequent changes of teachers and rooms. In secondary school the students learn that they are to be treated as members of a group rather than as individuals. The hidden curriculum of the Western school is therefore one of teaching acceptance of the authority and impersonality of a formal organisation. Not all students adapt successfully to the timetabled, disciplined atmosphere of the Western school, but it is the goal of such schools to make every student conform.

According to Fafunwa (1974, p. 62), Koranic schools of the elementary type have a less impersonal atmosphere. They are usually at or near the house of the teacher. Lessons are often held in the open air. Their size may vary from a dozen to fifty pupils, but attendance is not as strictly monitored as in the Western school. The Koranic school day is not divided into strictly timed periods, as in Western schools, and arriving late for school is usually tolerated if proper excuses are given. Although part of the Koranic school's hidden curriculum is to learn to respect the authority of the teacher, there is a greater possibility than in the Western school for personal relationships to develop between the teacher, the student and the student's relatives. However, such close personal relationships between teachers and students' relatives may not continue once the student has entered higher levels of Koranic education.

Although Western, Koranic and traditional initiation schools vary a great deal in organisation and goals they all involve a considerable degree of discipline and subjugation to the teacher's authority. They also share the characteristic of attempting to remove students from the ordinary world to teach special knowledge and instil special disciplines.

Schools are not completely divorced from society, however, and the continuation of strict discipline in African schools must in part be a reflection of parental wishes. Nigerian parents commonly believe that beating is necessary to ensure learning (Onwuka, 1968, p. 35). Although flogging and strict discipline are often unpopular among students and some parents, it is unlikely that teachers would be allowed to enforce discipline so strongly unless parents and relatives agreed with their practices. Changes in the organisation of schools towards a more relaxed style of discipline, learning by problem-solving rather than by drill and other kinds of reform are likely to meet with resistance from society at large as well as teachers in schools.

School Goals

Schools can be compared with other kinds of institutions which care for people or provide services: for example, hospitals. Schools and other kinds of institutions share the following basic characteristics:

(a) A set of goals which define the aims of the institution.
(b) A set of rules (both official and unofficial) which regulate or at least influence the behaviour of staff and members of the institution.
(c) A standardised treatment of the institution's inmates or clients. Some institutions are very standardised, treating all individuals in exactly the same way, whereas others allow officials and clients considerable leeway in behaviour.

When a patient is admitted to hospital, or a student begins secondary school, certain routine procedures take place. New members of the institution may have to wear a special uniform, will have their personal histories recorded on files and will be subject to commands from the staff. The entrants are processed according to the rules and goals of the institution.

Like other types of care and control organisations, schools have goals which reveal the aims of the staff and clients. Three types of school goals can be distinguished. Each type may occasionally be in conflict with another, so teachers and students sometimes have to make difficult decisions about which are the most important.

Instrumental Goals
These relate to the outside world – they are the goals of examination success and academic competition. Such goals are called instrumental because students are using the school as an instrument or a means to

attain success in the outside world. The school organisation encourages academic competitiveness.

Expressive Goals
These reflect the authority of the group over the individual. They aim to strengthen the unity and common identity of staff and students. Expressive goals express or symbolise unity and consensus. Examples of expressive activities, which follow expressive goals, are sports events, school assemblies and other rituals which emphasise the importance of the school's reputation and unity.

Sometimes expressive goals give students who are not very good academically a feeling of equality with their classmates. But there is always a potential conflict between expressive and instrumental goals. This is because the school is trying to do two opposing things: to encourage competitiveness and individualism through academic work, but at the same time trying to promote cohesiveness and equality through expressive goals and actions.

Normative Goals
These are reflected in the aspirations of teachers to instil norms in students. Norms are beliefs or standards of how behaviour ought to be. Teachers often hope that their efforts will not only lead to normative behaviour in school, but will also have an effect on students' behaviour when they have left. Thus schools are organised as a society within a society so that ideal, moral aspects of the world can be stressed in isolation from the supposedly corrupting influences of the outside world. This is as true of the traditional Poro initiation school of the Mende people of Liberia and Sierra Leone as it is of the modern secondary school. Both attempt to remove their students from the real world to some extent, and try to teach values such as responsibility, honesty, physical strength and stamina, courage and initiative.

Needless to say, the normative goals of schools are usually the most irksome and tedious as far as students are concerned. Sometimes normative goals conflict with instrumental and expressive goals. We all know of the tiresome narrow-minded kind of teacher who spends more time punishing students or correcting their behaviour than actually teaching them (conflict with instrumental goals), or interrupting a school assembly, prize day or concert because students are not wearing school uniform correctly or have broken some other school rule (conflict with expressive goals).

The School and Bureaucracy

While factory work is relatively uncommon in African societies, work in bureaucratic institutions is a very common source of employment for the educated. So if school is not so much a preparation for industrial work, it can be thought of as training for participation in bureaucratic organisations.

Higgins (1976) found that in one developing country (Iran) negative characteristics of bureaucracy, such as authoritarian relationships between staff, adherence to rigid rules and reluctance to accept change, were mirrored in that country's education system. Schools can play an important part in teaching people how to act as bureaucratic employees or how to survive in bureaucratic institutions. This may be thought of as one of the hidden goals of the school.

As there are close parallels between schools and bureaucratic institutions such as offices or government departments the next section will be devoted to looking at what bureaucracy is and in what ways schools are non-bureaucratic as well as bureaucratic.

What is Bureaucracy?

Every kind of social organisation, including the school, must solve two major problems:

(a) The tasks to be performed by the organisation's staff and members must be divided up and allocated in some way – this is the problem of the division of labour.
(b) The organisation's members must agree on the way tasks are allocated to each person, or must have tasks forced upon them – this is the problem of authority and power in organisations.

Max Weber, one of the founding fathers of sociology, defined bureaucracy according to the special way it solves these two problems. Weber suggested that there is a gradual trend towards bureaucratisation in most areas of human life. This is evidenced by such things as growing conformity to written rules, the rise of the government official over the traditional ruler or chief, and the development of impersonal relationships in organisations. Thus problems of authority and the division of labour are increasingly solved by reference to written rules and bureaucratic authority rather than obeying the orders of a traditional ruler, chief or king.

Weber saw the growth of bureaucracy as a very gradual process. Some institutions become more bureaucratic than others, and some resist becoming bureaucratic. An example of resistance to bureaucratisation is the Aladura Church in Nigeria, in which the authority of the church's leaders is believed to flow from their faith in God or their spiritual gifts rather than from their position on a career ladder in the church or their administrative competence. It is possible to find churches, usually long-established denominations, which are much more bureaucratic than the Aladura Church in their organisation.

An example of increasing bureaucratisation can be found in the world of military organisation. No one could describe the army of Samory, the West African slave-trader and conqueror of the late nineteenth century, as a bureaucratic organisation. Yet it was a formal organisation. It had goals, a division of labour and a system of authority based on Samory's power and personal qualities of leadership. The modern army, by contrast, is much more bureaucratic. It has a set of written rules and procedures, a hierarchy of officers and soldiers with established career patterns, and special facilities for training.

So churches and armies provide just two examples of organisations which may resist bureaucracy, but have nevertheless been susceptible to growing bureaucratisation in the twentieth century. Similarly, schools in African societies have been brought progressively into a bureaucratic state system in recent years. Beginning as isolated mission schools, scattered government schools or bush schools built by local people, the education systems of Africa have gradually become more centralised and subject to bureaucratic rules and regulations. Islamic schools, however, are an exception to this. Partly as a result of local suspicion of Western educational influence in northern Nigeria, and partly because of colonial government's unwillingness to expand educational facilities in northern areas, Islamic schools were not absorbed into the official system of education in the same way as Christian mission schools. There are now signs that Islamic schools receiving government grants and official inspection will increase in number. In 1975 in the Kano area, for example, there were twenty-two *Islamiyya* schools, while a smaller number were also recognised but did not receive government grants (Kelleher, 1975, p. 250). This suggests that Islamic schools will become increasingly subject to central authority and bureaucratic regulations.

How Bureaucratic are Schools?

In order to answer this question we should remember that in real life no organisation can be completely bureaucratic. Bureaucratisation is a matter of degree. Weber suggested that we consider the essential characteristics of bureaucracy and, using these as a measuring rod, judge how bureaucratic organisations such as schools have become. Weber termed the essential characteristics of bureaucracy the 'ideal type'. By this he did not mean that they are ideal features of an organisation in the sense of being good or highly valued. He only meant that such ideal type characteristics represent the essence of bureaucracy.

Some of the key features of bureaucratic organisation are as follows.

Each will be considered in relation to the school:

(1) Bureaucracies consist of a hierarchy of offices.
(2) Tasks are performed according to written rules.
(3) Officials perform their tasks in an impersonal manner.

(1) *Bureaucracies consist of a hierarchy of offices*
Perhaps the most obvious resemblance between schools and other bureaucratic organisations is the existence of a hierarchy of offices or positions. Headteachers or principals are responsible to a body of officials (in the educational administration), beneath the headteacher are other teachers of descending rank, each with special skills and training, and at the bottom of the ladder are students themselves.

On closer examination, however, the school hierarchy is not quite the same as other bureaucratic hierarchies. To begin with, the students are not employees of the organisation as clerks in an office are. The students are clients of the school bureaucracy rather than members of it. Considering the teachers next, it would be difficult to say that they occupy a single or simple hierarchy in the school. In secondary school, the work of the physics teacher cannot be supervised very closely by other teachers or even by the headteacher if none of them knows about physics. The headteacher can supervise teachers' general conduct and make sure that they keep order in their classrooms, but beyond this the head has to allow subject teachers some discretion to plan the year's work and decide how to teach the students. Each subject group of teachers (for example, sciences, languages, geography and so on) usually enjoys a degree of autonomy within the secondary school and, under its head of department, forms a separate hierarchy. As with many bureaucracies, therefore, schools have a division between specialist (the subject teachers) and administrative positions (for example, the head, deputy head or bursar). There is always a possibility of conflict between these positions because the specialist often resents interference from the administrator, and the administrator wishes to impose bureaucratic rules on the specialist.

Teachers may attempt to reduce this conflict by emphasising the professional unity of all the staff. The head and deputy head might share a similar training background and outlook with other teachers. The gap between headteacher and other teachers is usually narrowest in primary schools because the head may be teaching to a greater extent than the head in a secondary school, and the staff are not divided into specialist positions according to subjects.

Perhaps it is better to view the school as 'a loose confederation of classrooms' (Bidwell, 1965), each classroom being managed by a relatively autonomous teacher, than as a hierarchy of the bureaucratic type as outlined by Weber. This is not to say that teachers are completely free to act as they wish or that schools are free from bureaucratic control. Some of the bureaucratic constraints on teachers and schools will be considered shortly. But the teacher is dealing with young people whose behaviour is sometimes unpredictable and who often have unforeseen learning problems. The teacher's task therefore contains elements of unpredictability and is to this extent non-bureaucratic. The teacher must have some autonomy to do his or her job.

There is another problem in viewing schools and their staff as part of a bureaucratic chain of command. This is the amount of freedom that the headteacher or principal may have. This varies from country to country. In many African states the headteacher is technically the agent or bureaucratic official acting for the local education office; he is supposed to follow its instructions and officially has little responsibility beyond this. In the author's experience of primary schools in northern Ghana, for example, headteachers would receive notice from the district education office that perhaps one or two of their staff were to be relocated in another school, perhaps over a hundred miles away, without any explanation or consultation with the heads or the staff being moved. One study (CESO, 1969) found that the number of transfers of primary teachers is excessive, causing a great deal of uncertainty and insecurity among staff.

However, the headteacher of a small primary school, who appears to have very little official power and seems to be firmly controlled by the education bureaucracy, has more autonomy than clerks or other minor officials if for no other reason than that the school is physically separated from the education offices which contain his superiors. This freedom from direct control means that despite the bureaucratic control of appointments and promotions the head is often free to take all sorts of local decisions about how teaching is to be carried out, whether to try to involve the local community in school affairs, and so on. Sometimes teachers' freedom from direct bureaucratic control is abused. Inspectors who visit distant primary schools unexpectedly may occasionally find that classes have been dismissed so that teachers can visit friends or go to the local town.

Secondary school heads and college principals usually have more autonomy and responsibility than primary headteachers. This is because they may have as many qualifications as most of the officials in the educational administration. Therefore it is difficult to apply the concept of a graded bureaucratic hierarchy to all schools. Secondary heads often have considerable freedom to decide such matters as the way resources are to be spent in a school (although they do not decide the overall budget or allowance for the school), how the staff's tasks should be divided up and which teachers should be recommended for promotion.

(2) *Tasks are performed according to written rules*

The second main characteristic of bureaucracy is the tendency for tasks to be specified in writing, and for bureaucratic personnel to be trained to perform their jobs in accordance with written rules.

These characteristics appear to correspond to the organisation of work in schools. Teaching is divided into areas of competence, or subjects. The syllabus specifies in writing what the students and teachers must cover in the performance of their tasks. But there is a problem in describing teaching as an activity in which all the tasks are neatly divided up. In reality, the teacher has some professional freedom to alter the course of the curriculum and to decide how to present material. However, most students are very anxious to be taught the standard ways of passing examinations and resist teachers who try to vary teaching methods or interest them in anything else. In every education system there is conflict between the centralised, bureaucratic nature of the syllabus and examination system, and teachers' professional desires to do the job in the way they think best.

The continued existence of high proportions of untrained teachers in many African education systems also calls into question the idea that teachers, as professionals, can oppose bureaucratic constraints. As a result of the rapid expansion of the primary school system in Nigeria, for example, there are severe shortages of well-trained teachers. As they gain experience, untrained teachers acquire routine skills of teaching. This is a kind of training, but it is limited, and uncertificated teachers do not have the insights of a professional education. The lack of job security for untrained teachers and their inability to claim professional status weakens the political power and prestige of teachers as a whole (see Chapter 5). Therefore it is likely that wherever untrained teachers are found in significant numbers schools are subject to closer supervision and more bureaucratic control than in education systems in which all teachers are trained.

(3) *Officials perform their tasks in an impersonal manner*

A final comparison to be made between the ideal bureaucracy and the school lies in the field of the impersonality of social relationships. Impersonality is not very characteristic of teachers' relationships with one another or with students, perhaps because school is often a small community which encourages personal contacts, friendships and animosities. Gossip about school politics – for example, the decisions of the headteacher or the latest news of promotions – is common. Consequently, personal bias and favours enter teachers' dealings with one another and with students. An exception to this is the headteacher, who tries to administer his school impersonally and bureaucratically, and this will be discussed in the next section.

In relations with students, teachers are formally obliged to act impersonally and impartially. Teachers can sometimes carry impersonality too far by becoming cold, aloof and rule-bound in manner. However, most teachers strike a balance between giving students individual attention wherever possible and yet trying not to let too many personal feelings and biases affect their relationships with students.

A study of teaching methods in a sample of African primary schools discovered that 'it was considered a virtue [by teachers] to treat all children alike' (CESO, 1969, p. 121). Primary teachers are more interested in the academic performance of their pupils and in making sure that they all work hard than in looking for individual differences in ability among children. Thus success in examinations is seen as dependent on hard work and motivation, rather than on pre-existing differences in ability, intelligence, personality or other individual traits. This finding supports the view that African teachers tend to assess students impartially. Apparently, little use is made of concepts derived from professional training (for example, the psychology of achievement or intelligence) to assess individual students' characters or performance.

From our brief comparison between schools and the ideal type of bureaucracy, it should be clear that schools have bureaucratic characteristics, but there are also some important non-bureaucratic aspects of the teaching task and social life in schools. As Banks concludes (1968, p. 163), 'there is no evidence that schools and colleges are organised along rigidly bureaucratic lines'. This generalisation must be qualified, of course, because some teachers in African countries (for example, primary schoolteachers) do have to work in a rather rigidly constrained bureaucratic framework, while others, such as secondary teachers, may have considerably more autonomy than this.

The Role of the Headteacher

Teachers usually form a relatively close-knit social group in the school. Although teachers spend much of their working day in the classroom, they also interact a great deal with other teachers – for example, in staff meetings, school events, discussing students' work or meeting socially outside the school. Even teaching itself, usually an individual activity, is heavily influenced by the actions and attitudes of fellow teachers. The individual teacher depends on colleagues' co-operation in such matters as sharing the school's workload.

Sometimes teachers democratically discuss the organisation of the school. In other schools, the headteacher or principal may take all the important decisions, passing them down to a group of teachers who are either too divided among themselves and unable to challenge the head or are simply willing to accept the head's authority. And in other cases the headteacher is himself restricted to the role of interpreting and carrying out orders from the educational administration. In such a position the headteacher may feel himself to be very much a part of the ordinary teachers' group because they may all have to unite in opposition to the education office from time to time.

If they are given a measure of freedom from administrative control headteachers tend to behave like other people in leadership positions, such as bank managers or chiefs. A general tendency in such roles is for the occupants to try to create social distance between themselves and the people they lead or give orders to. Social distance is marked by a special kind of behaviour which emphasises aloofness from ordinary people and which creates an air of authority and responsibility around the officeholder. When approaching a bank manager, a chief or a secondary school principal, for example, those of lower social status must remember to be polite or deferential in their speech; they may have to make appointments to meet such people; and when they meet, the conversation may be more like an interview than an informal discussion. These are all devices for the creation of social distance. Social distance appears to be necessary in most societies because it enables holders of authority to avoid uncomfortable changes from being close and friendly one moment to distant, superior and commanding the next. Aloofness also enables those with some authority to act impersonally and not favour the interests of one person over another.

Sociologists (for example, Bidwell, 1965, and Corwin, 1965) have done a great deal of research to discover how decisions are made in schools and whether headteachers really adopt the pattern of aloofness just described, or whether they try to implement their decisions by using a close, personal approach to their staff. Headteachers also have to decide whether to delegate their responsibilities to their junior colleagues or whether to try to monopolise decision-making themselves. In addition to choosing whether to be personal or impersonal leaders, and whether to delegate authority, headteachers are also presented with a choice in terms of which aspects of their job they wish to concentrate on. A typical secondary headteacher, for example, must cope with all three roles below, but each head will resolve for him or herself exactly how much time should be spent on each.

(a) *The public role*. This involves liaison between the school and the local community, and particularly with representatives of such bodies as the town or district council, local churches and other prestigious organisations. The head is responsible for the public image of the school, and those heads who spend a lot of time on this role organise many showpiece events such as school concerts, plays, prize days and sports events.

(b) *The organisational role*. A headteacher who takes this role seriously often sees himself as an administrator or business executive rather than as a teacher. Such heads spend most of their time working at their desks with school timetables, plans for school budgets and requisitions and with correspondence to the educational administration. It is important to remember that not all headteachers like this kind of role or have been trained in management to deal with it, but some are nevertheless thrown into organisational roles because their schools have expanded and demand efficient organisation, or because their school has merged with another.

(c) *The teaching role.* Pressure of expectations to perform the previous two roles usually cuts down the amount of time a headteacher can spend in teaching (although primary headteachers may do a lot of teaching). Some secondary headteachers are relieved to leave the classroom, while others cling to this role because they wish to maintain face-to-face contact with as many students as possible.

Whether a headteacher carefully balances his time and energies between each of these three roles, or whether one or two are neglected at the expense of the other(s), will clearly affect the teaching staff's attitudes towards the head and the running of the school. But these attitudes will also be affected by the headteacher's *style* of leadership – whether he is an impersonal bureaucrat or a personal leader, for example.

Moeller (1964), in a study of twenty high schools, asked a sample of teachers about their schools' organisation and whether they shared in school decision-making. Surprisingly, Moeller found that teachers who felt that they had a greater than average say in the affairs of their schools, and had a sense of power, were those who worked in highly bureaucratised schools.

Moeller's findings that teachers are favourably disposed to working in bureaucratic schools become less surprising if we remember that bureaucracy has the advantage of *predictiveness*. The fact that rules of procedure are known to all and that the headteacher himself abides by these rules means that teachers can predict how decisions will be made. This apparently gives a greater sense of power, perhaps because teachers know when it is possible to intervene to alter decisions, or at least know that decisions have not been arrived at behind their backs in an unfair or undiscussed way.

Typical problems to be resolved in school administration are who shall teach which classes, how school resources and accommodation are to be distributed and who is eligible for promotion. Schools which do not have a bureaucratic method for resolving these problems, according to Moeller, make teachers feel insecure and uncertain about what the rules of school policy-making are. Teachers in less bureaucratic schools may try to take decisions, but find that the head has already made them or has reached decisions after consultation with a select few of the staff with whom he has close relationships. Thus headteachers who are friendly with their staff and who try to develop personal relationships with them may find that teachers become hostile and dissatisfied with the running of the school if it is not clear how decisions are reached.

Therefore it is wrong to see all headteachers who use the personal or 'human relations' style of leadership as liberal and democratic leaders. At the same time, not all those who use a firm, rule-bound approach are necessarily ruthless or undemocratic. As Richardson found (1973), the reverse may be true. In a case study of one secondary school she found that the headteacher's use of structured staff committees, bound by rules of procedure, led to the head being perceived as a fair and able leader. But the earlier use of an approach based on personal consultation was seen by staff as unfair and unpredictable management.

It is clear that the role of the headteacher is crucial to the way in which a school develops and a body of teachers is organised. One survey of African primary schools concludes that school quality is more influenced by the policy of the headteacher than by anything else. Successful schools showed 'the far-reaching and good influence of a stimulating personality at the top' (CESO, 1969, p. 122). Schools considered as successes in this study were those which obtained immediate replacements for departing teachers, held regular staff meetings, had established local committees in their surrounding communities to raise funds for school activities or to discuss school management, and had an orderly and purposeful atmosphere in their classrooms.

It follows that neglectful heads or those who are less able have severely negative effects on school organisation. This can be seen when an effective headteacher is replaced by someone who takes less interest in the personal development of the teachers and students, or who tolerates absence from duty, staff shortages and lax timekeeping, or who sets a bad example by his own absenteeism and lack of professionalism. The strong authority invested in the role of the headteacher therefore has the advantage of enabling reform from the top in a school system, but it also carries the danger of allowing some headteachers to abuse their authority and to exploit the deference shown to their position.

Students as a Social Group

The way in which a school is organised affects the students as much as the teachers. The quality of teaching and academic performance, the efficiency of the administration, the size and ethnic composition of the school are all important social influences on the life of the student. But students do not accept schooling entirely passively. Unlike factory products, students interpret and pass judgements on the way they are processed through the organisation.

In some schools these interpretations and judgements are shaped by student culture. Such subcultures are more likely to form in boarding schools, where students share all aspects of life, than in day schools. But even if a fully developed student culture does not form in a school there are still likely to be a variety of adjustments to school life and differing attitudes towards the school among groups of students. Sometimes these groups share ties of friendship, ethnic origin, or similar age, interests or abilities. Such groupings and the formation of a student subculture provide students with rules and expectations which are alternatives to the official rules. This is illustrated by the following extract from K. Elliott's book about a secondary school in Nigeria. It shows how the student's social groupings and rules are as much a part of school organisation as the teacher' group and rules (1970, p. 98):

No matter how muddled the administration became they went peaceably to their classes, worked hard and carried out their work without supervision. The prefects and senior students ran their own republic, and overt disorder which threatened their studies, and therefore their examination results, was firmly controlled. . . . The students followed their own inclinations without hindrance. They went into the village. They took taxis to Bukuru. They occasionally got drunk. Uniforms were occasionally unwashed, unrepaired or, in the senior forms, not worn at all. The bigger boys, in particular, slept late in the mornings and stayed up late at night. They set up their own systems of authority, each one a patron, with his own clientele of juniors who washed for him, copied up his notes and received his protection. Such systems were built up within each tribal group, and unhappy were those outside it or those who had no one of their own tribe to protect them.

Elliott's account of these events in a secondary school shows a number of interesting things about the nature of the student subculture. First, it is clear that the most important goal of the students is the instrumental one of passing examinations. The students virtually keep order in the school themselves so that academic work is not disrupted too much. They are willing to tolerate the poor organisation of the official school community as long as they are not deflected from their main goal. However, it is apparent that they are not particularly loyal to the school's official traditions and values (evidenced by the reluctance to maintain their uniforms), or the expressive goals of the school community.

Elliot's description of this school also shows how social groups form among students. Ethnic origins seem to be particularly important in deciding membership of cliques or subgroups in the school, although one can imagine other schools in which most students come from a single ethnic group or local district, in which case other criteria (friendship, age, ability, village of origin) would presumably become important in group distinctions among students.

Foster (1965) found that ethnic imbalances in secondary school enrolment in Ghana (the overrepresentation of some ethnic groups and the underrepresentation of others) are not marked, except for an underrepresentation of northerners. Such equality between ethnic groups is likely to be found in other African countries where access to education is relatively open (see Part One). But certain schools tend to become dominated by a particular ethnic group, even though the education system as a whole is fairly representative of all groups in a country. High-status schools, which have a national reputation for high academic standards, tend to be ethnically mixed because they attract students from all over the country. Low-status schools, however, are significantly more ethnicised because their students are mainly drawn from the surrounding district or region.

Foster also found that ethnic concentrations in girls' schools, whether high- or low-status, tend to be more marked than in boys' schools. This is explained by the facts that educational opportunities for girls and the willingness to educate them lag behind the development of secondary education for boys; the most urbanised and advanced ethnic groups are most willing to send their daughters to secondary school, and so girls' schools are dominated by these groups.

The School Culture

The previous section describes some of the characteristics of the unofficial culture of the students. This subculture binds students together with ties of loyalty and constrains their behaviour to some extent with unofficial rules. The formal organisation of the school also makes a bid for the loyalty of the student.

There is no clear dividing line between the official and unofficial cultures, or between the official and unofficial rules which represent these cultures. When teachers or students know that they are acting either formally or informally, rules of behaviour are usually clear and therefore roles are clearly defined. For example, a teacher may work in the classroom (formal role) or drink with friends in a local bar (informal role). In both situations the teacher is likely to feel secure. But if students from the teacher's school walk into the bar late at night should the teacher act formally and reprimand them, or act informally and try to ignore them? Whatever the teacher decides to do he will feel uncomfortable because he does not want to put on the stern face of the schoolmaster in an informal setting, and yet probably feels obliged to maintain the formal rules of the school which state that his students should not be out of the school compound so late.

Sociologists who have studied institutions of various kinds (for example, Dornbusch, 1955, and Goffman, 1968) comment that there is a tendency for the staff of institutions to turn a blind eye to the misdemeanours of inmates. Up to a point the staff are prepared to let the inmates run their own affairs. This is because the staff want to avoid those uncomfortable situations which are not clearly formal or informal, such as the incident in the bar just described. Avoidance of undefined situations appears in schools as well as other institutions.

The official culture of the school defines the roles of teachers and students. It reduces some of the anxieties about undefined situations and provides a clear guide to behaviour. The school culture includes such things as symbolic communication: for example, a distinctive use of language and particular ways of addressing teachers, or visual symbols such as school uniform. It includes expressive activities of the sort mentioned above, such as morning assemblies or sports days.

The extent to which school cultures are internalised or adopted as a design for living by students will depend on a number of factors. Changes in the organisation of schools and society at large can change or threaten the stability of official school cultures. Therefore, as school cultures change, students' experience of schooling in general changes. If a school gradually changes its intake of students – for example, by drawing in proportionately more local students than before or becoming less selective in admission procedures – then the newer students may be less willing than the former to accept traditional school rules and customs. Rapid staff turnover can also destroy long-lasting school traditions. And if prevailing social attitudes towards the nature of schooling change then it is likely that old school traditions will die out to be replaced by new ones. Elite schools which were patterned on English public schools have changed many of their customs, songs and activities since independence. The teachers are now generally local graduates rather than expatriates, and these schools must share resources with newer schools.

School Quality

In addition to the informal culture of the students and the official culture there are other aspects of school organisation which affect the experiences of students. These aspects can be summarised as school quality, although this is sometimes rather hard to define. Nevertheless, the quality and status of a school is often well known by students and teachers alike. As mentioned, the role of the headteacher has a significant effect on school quality.

Foster (1965, p. 231) found that secondary school students have 'a very realistic perception of the school hierarchy which corresponds remarkably with our ranking of schools'. Foster's study shows how schools can be classified into two divisions, rather like football teams. In the first division are the better-quality government and government-assisted schools which have good examination records. The second division are the lower-quality or lower-status private and non-assisted secondary schools. A number of factors seem to influence the reputation of secondary schools: the examinations, the range of examinable subjects offered at a school, the proportion of graduates on the staff and the quality of teaching.

The characteristics and rating of secondary schools are well known and much discussed by students seeking entry to secondary education. However, the amount of knowledge about the quality of many secondary schools may be restricted in rural areas, where only the reputations of local secondary and elite national schools are known.

The higher-quality schools, which are often the longest established, are usually significantly larger than lower-quality schools. The larger schools are able to maintain a large, well-qualified staff and can organise a full curriculum, whereas smaller schools often experience difficulties in maintaining an effective staff. Sociological studies of the effects of school size on students' experience of education have not produced clear evidence of any advantages of the small school. A study of British secondary schools (Lynn, 1959) found that on strictly academic criteria the larger school has a clear advantage over the smaller school. This finding parallels Foster's conclusions about the larger size of the better-quality African schools.

It is wrong to isolate a single factor such as school size as a determining cause of difference in students' experiences of school life. The impact of a school's quality on the individual student is more likely to be the result of a combination of social factors – the characteristics of its staff, the efficiency of the headteacher and school administration, and its culture and traditions.

The Sociology of the Classroom

So far the school has been discussed as a single entity – as an organisation composed of groups of teachers and students. The school can also be considered as a set of smaller entities, or classrooms, each with its own particular characteristics. The classroom is not a completely separate or independent unit. The preconceptions and attitudes teachers and students bring into the classroom affect their behaviour there. But it is still true to say that classrooms are partly independent of the social conditions which surround them. Each class contains a group of students who may be well disciplined and studious with one teacher but rebellious and bored with another.

Over time, a history of interaction between each teacher and each class builds up – a history of understanding and friendliness, and possibly of conflicts and disagreements as well. In short, a gradual learning process takes place, a process in which the students assess the teacher and the teacher learns about the class. Some classes develop a reputation among the teachers, so that one may hear in the staffroom that 'the fifth form seem to be good academically this year' or 'the third form haven't settled down to working steadily yet. I can't remember a class as lazy as this one.' Similarly, teachers earn a reputation among the students. Mr Amankwah, the mathematics teacher, might be known as a strict disciplinarian, and so on.

It is important to understand the nature of classroom interaction because as soon as a teacher has built up a certain reputation or an individual student has become publicly known as clever or dull this reputation tends to influence future classroom interaction and other relationships between teachers and students. A particular student who is struggling with her mathematics lessons, for example, may be unwilling to ask questions of Mr Amankwah, the strict maths teacher, or approach him individually for help, because he has a reputation for being unapproachable. Thus the progress of the student is held back by a publicly defined reputation of the teacher. At the same time, Mr Amankwah may have written off this student because she has a reputation for being slow in mathematics; although the girl may well have some potential for improvement in the subject the teacher decides that it is not worth the effort.

It should now be clear that classroom interaction, and the social relationships between teachers and students at this face-to-face level, have considerable effect on the academic performance of students. Progress at school cannot be explained solely by the intelligence of the individual student, by his willingness to work hard, or by his home background. All these factors are important, but classroom interaction can also have a decisive effect on the student's academic performance.

Classroom Interaction and Ability

As far as the teacher is concerned, educational ability means the correct performance by students of the tasks set. Knowing how to answer a teacher, when to ask a question and what to do when a teacher sets a problem are as much social as intellectual skills. Thus the bright student who is shy and withdrawn in class, or is perhaps ridiculed by fellow students because he comes from a minority tribe, may well earn the reputation of being dull.

Part of the teacher's task, therefore, is not simply to instruct students but also to apply some sociology to understand the group structure of the class. The teacher should try not to see the abilities of individual students in isolation from the social context of the class and the effects classroom dynamics have upon academic performance. What the teacher expects from a student in terms of performance can be a powerful influence upon a child's academic progress, so it is important for the teacher to be as objective and unprejudiced about individual students as possible.

A famous study of the effects of teacher expectations was carried out by Rosenthal and Jacobson (1968). This experimental study of one school involved the intelligence testing of a sample of pupils. A number of the sample were selected at random, and the teachers were told that these particular children showed greater than average intellectual promise and that in the coming year they would bloom in ability at school whether or not the teachers gave them any extra tuition.

A year later, all the school's children were re-tested for intelligence levels and performance in schoolwork. It was found that the children who had been randomly selected and falsely identified to the teachers as potentially bright had in fact attained significantly higher levels of academic performance and intelligence. There were some exceptions to this finding: for example, teacher expectations did not have much effect on older pupils. Younger pupils, and pupils from a minority ethnic group, who were usually thought of as dull, profited the most from the revised expectations of their teachers.

Rosenthal and Jacobson's study shows dramatically that what teachers expect of students has a strong influence on actual performance. But there have been some criticisms of this study. This was a study of only one school, and other studies of teacher expectations (Claiborn, 1969) had different results. Perhaps the influence of teacher expectation varies, being weak with some types of teacher and some kinds of student populations, but much stronger in other situations. As far as African classrooms are concerned it is probably worth while for teachers to remember that their expectation may influence their students, by way of subtle forms of encouragement given to some, discouragements given perhaps unwittingly to others, and by the way questions are directed to the class.

Language in the Classroom

Student ability is influenced by classroom interaction and a vital part of this interaction is language. For some students of lower ability the lesson is often an attempt to appear inconspicuous to the teacher and to avoid being asked to speak, while at the same time trying to understand what the teacher and other students are saying. For other students (not necessarily the most able) the lesson is an opportunity to show off language skills and dominate the class.

It is the teacher, however, who typically dominates most of the time given to conversation in the classroom. Attempts to measure the amount of time given to teacher talk as compared to student talk often show that the teacher speaks for a longer time than all the students put together. This is surprising if we consider that the person who already has proficiency in verbal skills – the teacher – has much more practice in explanation, questioning and verbal reasoning than those who presumably need to improve the most – the students.

The typical teacher's misuse of language is not simply one of dominating classroom discussion time. There are other problems of teachers' style of classroom language. Barnes (1969) describes a language of secondary education which teachers use. This is a style of expression which mystifies students and holds back their verbal development: teachers use scientific or specialist terminology even in the early stages of teaching a new subject rather than using more common or homely words to define objects and ideas. Thus lessons can become recitations of terms rather than an opportunity to learn and use concepts in everyday speech. Teachers' reliance on drill and expecting students to learn by rote is partly a reflection of their own insecurity or lack of knowledge, according to one study of African primary schools (CESO, 1969).

Another characteristic of the language of secondary education is the teacher's tendency to use what Barnes calls closed questions. These require the student to anticipate what the teacher wants and to finish a sentence the teacher has started. The learning difficulties which result from this approach are illustrated by Gay and Cole:

> It is common for children to shout out answers to the teacher before he has finished stating a problem. They try to outguess each other to show the teacher how smart they are. For example, the teacher gave the problem, 'Six is two times what number?' When the children heard the words 'six', 'two' and 'times', they shouted 'twelve'. Their experience with the teacher showed that he was always asking the times table, and they guessed he was asking it again. They were wrong – and were probably never quite sure why. They were told the answer was 'three', which probably confirmed their idea that school made no sense whatever. (1967, p. 34)

This example refers to a scene in a primary school classroom. The tendency for teachers to use closed questions is as common in secondary schools as in primary, although the kinds of mistakes made by secondary school students would probably be more complicated than the simple mathematical mistake described.

Another common criticism of the use of language in the classroom is that teachers rarely expect questions from their students beyond routine inquiries about how to complete a task. Unexpected questions about ideas or information contained in the lesson often catch teachers off their guard. They prefer students to give them expected answers. As one report about primary teachers puts it, 'they seemed to feel safest at their desk, marking work with the help of a teacher's book that has all the answers' (CESO, 1969, p. 126).

The amount of ethnic variation in language can also affect the students' academic work. African teachers are often unsure which language should be used in the classroom – the local language of the majority of students (this might alienate and hold back the development of minority group children), the official language of the country, or some teaching arrangement alternating both local and official languages. There are advantages and disadvantages to each course of action as far as the choice of the appropriate language for the classroom is concerned. This problem will be discussed further with regard to the issue of literacy (see Part Three), but for the time being the special disadvantages of children from minority ethnic groups in the classroom should be noted.

Social Control in the Classroom

One of the main reasons for the dominance of classroom discussion by teachers is the use of language for social control. One of the best ways to ensure a quiet, obedient class is to fill as much time as possible with commands, dictation and questions.

Social control, or the maintenance of discipline in the classroom, is one of the major preoccupations of teachers. While there is a great difference between the sixth-form teacher who hardly needs to reprimand his class and the primary schoolteacher who beats the children every day, it is true to say that all teachers must face the problem of control from time to time. Teachers know that effective control of their class depends on establishing a reputation as someone who will not tolerate classroom disruption. Experienced teachers often advise junior colleagues to be extremely strict with their classes in the first few weeks of teaching a new class. This way, students are given the impression that the teacher will always expect them to be obedient.

Teachers are not always successful in imposing control on the classroom, however. The fact that classroom discipline does occasionally break down and that students can become unco-operative or rebellious means that the teacher's enforcement of control is not an automatic thing. The teacher has to make periodic attempts to reinforce control. Waller (1961), in a classic study of the sociology of teaching (first published in 1932), describes how a teacher must practise 'impression management' in order to make control effective. In other words, teachers become practised actors who are able to give the impression of being stern or kindly, angry or peaceable, patient or exasperated, as the situation demands. Learning to put on an act is an essential part of the teacher's task of control.

The students themselves do not simply listen to the instructions of the teacher and obey like robots. The lesson is for them partly a game in which they must try not to appear ignorant and, as Gay and Cole comment above, 'show the teacher how smart they are'. Thus students are very active in the classroom. They must continually try to interpret what the teacher wants next. They might also be tempted to let their attention wander from the teacher, particularly towards the end of a tedious lesson, and therefore pose a threat of disruption or disorder to the class. Even the student who falls asleep in class is, in a sense, actively flouting the teacher's authority and must be corrected. It is not unusual to find that teachers design their lessons with distinct phases of activities, so that the variety of tasks the students have to do will hold their attention and prevent the possibility of boredom and disorder.

Interruptions, questions and other challenges to the teacher will be particularly frequent when a teacher is a newcomer to the class. The students will test to find out how far he or she will yield before punishing or correcting them. Once students know how strict a teacher is a kind of bargain is struck between them.

This bargaining process and the way it is resolved is known as 'defining the situation'. If a teacher successfully defines the classroom situation as one in which quietness and hard work prevail then the students will accept this as reality. Some primary headteachers are so good at defining the situation for their pupils that they can bring quietness to a room simply by tapping a ruler on a desk. While such teachers would probably have had to correct the pupils continually at the beginning of the year, they will gradually have refined their control over the children so that eventually only minimal correction is necessary. The children in such classes do not think of disrupting them because the teacher's authority has become a reality to them. With another teacher who has not been so effective in defining the classroom situation, however, the same children might well contemplate not paying attention to the lesson or even disrupting it.

Students' acceptance of a teacher's authority does not, however, depend entirely on the strictness of a teacher, or the effectiveness of his techniques for controlling the class. A teacher who tries to enforce discipline for discipline's sake, or for the satisfaction of wielding power over others, or to hide his own ignorance, will find considerable difficulty in maintaining classroom control. This is because students interpret teachers' abilities and fairness, and their response to the teacher's instructions will depend on their assessment. An example of the difficulties experienced by a strict, but ignorant and biased, teacher is given in Ngugi's novel, *A Grain of Wheat*:

> Kihika left Mahiga school a little disgraced. It happened like this. During a session one Sunday morning, Teacher Muniu talked of the circumcision of women and called it a heathen custom.
> 'As Christians we are forbidden to carry on such practices.'
> 'Excuse me, sir!'
> 'Yes, Kihika.'
> The boy stood up, trembling with fear. Even in those days Kihika loved drawing attention on himself by saying and doing things that he knew other boys and girls dared not say and do. In this case it was his immense arrogance that helped him survive the silence and blurt out:
> 'That is not true, sir.'
> 'What!'
> Even Teacher Muniu seemed scared by the sudden silence. Some of the boys hid their faces, excited yet fearing that the wrath of the teacher might reach them.
> 'It is just the white people say so. The Bible does not talk about circumcising women.'
> 'Sit down, Kihika.'
> Kihika fell to his seat. He held on to his desk, and regretted his impulsive outburst. Teacher Muniu took a Bible and without thinking asked the pupils to look up 1 Corinthians 7, verse 18, where St. Paul discussed circumcision. Muniu triumphantly started reading it loudly, and only after a couple of sentences did he realize the mistake he had made. Not only was there no mention of women, but circumcision of the flesh was not even specifically condemned. He closed the Bible, too late. For Kihika knew he had won the contest and could not help trying to seek approval from the eyes of the other boys, who secretly rejoiced to see a teacher humiliated by one of themselves. Muniu rather awkwardly explained the verses away and then dismissed the children.

This extract illustrates how even the teacher who appears to be completely certain that he has the right answer can be caught out by his own pupils. Challenges to a teacher's classroom authority may not be as direct as in this example, however, because sometimes students resist in ways which are safer for them: for example, by pretending never to know the answer to a teacher's questions, by remaining silent for as long as possible, or by doing written work extremely slowly. The students do not break any overt classroom rules this way, but nevertheless manage to communicate hostility and passive resistance to the teacher.

A study of passive resistance in Indian mission schools in America found that the children there are in many ways model pupils because parental discipline is strong and the children are generally polite and restricted in the presence of adults (Dumont and Wax, 1969). But the Indian community considers Western education irrelevant to their needs, so the children have found ways of controlling their teachers by remaining silent and unco-operative.

This situation is very different from the classroom atmosphere in most African schools, where enthusiasm for education is high and the students are usually co-operative with teachers because they are highly motivated to pass examinations. The study is useful, however, because it illustrates the fact that in classrooms the world over the teacher's authority rests partly on the goodwill of the students. If teachers enforce discipline unfairly, appear to be ignorant, or stray from the syllabus, African students will also challenge their authority.

Changes in Classroom Organisation

It has been common in many countries recently to question the characteristics of the traditional classroom and to ask whether they can actually impair the educational progress of children. Is it desirable, for example, for the teacher to monopolise classroom interaction and be preoccupied with control rather than education?

Some educationists argue for a more equal relationship between teachers and taught, with the teacher playing more of an adviser role than an instructor role. The teacher should aim to stay in the background while students work and discuss together in small groups. In theory, the social structure of the class becomes more open in the sense that students are able to move fairly freely about the classroom and develop learning relationships with a wider range of fellow students than before. Instead of the teacher setting the pace of the lesson by standing in front of the class and instructing them as a group, the teacher in the open classroom is supposed to work with students individually and to develop individualistic relationships with them.

It should be remembered that there is always a gap between the theory of education and social reality. In practice, teachers may work much as they always have done while subscribing to new ideas in order to appear progressive to others. Sociological studies of changes in classroom design and educational philosophy suggest that teachers often continue to dominate the classroom and exercise control in traditional, if slightly modified, ways.

In Britain and the USA, the open classroom idea seems to have spread only among a proportion of primary schools. Secondary education, where instrumental goals and activities are more common than in primary education, seems to have resisted the open classroom and discovery methods because they do not constitute appropriate preparation for standardised examinations. In Africa it is likely that examination-oriented students will prefer the traditional classroom to open classroom methods, which have vague goals of discovery rather than drill in knowledge to pass examinations.

The open classroom also conveys certain cultural expectations which may be resisted in many African societies. One of the assumptions of progressive teaching methods is that the child will discover knowledge for him- or herself, and will ask questions of the teacher out of curiosity. Although children obviously do ask questions and are curious, even in very strict, traditional classrooms, they might only be willing to show curiosity in polite culturally defined ways. In many societies it is impolite for children to go on asking questions of adults, or to interrupt adults when they are speaking. The philosophy of the open classroom, which imagines that self-awareness, discovery and inquisitiveness will develop in some kind of cultural vacuum, may well contradict the socialisation patterns of African children. And it is not at all certain that parents would willingly accept a change from the traditional classroom atmosphere in which children are well disciplined, and punished if they are lazy, to one in which children are given freedom and encouragement to question the teacher.

Another social obstacle to the development of open classrooms in African schools is cost. Changes in teaching methods have to be financed by extra teacher training (for example, in-service courses for existing teachers), and open classroom methods usually demand more expensive teaching materials, visual aids and so on than traditional 'chalk and talk' methods.

Conclusion

Classroom interaction should not be seen in isolation from society outside the classroom. Influences on classroom interaction can be thought of as divided into a number of spheres. First, there is the sphere of influence of the school itself: things like the physical layout of the school and classrooms, the provision of, or failure to provide, teaching materials, the quality of the school administration and the role of the headteacher. Secondly, there are the influences of the education system on the classroom – the type and level of curriculum, the quality of training that teachers have received, the number of examinations students must sit, and the amount of educational innovation (for example, educational broadcasting), are examples of the system's influence on daily life in the classroom. Thirdly, there are the social influences represented by attitudes of teachers, students and parents towards the school. Teachers and students enter the classroom with preconceptions of how to behave and what to expect. Students, for example, form a mental picture of school life which is shaped by the experiences of educated brothers, sisters and educated relatives. These traditions, along with parental expectations that schoolchildren should be well taught and disciplined, influence classroom interaction.

Given all the above influences, however, we must remember that classrooms have their own dynamics or chemistry of interaction. Although we can look at a whole range of social influences on a class of students, no one can predict precisely how that class will develop, or how individual teachers will respond to it. Only by examining face-to-face interaction – how teacher expectations of an individual student are formed, how language is used in the class, and how teachers and students bargain for control – can we fully understand the nature of classrooms and academic achievement.

Questions and Discussion Topics: Chapter 4

1 What does the social life of school teach students, and why is this social life described as the 'hidden curriculum'?
2 Compare and contrast the work of the following, paying particular attention to the amount of rule-following expected of each: (a) the teacher, (b) the lawyer, (c) the doctor. (See M. Peil, *Consensus and Conflict in African Societies* (1977, pp. 108–9), for a brief comparison of the status of these groups.)
3 What are the advantages and disadvantages of giving headteachers considerable freedom from bureaucratic control?
4 Discuss the reasons for school strikes by students and the part played in such conflicts by student subcultures or groupings.
5 What characteristics of students' appearance might lead a teacher to expect less of one student than another?
6 List in order of quality the secondary schools in your town, district or region. Compare your list with another's (this is an instructive group exercise), and discuss the reasons for choice of which schools are high, medium or low quality.
7 As a practical exercise, observe a school lesson, or a discussion group or seminar in your own college/university. Time the lecturer's or teacher's contribution and each student's contribution to the class discussion.
8 'Order in the classroom does not depend on the strictness or power of the teacher as such, but upon whether his/her claims to authority are perceived as legitimate by students.' Do you agree? Give reasons for your answer.

Chapter 5

Sociology and the Teacher

Introduction

Society expects many things of teachers. Students expect them to relay ideas and information effectively. Parents and students' relatives expect teachers to discipline their classes, to instil moral values and promote academic achievement. Development planners expect teachers to become key figures in plans to revitalise villages or begin some sort of co-operative effort. Curriculum reformers expect teachers to adopt new ways of teaching and new syllabuses. Adult literacy schemes expect teachers to play a part in helping local people to improve their reading. And governments expect teachers to introduce to their students ideas of national unity and respect for state institutions.

While society is all too ready to heap expectations and obligations on to the shoulders of teachers, it is surprising to find that teachers are not usually given the material rewards, training or social prestige to match their supposed importance. In this chapter we will examine the reasons for this state of affairs, particularly with regard to primary teachers, although the status of secondary schoolteachers will be discussed as well. When considering the work of the teacher and the place of teachers on the social scale, it may be useful to refer to Weber's ideas on social inequality.

Weber distinguished three elements of social inequality: social status, class position and power resources (see Part One). Traditionally, teaching enjoyed relatively high status and prestige. Teachers opened the door to the world of literacy in many African communities at the beginning of the century; they were often the only people able to read and write. As the number of teachers and the proportion of literate people grew, teachers' scarcity value declined. In Weber's terms, teachers' class position – the worth of their skills and their value in the labour market – fell. Although teaching still has some prestige because it is considered a rewarding vocation by many, the low income of teachers compared to other professionals often prevents them from appearing prestigious to others. Owning a house of modern design, a motor car or smart clothes are out of the reach of most teachers, particularly at the primary level. Secondary schoolteachers and most involved in higher education do enjoy professional status and relatively high financial rewards, but even the better paid feel deprived of what they think are their just rewards and, like less well paid primary teachers, have taken political action to improve their position. Union activity is an attempt by teachers to strengthen the third element of their ranking in society – power. Taking the Nigerian Union of Teachers as an example, we will discuss teachers' attempts to upgrade their status.

The Teacher's Public Role

Religious Influences on Teaching

The religious roots of education have established the idea that teaching is a vocation for which relatively low material rewards can be expected. This still applies nowadays, even though many teachers are not overtly religious and few work for mission schools. Although modern teachers may be fighting for higher pay, there has remained a public expectation that teachers should be self-sacrificing.

Islamic and Christian influences have affected the role of the teacher. As Fafunwa (1974, p. 56) notes, there was an early link between Koranic teaching and dependence on charity. Thus teachers in the Islamic tradition were much respected (high social status) because they were men of knowledge who cared enough about the Koran to teach it to others, but at the same time they were expected to be poor (low class position). According to Islamic tradition, local teachers do not receive fixed salaries or set fees, but depend on gifts and charity from students' relatives.

Christian influences on the teaching role were similar to Islamic influences in that relatively high status and low economic standing became confirmed characteristics of mission schoolteachers. Preachers, catechists and mission teachers shared the prestige of being associated with the coming of European knowledge, technology and overrule. In some cases, teachers were the go-betweens of colonial administration and village communities. Teachers had great prestige because they could provide the rare skill of literacy in the new official language. In addition to this, mission teachers were expected to be strongly religious and to have good moral character.

European missionaries therefore defined the teacher's role as one of self-sacrifice and subservience to paternalistic moral control. A teacher's suitability for a post was not assessed just on ability but also on personal habits, sobriety, dress and other characteristics that the missionaries considered appropriate.

The fact that teachers in the early days of colonial rule did not exploit their market position and their rare skills becomes less surprising therefore when we realise how strong were the moral pressures exerted on them. If a teacher did not show the expected behaviour of deference and self-sacrifice he could be deprived of work. Inter-denominational differences and hostility undoubtedly acted as barriers to collective action by teachers to improve their class position. As Fajana points out (1973, p. 392), missions were very hostile to the formation of teachers' unions in the 1920s. In 1926, for example, missions in Nigeria cut teachers' salaries before this was actually required by the colonial government. Any group action by their teacher employees threatened their policy of paying such low wages. Teachers' attempts to group together also threatened the religious distinctions of the various missions: missionaries feared co-operation between Catholic and Protestant teachers, for example.

Teachers are usually expected by parents to have high moral standards and to set a good example to children. As Roberts (1975) points out, it may be difficult for village schoolteachers – particularly young men – to live up to these expectations. Male teachers might be regarded with suspicion as outsiders who could seduce local girls, and so their behaviour is often closely watched and subject to gossip. Roberts mentions the high cost of compensation payable by teachers accused of such wrongdoings, and the withdrawal of food by people who normally cater for the village teacher.

Young teachers may find that they have to be particularly careful not to offend their elders in such things as smoking, drinking and enjoying the company of the opposite sex. These constraints, and the difficulties experienced by a teacher trying to gain acceptance in a local community, are well described in Ngugi wa Thiong'o's novel *Petals of Blood* (1977).

Although there have been some changes in public attitudes in recent years, with less strict ideas than before about teachers' conduct, it would still be true to say that teachers are more constrained than many other people by society's moral standards. Traditionally, teachers were expected to show some self-sacrifice and a concern with moral virtues rather than with financial rewards. The continuation of these expectations, albeit in a diluted form, affects teachers' own perception of their work and may explain some teachers' reluctance to strike or to demonstrate their desire for better pay and working conditions.

Structural Weaknesses

Teaching is an occupation which yields certain rewards: for example, the personal satisfaction of teaching the young, some of whom may eventually become important, or the relatively large amount of free time and holidays compared with office work. But there are other negative aspects of the teacher's public role. These might be termed structural or in-built weaknesses, and they apply to primary and secondary teachers alike.

The first and perhaps most significant problem is that the teacher spends a lot of time with the young. There is a saying that a teacher is 'a boy in a man's world and a man in a boy's world'. Teachers are believed to be without much knowledge of the real adult world, to be immature and inexperienced. This belief may be misguided as far as individual teachers are concerned, but the belief prevails and all teachers have to deal with it to some extent.

Sometimes people are quite accurate when they perceive teachers to be out of touch with other adults. Years of classroom teaching may make it difficult for teachers to turn off their teaching manner when in adult company. They sometimes become known as pedants who are for ever correcting opinion or spouting unwanted information.

Low prestige which results from working with the young is accentuated by the fact that many teachers are comparatively young themselves. The youth of teachers is particularly marked where pupil teachers are used to a great extent, or in countries like Nigeria which have recently expanded the output of teachers, or in rural areas, to which the newly qualified staff are often directed before being allowed choice jobs in urban areas. Age is still a strong status factor in African societies, and the literacy or training of a young teacher may not persuade the elders of a community that he has much status. Many young teachers are unmarried, and not having children of his own, a house or a farm detracts from the prestige of the teacher.

In rural areas, as Roberts notes, not only is the teacher in many cases thought of as young and inexperienced, but he is also in a dependent position. The teacher cannot cut himself off from village life or act independently of the elders. This is because food and shelter are usually provided by the villagers, and it is difficult for teachers to fend for themselves if they are teaching all day. The junior, dependent status of teachers is emphasised.

Another structural weakness of the teacher's role is the common idea that teaching, particularly at the primary level, is considered more suitable for women. Most societies have entrenched beliefs that men are superior to women, so that an occupation which involves childcare (traditionally a female activity) has low prestige. And in fact, because they usually have difficulty finding other professional or clerical work, primary schoolteaching is an attractive alternative for many educated women. It is interesting to note that inequalities between the sexes are perpetuated within teaching: although women are a large proportion of the teaching force, headteachers are usually men.

Another reason given for women's interest in teaching is that it is an occupation which allows free time to bring up children, and that the teaching service is sufficiently flexible to allow women to drop teaching for a few years and return to it later. In the eyes of other professionals the status of teaching is sometimes regarded as secondary: the husband earns more money in his profession, while his less educated wife supplements the household income through teaching. Of course teaching is the principal occupation of many households, but the image of it as less prestigious than other professional occupations is thereby established.

A major structural weakness of the teacher's role is that teaching is considered an occupation for failures. As Bernard Shaw put it: 'Those who can, do, while those who can't, teach.' Student teachers often add another remark: 'Those who can't teach, teach teachers.' Both remarks indicate the idea that teachers and college lecturers would be unlikely to succeed in any other occupation, and that the only success they can enjoy is in the world of children or students.

This view seems unfair to those who have successfully completed examinations and courses to become teachers and who are committed to the profession. Nevertheless it could perhaps be applied to pupil teachers who teach because they cannot find any other opportunities. Many teachers view their occupation as a stepping-stone to another career, so that in one respect they cannot be seen as failures, but as people who aspire to other kinds of work or to further education. At the same time, the desire to move out of teaching means that it is regarded by some as a second-best job. There must also be a proportion of teachers who never really wanted to teach, but who became trapped in the occupation because they failed to find another.

Lack of commitment to teaching among teachers and the perception of some teachers as failures therefore lowers the social status of teachers in general. There is disagreement, however, about the degree of lack of commitment among teachers. From a survey of primary and middle schoolteachers, Bame (1974) found that over half of the men and nearly three-quarters of the women teachers interviewed were satisfied with teaching. However, almost 75 per cent of the men and 45 per cent of the women teachers did not plan to make teaching their long-term career.

Low commitment to teaching or to a particular school is reflected not only in teachers' attitudes and plans for themselves, but also in the way they carry out their work. Absence from school, poor timekeeping and badly prepared lessons are noticed by students and their relatives and are evidence of low commitment which lowers the prestige of teaching generally. Perhaps the policy of removing teachers from one post to another within relatively short periods of service aggravates the problem of low commitment; people in the local community feel that it is not worth while getting to know the teacher, while the teacher is not too worried about poor performance because he or she will move to another post within one or two years.

Primary teachers often find themselves in rather lonely situations, therefore, if local people are not very interested in co-operating with them or in establishing social relationships. Sometimes teachers are posted to areas in which they do not speak the local language, and this problem increases the social distance between teacher and community. As Roberts points out, teachers are in a very unusual position because, unlike most other professional or educated people, they are expected to work and live in isolated villages as well as in larger urban centres. Low commitment to teaching, difficulties in getting on with local people, and the possibility of postings to rural areas all combine to reduce the prestige of teaching. It is not surprising that teachers who are working in villages often complain about their conditions of work and the lack of social contacts with other educated people.

Parent–teacher relations contain many problems for teachers. Teachers are in some ways very skilful at keeping parents or relatives of their students at arm's length. Most parents know little about schoolwork and usually do not wish to know about it. However, when the local community decides that the school is not being run properly or that a teacher is misbehaving this lack of communication between teachers and parents is a handicap. Stereotypes of teachers as young and irresponsible, or of local people as old-fashioned and interfering, easily develop. Roberts (1975), discussing this problem, shows that there are no established channels for local people to take action against a teacher. If they have a complaint they have to shun the teacher or withdraw their children from school. When incidents such as these occur, the failures of the arbitration system are shown up. The public role of the teacher is defined rather vaguely. There is a need to establish closer links between communities, teachers and education authorities.

While we have concentrated on the problems experienced by teachers in relations with parents, and the structural weakness or vagueness of teachers' roles, it should not be forgotten that some teachers adapt very successfully to community life. Teachers often chair meetings, or are secretaries or members of village committees. The prestige of such teachers is high, at least locally. As mentioned in the chapter on school organisation, well-organised schools have regular and purposeful meetings with parents. Older teachers sometimes settle in the villages or towns to which they are posted. As a teaching force becomes more balanced in its age structure – that is, with an increasing proportion of older teachers – some of the problems of relations between parents and young inexperienced teachers can be expected to disappear.

However, one weakness of primary and secondary teachers' roles that is more likely to grow than disappear is the tendency for their knowledge and skills to become commonplace. As increasing proportions of parents are educated themselves, it is likely that they will be more willing to challenge the teachers' opinion and wish to know more about the content of their children's education than their illiterate forebears did. It is also possible that some educated parents, remembering their own schooldays, will have a disdain for schoolteachers even though they continue to respect education. Teachers, particularly those who use strict methods of discipline, are remembered as killjoys. Many parents wish teachers to be strict with their children, but at the same time they have mixed feelings about the discipline that teachers have to enforce. Educating students or helping to build national unity are the psychological rewards which some see as attractive aspects of the job, but having to control and discipline large classes of children is perhaps a less prestigious aspect of teaching.

Secondary Teachers' Status
Many of the structural weaknesses in the primary teacher's role apply equally to secondary teachers, except that they are less subject to rural isolation. As we have already mentioned, secondary teachers are also better paid and enjoy a professional or at least semi-professional status. Secondary teachers should not be considered as a single group, however, because there are significant status differences among them according to qualifications, length of teaching experience and subject or specialism.

We must distinguish, for example, between graduates and nongraduates, between graduates with or without teacher training certificates, and between all these categories and those without either degrees or teaching certificates. Some would argue that it is this variety of levels of qualification and competence, and the sometimes petty animosities and status distinctions which teachers engage in, that add another structural weakness to the occupation of teaching. Secondary teachers are certainly aware of the differing statuses of subjects taught, as well as of qualifications or seniority. Vocational or technical subjects (home economics, metalwork, arts and crafts) are traditionally held to be less prestigious than academic subjects such as science or languages, so that teachers of the latter often have a higher status in the pecking order of the staffroom. Such status distinctions by subject or specialism are often compounded by the type and location of training of teachers. A graduate of a university education department usually has a lot more prestige than a graduate of a teacher training college, but there may also be further distinctions according to which particular college or university a teacher graduated from.

Although secondary teachers have a much higher social status than primary schoolteachers, their claims to a fully professional and influential position in society are not wholly recognised by the public or by governments. From a survey of a group of secondary teachers Morrison (1976, p. 102) found that more than half (59 per cent) thought that teachers had no impact on governmental education policy, and that only a fifth thought that teachers had much say in policy. As African

Table 5.1 Vocational Expectations and Present Employment of ex-Grammar School Students

	Percentage wanting to become	*Percentage who really became*
Primary schoolteacher	2	0·5
Secondary modern schoolteacher	3	6
Secondary grammar schoolteacher	11	31
Doctor	20	4
Lawyer	12	3
University lecturer	13	4

Source: This is a shortened version of the table presented by Adeyinka (1973).

education systems and their administrations tend to be very central-ised, particularly in francophone countries, secondary teachers lack the power to influence the educational process they are involved in.

Perhaps this lack of influence in society, the difficulties of claiming a fully professional status, and lower financial rewards than other pro-fessional groups enjoy, all combine to make secondary teaching a second-choice occupation for graduates or other well-qualified people. From a survey of 723 ex-students of grammar schools, Adeyinka (1973) found that a lot more people become secondary teachers than really want to, whereas the situation is reversed for popular profes-sions such as medicine and law (see Table 5.1).

Another reason for the public estimation of teachers as semi-professional lies in the separation of teacher training colleges from the mainstream of professional training and socialisation, the universities. Being trained in a college, even the higher-status advanced teacher training colleges which recruit for future secondary teachers, is unfor-tunately regarded as second best, though there is some evidence to suggest that college-trained secondary teachers are more progressive and professional in their approaches to teaching than graduates with-out any teacher training (Ferron, 1969). Of course, a high proportion of secondary teachers are university graduates; but, as Fafunwa (1970) notes, because university education departments usually have the lowest status a professional teacher training qualification gained after a first degree does not confer any additional prestige, compared with that of other professionals. Fafunwa suggests that one way to improve all teachers' standing and professional status would be to centralise and enlarge teacher training colleges, so that student teachers could enjoy better facilities and really effective training. Another possibility would be to abolish teacher training colleges altogether, and to merge student teachers with university students. In America, for example, the education of teachers is not separate from other university courses, so that intending teachers may study a wide variety of degree courses as well as those required for their professional training. This solution not only reduces some of the artifical status distinctions between teachers and other professional groups but also has a healthy broadening effect on the education of student teachers.

Teaching – a Profession?

Professional work is partly defined by the objective characteristics of an occupation – whether a particular group has a complete set of skills or knowledge, a long period of training, some freedom to decide how to carry out its work and enforce its own standards or code of ethics. These characteristics are, very briefly, definitions of professional work, but public acceptance of what is professional is also a matter of tradition and the ability of a group to persuade the public that its work is professional. Doctors, for example, have come to be regarded as professional in the last hundred years or so, but before this time their status was not so high. In parts of the world today (for example, the USSR), doctors do not have such a high status as they enjoy in Africa or Western Europe.

Teachers have difficulty in establishing themselves as a fully professional group. In the first place, teaching lacks the mystique and reverence associated with medicine, the law and other traditional professions. Schooling is now commonplace, and teachers are regarded as ordinary workers with commonplace skills. A teacher's knowledge, particularly at the primary school level, is not a special kind over which they have a monopoly, as do doctors and lawyers, but is composed of many different aspects of knowledge such as mathematics, history and chemistry. These subjects are often learned and relayed by teachers at a simple level only. Teachers do not have their own well-developed body of skills or expertise. Educational theory, which could be considered as an example of professional knowledge, is often disregarded by teachers after training (assuming they are given theory training in the first place). Teaching skills are seen as commonsense knowledge about controlling children, which almost any literate person could master with practice.

The professional is often regarded as a highly responsible person whose decisions are crucial to the well-being of the client. Thus the doctor is seen taking life-and-death decisions, the pilot is entrusted with the safety of passengers and the lawyer has to deal with intricate arguments in the courtroom. Teachers are not usually seen as people who have to take such crucial decisions, or whose ability is all that important, beyond a certain basic competence. This view is unfair, given teachers' influence over the welfare and academic progress of their students. Examination success, for example, is dependent on the teacher's skill in helping the student beforehand. But most of the credit for successful academic performance goes to the bright student, not the teacher. The teacher can assist or delay the progress of a student, but he or she is not often perceived as a decider of fate in the same way as a surgeon performing a difficult operation, or a lawyer presenting a complicated case in court.

In the 1950s, when two-thirds of Nigerian teachers were untrained (Howell, 1958, p. 106), there developed the view that no special skills were needed for teaching. There are still significant proportions of teachers in most African countries without any formal teacher training or professional qualifications.

As we have already mentioned, teacher training does not have such a high status as the higher education of other professionals. Training colleges, particularly those supplying primary schoolteachers, have a history of admitting students with lower academic qualifications than university entrants. Training colleges also tend to be more school-like than universities: college students often have to study a wide variety of subjects, as at school, and may have to tolerate stricter rules concerning dress and behaviour than other students. Such downgrading of teacher training students' status is unnecessary, and many institutions now have a freer, more adult atmosphere than before.

Teachers' claims to be professionals are also weakened by the authority structure of education authorities and schools. Teachers are subject to bureaucratic rules and regulations, and their work conditions are mainly decided by the authorities rather than themselves. Teachers' unions, which will be discussed below, have played an important part in furthering the rights of teachers to influence such things as pay levels, school curricula, and relations between schools and local authorities. Such attempts to run their own affairs are signs of growing professional awareness among teachers, but they do not yet compare with the strength of lawyers' associations or medical councils.

The success of individual teachers in resisting the control and constraints of bureaucratic authority obviously varies according to how many qualifications a teacher has and how much authority these qualifications command. A headteacher with lower qualifications but more experience than his junior colleagues will have some authority, but not complete control, over them. And a teacher with a degree or certificate has authority over the ordinary illiterate villager in educational matters. However, it is difficult to see how teachers can resist the very strong constraints of the education system itself. Even the most highly qualified teacher must recognise that he or she is an employee of a bureaucratic organisation.

Within schools, the amount of conflict over decision-making has been found to be higher than average where teachers are well qualified or professionally oriented (Corwin, 1965). Better-trained teachers tend to feel more constrained by bureaucratic rules and regulations than their less qualified colleagues. They are more likely to question authority and to demand some freedom in arranging schools affairs themselves. This tendency is most marked in colleges and universities, where professional values are strong among lecturers and where bureaucratic officials (for example, the registrar, the finance officer) are supposed to be accountable to lecturers' representatives.

As yet, however, most teaching is regarded as marginally professional or semi-professional work. Primary schoolteachers have been found to have a status roughly comparable with skilled manual workers (Peil, 1977, p. 208), while secondary teachers are placed somewhat higher than this. Teachers' salaries are much below those paid to other professional groups, and few teachers receive extra allowances, research facilities or training abroad, which some doctors receive, for example.

Commitment or dedication to a life's work are supposed to be key characteristics of a profession and, as mentioned above, teachers' commitment is usually lower than that shown by other professionals. Teaching is often viewed as an insurance policy by those who wish to try another line of work, or sometimes as a short-term activity to finance study for further examinations and movement to higher-level occupations. These characteristics, though by no means typical of the majority of teachers, have tarnished their professional image. In addition, there is often less pressure on teachers than on members of other professions to keep up-to-date with recent changes in professional knowledge or research findings, which affect the job. Pilots, doctors and lawyers, for example, often have to re-educate themselves if they are to survive in their work. Teachers, on the other hand, can manage with the same yellowing notes and textbooks year after year. The difference is a matter of degree, and some teachers are keen to learn new material or indeed are forced to do so if the syllabus changes. Many so-called professional doctors also get by with out-of-date knowledge.

The question as to whether teachers are to be regarded as professional is therefore only answerable in relative terms. The answer depends on what is publicly accepted as professional behaviour or rewards. At the moment teachers enjoy some autonomy – for example, in deciding how to teach, and in having more free time than other professionals – but they are also constrained by influences from local authorities, the community around their schools, and by parents' wishes. The semi-professional image of teaching is accentuated by low commitment among some teachers to the job, its 'feminine' role in society and other structural weaknesses mentioned in the previous section. In the next section we will discover to what extent teachers may be successful in creating a more independent and prestigious role in society.

Teachers and Trade Unions

Trade unions are social organisations which seek to unite workers of a similar class position and to promote the economic and social interests of their members. Trade union activity has grown significantly among teachers in recent years, particularly in Nigeria. This is not surprising, given the strong sense of common feeling or occupational identity among teachers. They are one of the largest single groups of state employees in most African countries. Teachers have begun to realise their importance in implementation of government schemes to expand education, and have begun to exercise power as a group.

In the past, most teachers rejected the very idea of joining unions. Although they were often exploited by their employers, teachers saw themselves as a group apart from manual workers and were reluctant to bargain for better wages or conditions as workers do. Early this century, associations of teachers were formed to campaign for common interests but, as Fajana (1973) points out, 'they were little more than clubs for a certain class of teachers'. Modelled on the professional associations of doctors and lawyers, many of these early teacher groups restricted membership to headteachers or to teachers with suitable character references.

At that time teachers were divided by religion according to the various mission schools they worked for. These divisions, together with the reluctance of teachers to form a strong united union, meant that teachers' interests as a class group were neglected.

There are many examples of the way in which teachers were exploited, particularly during the period of colonial rule. In the 1920s and 1930s wage cuts were introduced in most African countries. New training requirements and conditions of employment were also introduced without much warning and without consulting the teachers' associations. Typical of such arbitrary changes of terms of employment was the phasing out of C-Special teachers in Nigeria in 1963. As Onwuka reports (1968, p. 34), experienced and able teachers without much training were registered as 'C-Special' in 1942. Good primary-leaver teachers were retained by the mission schools and some of this group did not receive further training. In 1963, when these teachers had devoted most of their working lives to education, a proportion were simply sacked without any compensation or pension. Some were allowed honorary teaching certificates, but their qualifications had to be renewed yearly and were dependent on good reports from head-teachers; not surprisingly, many who found themselves in this humiliating position had to buy their reinstatement yearly. Even today it is common to find that untrained teachers are sacked every June, usually but not always to be re-hired the following September.

These examples affect only a proportion of teachers, but they reveal the attitude of governments to teachers in general and to untrained teachers in particular. Shoddy treatment of teachers continues, with many having to tolerate inadequate working conditions, poor supplies of equipment, irregular or non-payment of salaries and overbureau-cratised management. This last is particularly irksome to teachers, who often find that they have to make expensive and troublesome journeys to education authority offices to inquire about salary payments or the non-delivery of school books or equipment. Non-payment of salaries is also humiliating because teachers are sometimes forced to borrow from local moneylenders to survive.

Before the Second World War, when Western education was in an early stage of development, teachers acceded to government and mission attempts to cut salaries or worsen working conditions, and any opposition was short-lived. Gradually, however, teachers' groups and associations began to communicate with one another and, realising their common interests, formed large unions. Thus the Nigeria Union of Teachers was formed in the 1930s and, according to Fajana (1973), had at least fifteen branches and an efficient executive office by 1936.

It must not be thought that the colonial government of this period was entirely opposed to the formation of a strong teachers' union. Unions are not necessarily groups which challenge governments. In the teachers' union of Nigeria it is possible that the colonial government saw an ally against the strong influence of the missions. Missionary bodies were certainly much more opposed to union activity than were the government. Government tolerance of unions also allowed potential conflicts between teachers and the authorities to be institutionalised; rather than letting conflict come into the open, or even erupt in a violent manner, unions can often channel feelings of conflict and deprivation into peaceful arbitration. It is quite likely that colonial governments saw the advantage of developing a single, relatively tame teachers' union rather than opposing and provoking extreme reactions from teachers. But Fajana (1973) goes as far as to say that in Nigeria in the 1930s the Director of Education encouraged the development of a union of teachers out of a genuine wish for teachers to share in government education policy-making, and not entirely for the cynical political reasons suggested.

In the post-independence era African governments have imposed many curbs on union development and the right of union members to strike. Some countries, such as Tanzania, have abolished unions and amalgamated them into a single, pro-government organisation. During Nigeria's period of civil strife a strike ban (1969) was imposed. Nevertheless, teachers' unions have continued to voice their interests in Nigeria, and in 1975 there were a number of teachers' strikes to press claims for higher pay, regular payment of salaries and better working conditions.

The fact that teachers are willing to strike shows that they have become conscious of their power and their common interests. Much of the deference earlier shown to employers, particularly mission bodies, has disappeared. As Sami (1977) points out, the reference groups to which teachers now compare themselves are teachers in other states of Nigeria, not teachers in the same church or missionary group.

The occurrence of strikes does not, however, mean that teachers are as yet a totally united group. Sami discovered that militant attitudes varied among different groups of teachers. Rural teachers, for example, were more concerned than others about public reactions, particularly as local parents were worried that students could not take examinations during the strike. Sami reports that many village teachers in Rivers State quietly allowed examinations to go ahead. Urban teachers, however, felt more able than rural teachers to adopt a militant approach, and women teachers in town were the most militant group. Perhaps this is because teaching provides only a second income for their households, so that they can afford militant attitudes. And women teachers are often of higher social background than men, and therefore more likely to compare their salaries with professional salaries.

Marked status differences also exist between primary and secondary teachers. It is significant that, during the Rivers State strike described by Sami, secondary teachers sought quite different benefits from those claimed by primary teachers. Secondary teachers were concerned about car allowances and other perks, and were reluctant to ally themselves with primary teachers. Thus teachers are far from being a single, united class of workers. Trade union activity of a highly political nature, the strike, is a temporary allegiance of different status groups – teachers of different grades, qualified and unqualified, junior and senior teachers, male and female, rural and urban teachers – rather than a representation by a solid group of employees who all think the same way and wish to press the same claims. Governments are usually able to play upon these internal divisions in the teaching service and the reluctance of many teachers to strike, in order to modify teachers' demands. By taking strike action, teachers also risk public assaults (usually verbal) on their position in society and are open to questions about their supposed importance. As discussed above, the teacher's public role suffers from certain structural weaknesses. It is only when examinations are set, perhaps, that teachers have enough political power to stress their importance to society.

In conclusion, teachers are a powerful group by virtue of their numbers, strong and growing sense of occupational identity and the fact that they are an articulate, educated group. Concerted action in the form of strikes or political pressure on governments is likely to raise their salaries, their class or market position and, in turn, their social prestige or status. But divisions between teachers, particularly between primary, unqualified and secondary teachers, will at the same time reduce the likelihood of such concerted action. The maintenance of a proportion of pupil teachers or unqualified teachers is indirectly in the interests of governments that wish to hold down all teachers' salaries. Added to this is the fact that many teachers subscribe to politically conservative beliefs. The very nature of teaching involves the relaying of established truths and knowledge to the younger generation. Teaching encourages teachers to think of themselves as guardians of the status quo.

The fact that they are in the business of controlling and disciplining the young means that some have conservative opinions. This is very much a generalisation, and it must be remembered that in the past the ranks of radical African political parties have been swelled by teachers. However, the lack of qualifications, of general education and awareness among some teachers, coupled with conservative attitudes, make it uncertain whether the teachers' cause will continue to grow in power sufficiently to establish all teachers as fully professional.

Questions and Discussion Topics: Chapter 5

1 Why is the teaching profession subject to status insecurity?
2 Should primary, secondary and higher education teachers all belong to a single trade union or association? What advantages and disadvantages might result from such a union?
3 Do you agree that teaching is fundamentally a socially conservative activity?
4 What suggestions can you make for improving relations between teachers and communities in rural areas?
5 It is sometimes suggested that teachers should be encouraged to develop a research attitude to their work (see, for example, Hawes's article mentioned at the end of Chapter 6, p.155). What does this suggestion mean? Discuss in relation to (a) teacher participation in designing and implementing new school curricula, and (b) how a research attitude might be encouraged during teacher training.
6 Discuss some of the common sources of conflict in school management and suggest how conflicts between teachers might be resolved.
7 Write an essay summing up the ways in which sociology could be useful to the teacher.

Chapter 6

Sociology of the Curriculum

Introduction

Without considering the curriculum, studying education is rather like watching a race without knowing anything about the difficulty of the course, the nature of the hurdles or the aim of the competition. In this chapter we shall try to relate educational achievement to the school subjects and knowledge which students fail or succeed at.

Every curriculum has the following characteristics:

(1) Like a race, a curriculum has an aim. A technical curriculum has the aim of producing competent technicians; a primary curriculum, that of providing general education and heightening children's awareness of the world. Students' and teachers' aims may, however, diverge from the official aims of the curriculum. Technical students may want an academic education, for example, and use their education to gain academic qualifications while neglecting technical subjects.

(2) A curriculum is a selection from a society's culture and available knowledge. No school curriculum could possibly include all fields of human knowledge. An attempt to do this would result in education at the most superficial level. It is therefore interesting to look at what is left out of a curriculum as well as what is included.

(3) A curriculum can be defined as the knowledge taught in school lessons or included in some other way in the timetable, such as project work. In addition to this official curriculum, there is also a hidden curriculum – the hidden aims of schools or teachers. School life teaches subservience to authority and timekeeping, for example, and these things can be regarded as part of the hidden curriculum. Teachers teach the official curriculum, but also give an idea of the techniques necessary to pass examinations. Not all teachers completely reduce their subjects to the bare bones, but most give hints on the best ways to answer examination questions. These messages, which students need if they are to be academically successful, are also part of the hidden curriculum.

Official curricula are to a large extent social influences – that is, they are ideas and knowledge which have been shaped by certain social groups (educationists, policy-makers, politicians) and which have effects on others (students and teachers). It is possible to study school knowledge sociologically, therefore, because it is part of society's general culture and ideas. Some people suggest that school curricula serve the vested interests of powerful social groups. Whenever we speak of ideas or knowledge serving such interests we suggest that knowledge is no longer neutral or objective but has an ideological purpose.

The ideological content of school curricula was very apparent during the colonial era. In those times students learned of European history, culture and science; African achievements and culture were played down. Certain areas of knowledge are rarely included in school curricula even today: for example, study of the inequality between richer and poorer nations of the world, racial and ethnic conflict, sexual relations, or political education. Although subjects such as these are usually considered to be too dangerous or politically sensitive to be included in school curricula, since independence some African countries have begun to include in their education programmes political education (often watered down to a subject called 'Civics') and social studies. As a result of the impression that school curricula seem either to distort knowledge or fail altogether to include vital topics it has been argued by some sociologists (for example, Young, 1971) that all knowledge is socially influenced or distorted in some way; curricula are just one example, and the knowledge we receive from newspapers, radio and books are other examples of this social influence. Young and others argue that teachers should recognise that they do not convey the truth as such because the knowledge content of school curricula has been filtered, censored and shaped in the interests of society's ruling groups.

However, there is a limit to the idea that all knowledge can be influenced by society. Some subjects in the school curriculum, like mathematics and the sciences, are less likely to be socially influenced than others, such as history, literature and geography. Mathematical and scientific principles are universal and, while they might be ignored by a society, cannot be distorted in the same way as subjects like history.

Even subjects like mathematics can be socially influenced as far as their use is concerned, so it should be remembered that while some knowledge is neutral and objective, the way it is taught will be influenced by the aims of the curriculum. Thus schoolchildren in Nigeria and Senegal might be taught the same basic mathematical principles, but the subject might be approached in different ways. According to the aims of a curriculum, mathematics might be taught in isolation from other subjects, or it might be used in an applied way with geography, social studies or technical subjects.

Types of Curriculum

When considering types of curriculum we should consider the following questions:

1 Is it a curriculum which attempts to integrate subject matter, or one in which the content is divided into subjects which are rarely connected?
2 Is it a standardised curriculum, or is decentralisation and experiment with content allowed?
3 Is it a self-contained curriculum which aims to provide a complete set of ideas and information with no idea of going further, or is it a curriculum which prepares students for a higher level?

(1) School curricula differ a great deal in content and aims, even between different levels of the same country's education system. At the primary level, content is usually wide-ranging, and some attempt is made to integrate all this knowledge. But as students progress to secondary and higher levels content becomes narrower, or specialised, and the subjects are taught in isolation from one another.

There is a basic distinction, therefore, between integrated types of curriculum and specialised or fragmented types. Some people believe that the secondary curriculum, particularly the kind inherited from the British system, is too specialised and that an integrated approach should be encouraged. It is argued that an overspecialised curriculum leads to gaps in understanding between the various subjects. The history or geography student, for example, may know little of what fellow students do in physics or chemistry, and the language student may know nothing of either of these fields. Rather than being shown the world as it is, some argue, the student is given a fragmented, artificial view of knowledge which does not allow him to make valuable connections between ideas.

Paulo Freire, a South American educationist, is a leading critic of established school curricula. Instead of passively learning subjects, Freire suggests that people learn to follow themes across subjects. He calls this approach 'problem-posing education', whereby learning is supposed to be stimulated by teachers and students working together to solve problems. The more traditional type of curriculum, specialised into subjects, is termed 'the banking concept' of education (Freire, 1972). Some of Freire's ideas are summarised opposite.

Freire is trying to convince us that the school curricula of most developing countries are outmoded and politically conservative. With regard to African education in particular, Makulu (1971) also argues that there is too much memorisation of meaningless facts – in languages, not enough verbal practice; in geography and history, not enough practical application; and in sciences, not enough observation

THE PROBLEM-POSING TYPE OF CURRICULUM	THE BANKING TYPE OF CURRICULUM
(a) Students and teachers participate as equals in the classroom, and the knowledge gained is collective property.	The purpose of schooling is to gain or bank knowledge and qualifications. Knowledge is the property of the individual.
(b) Teachers and students design and discuss the curriculum together; subject boundaries may be ignored.	Knowledge is set down in textbooks and the official syllabus, divided into subjects.
(c) The teacher is a guide to learning, and tries to relate ideas to the practical world of the student.	The teacher hands down knowledge as a gift to the student. The teacher's emphasis is on the mastery of words and set formulae, not on making students solve problems.

and experimentation. Both Freire and Makulu are therefore pointing out that, instead of encouraging initiative and the practical application of knowledge, the banking concept of education leads children to conform to the syllabus and to fail to apply school knowledge to the real world.

There would be many problems in trying to implement an integrated curriculum, particularly in secondary education. First, there are problems concerning the subjects themselves. While it may be illuminating to blend mathematics with geography or any other subject, for example, there is such a thing as overintegration. It has been argued that subjects need to be separated to some extent if students are to grasp the essentials or basics of each. Secondly, as society needs specialists of various types, an integrated curriculum might fail to provide the scientists, technicians and other experts thought necessary for development. Another difficulty in implementing Freire's ideas might arise from the difference in knowledge between teachers and students; Freire assumes that an equal relationship and dialogue between teachers and students is possible and, though this may be true as far as adult classes are concerned, one wonders whether children would be able to cope with the problem-posing approach of discussion between equals.

To be fair to Freire's argument, we must remember that the traditional, specialised curriculum does contain a great deal of irrelevant knowledge as well as essential facts and skills. Much of the knowledge we gain in school is never applied to work. Teachers rarely have enough time to teach fully or inform properly, mainly because of the constraints of a crowded syllabus and the pressure of the examination. Learning often becomes a matter of memorising notes or copying the teacher's instructions.

(2) Most African countries have standardised curricula: that is, the content of education is laid down centrally and the same things will be taught irrespective of which school is attended. Not all education systems are like this – some, like the American and British, have a degree of decentralisation which allows teachers to experiment with the curriculum. In Africa, however, education has always been the most important avenue of social mobility. African governments have tried to maintain standardised curricula so that students in different regions can compete on the same footing – it is known, for example, that the content of biology or history syllabuses will be the same in one school or one region as it is in another. Attempts to decentralise curricula, or to allow regional and interschool differences, are feared because students could be prevented from continuing to the next stage of education.

(3) Should curricula always prepare students for further education? It could be argued that most school curricula are not designed for the many who fail, drop out or only reach a basic level of primary education. Rather, it would seem as though the academic content of curricula is designed for the successful few. It is worth noting, however, that the introduction of a self-contained, limited curriculum which discourages notions of continuing to a higher level has never been received enthusiastically. Despite the irrelevance to many people of the academic curriculum and the dashed hopes of students who fail to attain post-primary schooling, the preference remains for a curriculum which is a stepping-stone to higher levels.

Who Defines the Curriculum?

School Knowledge and Common Sense

There is a tremendous gap between the school curriculum, or what is defined as knowledge valid for education, and common sense – the knowledge of ordinary life and the everyday world. This gap is partly a result of lack of knowledge and illiteracy among the uneducated, but is also caused by the nature of school knowledge itself; as has been pointed out, school knowledge is often far removed from the everyday, real world and, some argue, is too specialised and abstract for practical use.

It is not always true to say that educated people are the enlightened ones, and illiterates the ignorant. The teacher should not think of schoolchildren as lacking all knowledge, or as empty containers to be filled with information. The common sense which students bring to school is often useful and valid. If a commonsense explanation is incorrect, for example, if children believe that the sun revolves around the earth, the teacher should not totally ignore such theories but take them into account when correcting students.

The value of common sense is illustrated by a study of Liberian schoolchildren (Gay and Cole, 1967), who were given certain measuring tasks. It was found that performance of some tasks by the African children was superior to that of another sample of Americans. This was because the Liberian children had plenty of experience of judging weights, lengths and quantities in everyday life. When measuring rice or cloth, they had picked up commonsense skills from their parents, brothers and sisters. The Americans had less experience of these things. In other tests, which involved sorting cards according to geometrical designs, the Liberian sample did less well than the Americans. The experimenters concluded that the Americans had been given more reading materials and had more experience of picture puzzles than the Liberians.

The message for the teacher is clear. It is the experience and knowledge we have had out of school, or the experiences we have *not* had, which affect school performance. Unfortunately much of the school curriculum does not build on the commonsense knowledge and skills possessed by students. As Gay and Cole point out, much of the school curriculum consists of 'nonsense' material: symbols, drawings and formulae which do not relate to local ways of thinking. They argue that familiar materials – for example, rice or pieces of cloth – are essential if mathematics is to make sense at the primary school stage.

Although it is easy to say that teachers should pay attention to commonsense approaches and materials in their work, this can be difficult if a teacher is unfamiliar with an area or does not speak the local language. There is also a feeling that bookish knowledge has greater validity and higher status than common sense, even if information contained in books makes little sense to the student. The high prestige of bookish education is partly a legacy of the colonial period. Certain types of knowledge, and Western ideas in particular, were deemed to be valid educational material, but other sources of knowledge, such as Islamic culture, were mostly ignored.

The neglect of Islamic studies during the colonial period is a very good example of the way in which school curricula represent the interests of dominant groups in society. The official school curricula were defined by Christian, Western influences, and only a few isolated attempts were made to teach Islamic studies and Arabic in government schools during the colonial period. In northern Nigeria Arabic and Islamic studies were available in some schools, but were optional, fringe subjects in a basically Europeanised education system. As pointed out in Chapter 4, the number of schools teaching Arabic and

Islamic studies has grown since independence, and the curricula of some university departments also include subjects such as Islamic religion, literature and philosophy. At the school level, problems of modernising Islamic studies, of providing suitable textbooks and teachers, still remain; these can be attributed largely to the former neglect of Arabic and Islamic-influenced school curricula.

In general, therefore, school curricula often contain knowledge and ideas which are quite different from commonsense beliefs or the knowledge and values of local cultures and non-Christian religions. The low status of non-European knowledge is also illustrated by resistance to Africanisation of school curricula during and after colonial rule.

Colonial Influence
Africa's colonial past illustrates very well how the curriculum is subject to social and political influence. The impact of colonialism is not just a matter of historical study. The way curricula were defined in colonial times has much relevance to today's curricula.

As mentioned, much that seems wrong with present-day school curricula is attributed to the narrow-minded and European-based ideas of colonial governments and missionaries. It is suggested that Europeans imposed a bookish, irrelevant kind of curriculum on African schools: local social conditions, practical needs, cultural and religious differences were ignored. African students of the time knew more about the history of English or French kings than of African local rulers.

While it is undoubtedly true that much of the content of African education has been stifled by European-based curricula, examination boards and European ideas generally, the way this came about was not exactly one of imposition or transplantation by Europeans, as the first idea suggests. As Clignet and Foster point out (1966, p. 6), we should not see 'the development of colonial education solely as a process of thoughtless transfer of . . . curricula into African territories'.

Throughout most of the colonial period, the authorities attempted to change curricula from the academic type found in France and Britain to adapted curricula which they thought more suited to the limited needs of their subjects. This paternalistic attitude sometimes conflicted with the ideas of black clergymen and teachers, and with some white missionaries, who wanted to teach what they considered to be the best curriculum – an academic, general education as found in Europe.

The authorities, however, put forward many plans to introduce a more vocational curriculum, including subjects such as agriculture and handicrafts. Such a limited, self-contained curriculum would have blocked the African's chances of further education and the opportunity to compete with the European with equal qualifications.

An example of the obstructionist attitude of the colonial authorities to the spread of general, academic education can be found in this report from Watherstone, an administrator of the early colonial period: 'The leaving of education to missionary societies, biased as they are, and comparatively few of them providing for technical instruction, seems to me to be absolutely wrong' (1907, p. 360). This shows us that the colonial authorities did not simply transplant school curricula from Europe to Africa; indeed, they were often concerned with trying to prevent this happening.

Lugard, the first governor of northern Nigeria, who in 1912 was made governor-general of the north and south, saw the rise of an educated elite as a profound threat to the policy of indirect rule which he had attempted to introduce in the south of Nigeria. And primary education on a mass scale, in Lugard's opinion, could only lead to unemployment and social disruption.

According to Lugard, the curriculum was to aim to produce only useful citizens, loyal to traditional institutions and willing to co-operate with the colonialists. His recommendations for school curricula stressed the importance of moral training, manual work and the adaptation of education to African customs. As Abernethy puts it, the ideal students from Lugard's point of view 'should not be so highly trained that they threatened to take over the responsibilities of British officials or native authorities' (Abernethy, 1969, p. 84).

Lugard's policies to limit curricula in Nigerian schools were by no means fully implemented and brought about little change in mission policies. This was partly the result of lack of funds. Trade and industrial schools are usually much more expensive to establish than academic schools, and the great economic depression of the 1930s effectively put an end to this aspect of the colonial government's plans for educational reform. An equally important factor was the reluctance of Nigerians to subscribe to vocational schools and their preference for the general, academic curriculum. As Coleman notes:

> Despite protracted criticism and repeated resolutions of new purpose ... little progress was made before World War II in the substitution of a rural and vocational emphasis for the academic and literary bias in Nigerian school curricula. (1965, p. 119)

The following extract from the autobiography of Wellesley Cole, *Kossoh Town Boy*, illustrates the attitudes of those who aspired to further education in the colonial era:

> It was generally realised that a local African examination, however difficult or high its standard, could never achieve the same recogni-

tion in the outside world as the British one. We were a subject people, and our only chance of survival lay in maintaining these contacts with Cambridge, and with Oxford, London and Durham.

The colonial influence on school curricula was therefore twofold: on one hand, colonial governments tried to introduce vocational, non-academic curricula – usually without much success – while on the other hand, elite secondary schools were established and a tiny minority of the population were socialised in a bookish, academic kind of education.

Needless to say, the curriculum of elite secondary schools during the colonial period was highly irrelevant to the needs of development or the demand for technicians, scientists and agricultural experts. Classics (Latin and Greek), Hebrew and Divinity were the backbone of the curricula of most West African elite schools, and it was only when science became more popular in Britain during the 1950s that elite African schools followed suit. Even then, the proportion of students taking scientific or technical subjects was often smaller than those studying arts subjects or religious knowledge. The latter subjects are popular because they have a reputation of affording an easy pass (for example, religious knowledge) or demand memorisation.

The aim of curricula in elite secondary schools during colonial times was largely to socialise a privileged minority into an elite culture. Students lucky enough to have this sort of schooling were not just taught the formal curriculum, but also followed a hidden curriculum – that of European manners, values, aesthetic preferences in art and literature and beliefs in the superiority of British or French political institutions.

Although some colonial administrators criticised the irrelevant and Europeanised content of African school curricula, most colonial governments were highly reluctant to change the curriculum of elite schools. (Any changes towards vocational or technical subjects were attempted in less prestigious, non-elite secondary schools.) This policy was clearly supported by the most powerful section of the local population – the elite parents who stood to gain from having their children educated to the standards of the European ruling class. The fact that this type of education was of little practical value and completely unrelated to the sources of livelihood of developing countries was of less importance than the vested social interests of the elite and their colonial masters.

There was also much resistance to colonial attempts to introduce non-academic, vocational or practical curricula at the grass-roots or village level. The Phelps-Stokes inquiries into education, which took place all over Africa in the 1920s, are a good example of a colonial attempt to vocationalise education and of local resistance to this way of thinking.

The Phelps-Stokes reports arose out of a charitable fund set up by a rich American. We should remember that these educational inquiries and ideals were inspired by missionary and community workers in America and were meant to be progressive. There was a genuine desire to uplift the position of ordinary people by providing them with practical, relevant education. And the Phelps-Stokes Commission's first report criticised British colonial authorities for neglecting teacher training facilities. In the United States, however, the Phelps-Stokes Commission had been criticised for its experiments with education for blacks. By failing to stimulate criticism of the downtrodden social position of blacks and by omitting political education from the curriculum in schools Phelps-Stokes experiments in community education and teaching practical skills were seen as just another way of whites making American blacks accept their lowly position in society.

When the Phelps-Stokes Commission's suggestions were taken up by colonial authorities in Africa they also became a way of justifying the non-provision of academic education ⌐the only kind of schooling that could give qualifications equal to those held by whites. Abernethy (1969, p. 89) quotes the British government memorandum which recognised the Phelps-Stokes Commission's findings: 'Education should be *adapted* to the mentality, aptitudes, occupations, and traditions of the various peoples, *conserving* as far as possible all sound and healthy elements in the fabric of their social life, adapting them where necessary to changed circumstances and progressive ideas, as an agent of natural growth and *evolution*' (our italics).

As mentioned earlier, the economic depression of the 1930s led to cut-backs in educational expenditure, although there were isolated experiments with trade schools, community schools and vocational schools in many African countries. If the Phelps-Stokes Commission's recommendations had been fully adopted extra teachers would have been needed, together with considerable expense on new buildings and equipment. Sinclair (1976) gives an example of a village school curriculum which was introduced into a special school in Kenya during the colonial period. It shows what primary education might have been like if 'relevant' education had been introduced widely:

7.00 to 8.00   School gardens (tree-planting, grass-cutting, clearing gardens, making paths and drains and so on).
8.00 to 8.45   Arithmetic
8.45 to 9.15   Drill
9.15 to 9.30   Break
9.30 to 10.15   Reading (four days a week) or hygiene and morals (two days a week)

10.15 to 11.15   Handwork – baskets, mats, etc. (three days a
week) or writing and measuring (three days a
week)

As can be seen, the central part of this curriculum is non-academic
subjects. Assuming a six-day school week, the total time spent in
academic subjects (arithmetic, measuring, writing) was only seven and
a half hours, while non-academic tasks took up thirteen and a half
hours. Therefore it was an attempt to socialise children into a curriculum for labourers and simple craftsmen, not technicians, highly
skilled workers or managers. Rather than an attempt to adapt the
curriculum to the supposed needs of traditional African society, it was
a thinly disguised plan to provide white settlers in Kenya with a
semi-skilled workforce.

Agriculture and other practical subjects were also introduced into
the curricula of middle, technical and trade schools. But after a few
years these attempts to change the curriculum at the post-primary level
were mostly forgotten. The decisive factor in the rejection of adapted
education was the attitude of parents and students, who were not
interested in it and perceived that education of the academic type was
essential if they were to gain the wealth and social status of the
Westerner. Another reason for the failure of trade school experiments
was that some of the implements, materials and machines introduced
were only suited to European conditions: sometimes spare parts were
not available to mend equipment, or teachers had not been trained to
use it. To use a modern expression, inappropriate technology was
introduced.

We should not dismiss entirely the efforts of those teachers and
missionaries who sincerely believed that, through rural education, they
were speeding up the development of colonised countries. But as
Anderson says,

> regrettably, few missionaries realised that . . . they were demon-
> strating the advantages of western life every day . . . as they read
> books, wrote letters and gave orders to their labourers. Reading and
> writing were seen as the keys to success, not gardening, or to use its
> later euphemistic name, 'rural science', and still less 'educating the
> African along his own lines'. (1970, p. 21)

Thus, where schools with a vocational curriculum were established, the
teachers communicated a hidden curriculum of success through
academic education. This goes back to the earlier point that the aims of
students may diverge from the official aims of a curriculum; students in
trade schools were perhaps willing to tolerate lessons in woodwork and
other crafts in order the learn basic numeracy and literacy and thus
obtain clerical work.

Finally it is worth comparing modern attempts to introduce community schools, or practical rural-oriented curricula, with earlier attempts during colonial rule. It would be wrong to judge all modern attempts to make curricula relevant by the conditions and experience of the colonial period. But there are some similarities between the apparently progressive ideas of the Phelps-Stokes Commission and the apparently progressive ideas of those who support relevant or adapted education today. There are also some lessons to be learned from the past in terms of ensuring that teachers are trained to implement new curricula and that suitable equipment and teaching materials are provided. We will return to these questions about the need for relevant education in the section on education and development (Part Three).

Problems of Change

Before political independence from European colonialism Africans had begun to exert a strong influence on school curricula, either by voting with their feet (for example, ignoring vocational schools or setting up their own bush schools), or through the influence of black teachers, missionaries and representatives in colonial government. After independence, the question 'Who defines the curriculum?' became much more a matter of control by African governments, examination boards, African scholars and academics. However, the legacy of colonial rule and parents' continuing desire for academic curricula cannot be suppressed overnight. This is unfortunate, because there may be genuine academic or practical reasons for changing curricula. In Nigeria, for example, the secondary school curriculum has changed in some respects, such as revision of the content of history books, but the outward form of the curriculum with its Ordinary and Advanced level stages is still based on the British model and retains the disadvantages as well as advantages of this model. The curricula of most African countries except Guinée or Angola have similarly changed a little in content but not very much in structure.

Like all social institutions school curricula are supported by vested interests and are consequently difficult to change. Conservatism in education is also furthered by simple inertia – once things have been done in a certain way for a generation or two, people become reluctant to upset established traditions. The social forces which impede change in curriculum design will now be considered, but examples of successful change will also be discussed. Briefly, conservative influences on curricula can be listed as follows:

(1) The rapid expansion of school enrolment, which prevents the diversion of resources to curriculum change.
(2) The centralised and standardised nature of African curricula,

together with poor communications between the centre and the periphery (the schools and teachers).

(3) The link between established curricula and acceptable academic qualifications.

(4) The attitudes and abilities of teachers.

(5) The failure of earlier curriculum reform projects.

We will consider each of these influences in turn.

(1) *Quantitative Change*

No one can deny that African education has changed tremendously since independence, but most of this change has been in terms of rapid quantitative expansion of school enrolments. The impressive commitment to bringing education to as many as possible has held back curriculum reform. It is difficult enough to train sufficient teachers to manage the traditional curriculum; the cost of training teachers in new methods and of retraining teachers in post may be prohibitive.

New approaches in teaching such as discovery methods often require new books and more teaching materials than traditional methods, and these are additional costs to retraining teachers. Attempts have been made to introduce new methods of teaching without spending much on new textbooks or materials, but such curricular innovations are almost certain to fail. It is not much good for an education theorist to ask a teacher to 'use local materials' in the classroom unless adequate training and equipment are provided as well.

(2) *Centralised Curricula*

This factor also impedes curricular change because it holds back local experimentation. If basic changes or improvements in the curriculum are suggested the authorities have to be quite certain that such changes are desirable because they will have to be implemented throughout the country. Thus the centralised curriculum imposes caution on policymakers. As we have already mentioned, there are regional and ethnic imbalances in African school systems: an attempt to bring changes in one region (for example, towards discovery methods or a greater element of practical education) might be interpreted as a threat to education in that region. If changes are decided upon then implementation becomes a daunting task: as many teachers as possible must be retrained in the new syllabus; new books and syllabus outlines have to be circulated nationally; examination procedures affecting the new curriculum might also have to be changed. As such changes in curriculum cannot be introduced piecemeal, perhaps in different regions each year, it is no wonder that governments often draw back from the precipice of curriculum reform.

(3) *Curricula and Qualifications*

Qualifications, which signify knowledge or skills, can be seen as property. Thus attempts to alter curricula can often be seen as attacks on the prestige of qualifications and, in turn, the personal life-chances of the individual student. This was seen clearly with regard to colonial attempts to replace academic curricula with vocational education. It is likely that contemporary attempts to change the curriculum will also be resisted if they seem to tamper with students' qualifications – their personal property. Students may also worry that teachers will not be able to master the new knowledge well enough to prepare them sufficiently for examinations. Students' and parents' preferences are usually for the tried and tested syllabus.

(4) *Teachers' Attitudes and Abilities*

It should not be thought that teachers are always conservative in their attitudes towards curriculum innovation. A general study of curriculum change in Africa (Hawes, 1970) mentions that teachers are often enthusiastic about innovations and in-service training, particularly younger staff. But however enthusiastic teachers may feel about a new syllabus or a new method of teaching, such commitment to change is often weakened by the failure of educational administration to keep regular contact with teachers. Studies of curriculum projects repeatedly show that teachers are visited infrequently, are too isolated and receive too little guidance or in-service training to implement new curricula effectively. In short, teachers' reluctance to change the curriculum may not be a reflection of conservative attitudes in themselves, but of poor communication between the centre (the administration) and the periphery (schools).

We should also remember, however, that some teachers are undoubtedly conservative in attitude or are simply unable to put new teaching methods or content into practice. Those who are not committed to the profession or who cannot bring themselves to update their knowledge prevent change, even if communications between administration and schools are relatively good. For this reason it has been suggested (Hawes, 1970) that greater attention should be paid during teacher training to the possibility of curriculum reform: it is argued that teachers should be trained in research methods or ways of testing new curricula so that they can be brought into the process of curriculum design from the earliest stage of a project. In this way teachers would not be handed a finished product, but would be encouraged to make suggestions and amendments to a new curriculum.

(5) *Failure of Earlier Projects*

Attempts at curriculum reform which are ill thought out, badly administered or poorly financed can hinder future attempts. Education, like most fields of social activity, has fashions: in recent years there have been fashions in environmental or social studies, new mathematics, new approaches to language teaching, vocational and pre-vocational courses. It is not surprising that teachers and students become a little cynical about many of the curriculum changes advocated by education planners, especially as most of these changes are not followed up properly.

Examples of Change

Considering all the social forces against curriculum change it is a tribute to some governments, education planners and teachers that changes are possible, despite shortages of resources and the legacy of colonial systems of schooling.

An example of curricular change under rather special circumstances is provided by the education system in Guinée. When Guinée rejected a French plan to join a French–West African Economic Community in 1958, the French immediately recalled all technical advisers and administrators, most teachers and much of the equipment and records necessary for their work. This vindictive withdrawal affected education as much as any other government department.

The sudden break from France created the conditions for change in education (although the changes themselves demanded hard work and extra resources – particularly as far as curriculum reform was concerned) because new textbooks and extra teachers were needed.

Guinée represents one of the strongest attempts to Africanise the school curriculum. After independence students were no longer required to study French history and geography, Guinée and Africa became the focus of school subjects, and patriotism was encouraged in schools. At the same time there was a rapid expansion of the school system.

Guinée is therefore a good example of a radical break with the past as far as curriculum is concerned. But there are still links with the past: for example, French has been retained as the official language and the main medium of the curriculum. There are fourteen distinct local languages in Guinée and it is difficult to choose one for relaying the reformed curriculum. There have been attempts to write textbooks in local languages, but as there are three main languages (Foulah, Malinke and Soussou), a decision to write a standard book for all schools in any one language could revive old ethnic rivalries. The continued use of French may not in itself be oppressive because it has allowed Guinée to use an imported language to overcome local language difficulties. There is a disadvantage, however, in that French, a carrier of foreign European culture, cannot convey all the expressions and nuances of meaning contained in a local language. Therefore the thorough Africanisation of the content of education is not possible. While Guinée provides an example of an attempt to bring widespread change in education, Nigeria provides many examples of local experiments with curriculum design. Being a large country with a complicated system of state and urban council government, some areas have attempted distinctive changes. In Lagos, for example, there was an attempt to introduce modern mathematics to some of the primary schools (Alele Williams, 1974). Modern mathematics could be described as a kind of problem-posing education. Rather than being encouraged to bank or learn by heart the skills of addition, subtraction, division and multiplication, children are expected to discuss problems and 'write mathematical sentences which show logical steps in their thinking' (1974, p. 246). According to Alele Williams:

> In the Lagos experiment we have had all the necessary ingredients to produce a change – a Ministry that was convinced that a change to Modern Mathematics was necessary and desirable . . . the personnel to initiate the change, texts and other materials, and a carefully directed plan.

Note how Alele Williams has identified the necessary social ingredients for curriculum change. The changeover for the children – in mathematical knowledge and skills – is seen as less of a difficulty than social or institutional obstacles. Despite the success which Alele Williams claims, one wonders whether such localised attempts at change will have a significant impact on the nation's standardised primary curriculum. There has also been a swing away from the fashion in modern mathematics towards a fashion in basic numeracy: this is not to say that either method is wholly good or bad, but that social factors – such as changed decisions by the ministry – can adversely affect such projects.

Curriculum changes have also occurred at the secondary level of Nigerian schools. In 1971, for example, the West African Examinations Council introduced a new French syllabus. According to Obanya (1974), Nigerian French teachers were initially hostile to this change. The idea behind the new syllabus was to stress practice in speaking French, but teachers feared that students would not have enough experience in writing and translation. Obanya interviewed a representative sample of French teachers three years after the new syllabus had been introduced and found that resistance to it had largely disappeared. Teachers with fewer qualifications, and less experience of living in a French-speaking country than others, were found to be just as favourable in their attitudes: the overwhelming majority welcomed innovation in the French curriculum. This finding reflects the point made earlier: that teachers are not necessarily against changes as long as they are introduced effectively. Obanya concludes that the earlier resistance by teachers was a result of the fact that they had not been consulted in the initial design of the French curriculum.

Obanya's study seems to indicate a moderate success in curriculum innovation, and there are probably other examples in Nigerian education. We should remember, however, that this is a study of attitudes – not of the methods French teachers actually use in the classroom. It is quite possible that teachers, like anyone asked to complete a postal questionnaire, give favourable or positive responses in order to appear progressive. Whether real changes in classroom teaching have been achieved as a result of the new syllabus is still open to question.

It is generally important to distinguish between the impressive-sounding goals of governments, ministries and curriculum reformers and the social reality of the school. Those at the centre may often escape with the illusion that changes are occurring, while at the school classroom level teachers may be continuing to work in old ways while paying lip-service to new methods or a new syllabus. Perhaps one of the most important applications of sociology is to compare the official curriculum and planners' dreams with the actual work of teachers and students.

Conclusion

This chapter has mostly been concerned with the question, 'What kind of curriculum for African schools?' First, different kinds of curriculum were defined: problem-centred or subject-centred, centralised or decentralised, and self-contained curricula as opposed to those designed to lead up to higher education for a select few. Although curricula vary between these extremes, there has been a tendency for a general kind of curriculum to emerge in Africa – that is, an academic, subject-centred curriculum, usually very standardised and defined by a centralised administration, and the kind of education which aims to produce an academic elite.

From a study of curriculum development during colonial times it is apparent that the dominance of the standardised academic curriculum is in part a result of colonial influence and in part a reflection of local demand. In fact the demand by Africans for Western, academic-type curricula is also a result of the establishment of a certain kind of society under colonial rule – a society in which academic qualifications and general education were regarded as the keys to success, no matter how much colonial governments tried to impose relevant or adapted types of curricula.

Present-day governments face a dilemma. How can curricula be changed, perhaps made more relevant to local needs and to the common sense of ordinary people, without governments seeming to be as paternalistic or high-handed as colonial governments? It would appear to be politically dangerous for children of elite parents to continue to enjoy established, academic and prestigious education if a quite different sort of education were to be imposed on the ordinary mass of people. And in any case, as we have seen, it is difficult to change curricula because of problems caused by quantitative expansion, the centralised nature of curricula and the lack of training and resources for teachers.

There are also dangers in preserving the status quo, as far as curricula are concerned. This is not to suggest that there has been *no* change in school curricula over recent years. As mentioned with regard to Nigeria, some improvements in content and teaching methods have been made. However, the overall structure and academic aims of traditional colonial-influenced curricula remain. We now have to ask whether this kind of curriculum best serves the needs of economic, social and political development, or whether more radical changes should be advocated; this is the subject of the next part of the book.

Questions and Discussion Topics: Chapter 6

1 'It is the duty of every school to relate the whole curriculum to the life of the community it serves' (British Colonial Mission on Education in East and Central Africa, 1951). Do you agree with this statement?

2 Discuss any recent curriculum changes or projects which you know of (your lecturer may be able to provide information, or you may consult educational journals or periodicals). What are (a) the social and (b) the educational factors which explain the relative success or failure of the projects discussed?

3 Are Paulo Freire's suggestions of a problem-solving approach to learning suitable for (a) secondary schooling and (b) higher education?

4 How do secondary entrance examinations affect the primary curriculum and attitudes towards learning in primary schools?

5 Write a list of subjects or topics which you think should be included in the ideal secondary school curriculum. Now write a list of subjects which you think should *not* be compulsory, or not included at all. A group discussion of subjects selected may be useful. Justify your final list according to whether it meets the following needs:
   (a) The need for specialists? (For example, future doctors or engineers must study science subjects.)
   (b) The need to give all students a general, all-round education?
   (c) The needs of rural development?
   (d) The needs of industrial and technical development?

(e) The need to stimulate problem-solving attitudes, innovativeness and creative thinking among secondary school graduates?

6 It is often said that school curricula are full of information, but that ideas are rarely taught. Why do teachers usually find it easier to teach facts or information than ideas? Discuss the difficulties that a teacher might experience in trying to explain the following ideas in the classroom:

(a) democracy and party politics;
(b) development;
(c) gravity;
(d) prehistory;
(e) any others?

7 Write an essay summing up the ways in which school curricula are agents of social control.

Part Three

Education and Development in Africa

Introduction to Part Three

In Part Three we are concerned with the relationship between education and development. This introduction briefly defines the social, economic and political aspects of development. In addition, we discuss concepts related to development – social change, growth and progress – and their relationship to education, so as to prepare the way for the chapters which follow.

It is important to spend some time over definitions. In the next three chapters we will raise the question of whether or not education brings change or development but, first of all, what do we mean by these ideas?

Social Change

By social change we mean alterations in the ways of life and structure of a society over time. During the last hundred years many social changes have been brought about by colonisation and decolonisation, the growth of large cities, transport and communications, and the development of technology and commerce. In Chapter 7 we will pick out social and cultural aspects of change from economic and political aspects – that is, we will focus on changes reflected in the alteration of social customs, culture, ideas, values and social relationships.

We do not wish to imply from this division between social and political or economic that social changes are somehow independent of economic and political factors, or that cultural institutions and values cause change by themselves; we make this three-way division for purposes of convenience, recognising that changes in ideas and values cannot be understood apart from economic and political factors. The exploitation of oil resources and the way profits from them are distributed in Nigerian society or overseas have had profound effects upon the capacity of Nigeria to cause cultural and social change (for example, the expansion of schooling). At the same time, ruling groups or elites in Nigeria have been able to convince the majority – or at least enforce the view – that oil resources are best exploited in partnership with foreign companies in a basically free market economy. As oil resources dwindle in the next few decades, economic strains and shortages will undoubtedly challenge some of these ideas and values; thus economic and social aspects of change are intimately bound together.

As time passes, new patterns of behaviour and new rules of conduct come into being. One of the most commonly discussed kinds of cultural change is the decline of traditional cultures and the rise of so-called modern ways of life. For the individual this might mean a growing reluctance to accept the authority of parents and relatives; for example, the traditional idea of a marriage arranged by elders may be rejected. Nowadays the elderly complain a lot about the decline of respect for their position in society, the way that old customs and manners seem to be dying out and the apparent neglect of the elderly living in rural areas. We must remember that old people have probably complained about young people since time began, but there is little doubt that fundamental cultural changes have occurred this century.

Another way in which we might observe the scale of social change is to look at social values. These are beliefs and judgements which we apply in relationships with other people. Marriage is a good example of a social relationship much affected by changing values. People may now value choice of partner by the individuals concerned much more than they did fifty or a hundred years ago when compatibility of husband and wife was usually secondary to a union of two kin groups. Values regarding birth control may also be changing, thus affecting marital and extramarital relationships. In fact education may have a direct effect on attitudes to birth control, particularly among better-educated women.

Social change is also apparent in people's outlook – their knowledge and ideas. The individual of today is surrounded by information and news: the air is thick with competing radio broadcasts; newspapers and popular literature are available; and schooling has been much extended since the beginning of the century. Social change is therefore something which alters the inner personality, the outlook, the world-view of the individual – it is not just something which alters institutions and customs, leaving the individual untouched. The impact of education in changing people's minds – for example, in providing scientific explanations of such things as illness or other natural events – will be assessed in Chapter 7, but it is worth mentioning now that sociologists disagree about the causes of change, and whether formal education can ever be a primary cause of it.

Marxists argue that our cultural institutions – for example, schools, the family, the mass media – have strong socialising effects on the individual, but that they do not themselves bring about fundamental changes. Such changes occur if economic relationships (for example, between owner and worker), technology and resources, or the distribution of wealth change, thus allowing the so-called superstructure of society (that is, the cultural institutions) to change as well. This does not mean that Marxists believe that every economic change automatically brings a predictable cultural or social change. It is just that economic changes create the conditions which make other social or political changes likely; by the same token, any attempt to bring about social change or revolution through changing people's ideas (for example, by changing school curricula) will probably be abortive unless economic changes are brought about too.

Development

In Part Three we will consider economic, social and political development. In all these contexts, development implies some sort of change – a growing complexity and an increasing capacity to carry out ever more complicated tasks and functions.

Economic development suggests that economic institutions increase in complexity – for example, a society might change from a system of barter to a monetary system, and then develop more complicated institutions such as banks and insurance companies. At the same time the capacity of the economy to supply and produce goods may become greater than before.

Social and political development also imply increasing complexity – for example, the development of bureaucracies dealing with welfare, education and government – and greater capacity for the state to enforce its will through political parties, police, military forces and a civil service. Pye (1966) suggests that there are three main elements in political development: (i) the capacity of a state to carry out its goals, (ii) the development of political equality between citizens and (iii) the specialisation of political institutions and political roles.

Pye's scheme of development has an evolutionary tone: it suggests that relatively simple, undemocratic societies gradually acquire democratic political institutions and complicated organisations such as political parties. In short, Pye suggests that a process of modernisation takes place – an evolutionary development through a number of stages which have been pioneered by Western Europe and America. This view of development ignores significant political development in non-Western countries (for example, Cuba or China), and it also stereotypes traditional societies as simple and undemocratic. In fact, stateless African societies based on kinship rivalled any others in terms of democracy and complexity of political process. Traditional African states and kingdoms also revealed considerable specialisation of political institutions and roles; they may not have been fully democratic, but then neither were many European societies during the pre-colonial era.

The example of political development, therefore, shows that it is very difficult to trace a single line or path of development – whether economic, political or social – from traditional to modern stages. We will further criticise the 'tradition to modernity' model of change in the next chapter.

It is also difficult to ascertain the relationship between development and education. Economists who confidently predicted a positive relationship between educational growth and development are now treated more sceptically than before. Nor is it certain that expansion of formal education will bring social development, in the form of community development, social justice or a rational society in which enlightened social policies prevail. And an increase in education does not appear to guarantee increased political participation or the development of political institutions, to judge by a number of African states where schooling has expanded but which are under army rule.

Perhaps it is useful at this point to make a distinction between growth and development. Growth does not necessarily bring development. 'Growth without development' means that an economy produces more every year, but that the benefits and profits from this expansion do not trickle down to the mass of the population. Growth is often directed towards production for export, so not all sectors of the economy develop fully; at the same time, only elite groups or export companies grow rich from economic growth. This economic problem is typified by apparently prosperous countries such as the Ivory Coast.

An education system may be part of the process of growth without development: the totals of students and school-leavers may grow, but if there is a lack of suitable work economic underdevelopment and political apathy may result. In the following chapters we will discuss the extent to which this state of affairs has come about, and whether education can ever be a contributing factor to development.

Progress

A word often used by politicians and others in influential roles, 'progress', is rarely defined. For our purposes, progress can be taken to mean a particular view of social change in which the human condition is assumed to improve in every way – in terms of justice, equality, welfare and rational government. It is an optimistic view of human history and the future.

To twentieth-century man many things are possible. There are obstacles to progress but never before has human society had so much potential or so many opportunities to bring about progress. Unfortunately, however, progress is a problematic idea – it should not be taken for granted.

First, we should remember that to bring about improvements in one section of society or one part of the globe may result in exploitation of another part. Secondly, the idea of progress is relative – that is, one man's progress may be another man's poison. Birth control and Western standards of family size, for example, are assumed to be progressive by Westerners but may not be seen in this way by others. And thirdly, attempts to bring about progressive change may result in non-progressive, unintended changes. There has been progress in medical care and the eradication of serious diseases, but this has also resulted in an enormous growth of the world's population which has put a great strain on the supply of food and services such as education. We should be careful, therefore, before labelling as progressive all things which appear to be good – modern medicine, welfare services, education – before we have studied all the consequences of these supposedly beneficial things.

In the next chapter we will turn to the question of whether Western education is a progressive influence on society. Some argue that education enlightens and liberates a society, while others believe that schooling is oppressive and that society should be deschooled; we will try to strike a balance between these opposing views.

Chapter 7

Education and Socio-Cultural Change

In this chapter we wish to answer the question: 'What part does education play in social change?' To many education is a progressive or change-inducing force. It is usually supposed to be a thoroughly modern institution; after all, one of the main purposes of education is to give new knowledge, to enlighten, provide scientific, modern explanations and to teach a rational approach to problems. But we have to be cautious about this view of the relation between education and social change. First, does education really change views, values and customs? For example, do the educated always abandon supposedly traditional ways such as polygamy, or always prefer hospital treatment to traditional medicine? Secondly, is education itself a traditional influence in some respects? Perhaps authoritarian teaching methods or inefficient school administration are more likely to encourage conservatism or apathetic attitudes than positive attitudes about the future. Thirdly, the notion of change from so-called traditional society and culture to modern society is somewhat misleading in itself; of course, changes are occurring in society, but it is hard to define them as traditional or modern responses (see the section on modernisation below). And where schools have existed for fifty years or more, they have become part of established, traditional society.

To summarise, the relation between education and social change can be seen to correspond to any one of the following patterns or models:

(a) According to the first model, education can be seen as a direct *cause of change*. That is, the development of education has noticeable effects on ideas, levels of knowledge, values and ways of life generally. A slowing down of educational growth would, according to this model, limit change and hinder development.

(b) Education might have a *limited* effect on social change – it might cause some changes, but not have a clear effect on others. For example, it may increase knowledge levels among the population, but not lead to new attitudes or values such as individualism.

(c) Education might be a *neutral* factor which neither helps nor hinders change. Thus, according to this model, social changes are caused by other forces – for example, the growth of towns and cities – but at least education does not obstruct social change.

(d) Education could be seen as a *negative* influence on social change. According to this model, education's main function lies in transmitting accepted ideas, values and ways of life to the younger generation. Rather than challenging accepted ideas or stimulating achievement, schools encourage acceptance of authority, discourage innovative people and do not change the social structure very much by increasing social mobility.

These four different models are intended to show that we should not automatically associate education with social change, progress or modernity. We are not saying that any one of the four possible roles of education will exactly fit any particular society, such as Nigeria. But in the sections which follow, we will look at the influences of education and literacy to see which of the four comes closest to the realities of social change.

Education and Modernisation

Modernisation Theory
As we have already mentioned, the idea of change from tradition to modernity is one of the commonest ways of picturing social transition in Africa. The death of traditional values and ways of life and the rise of new, sometimes unwanted, ways are strong in the public imagination. This pattern of change is a characteristic theme of modern novels such as Achebe's *Things Fall Apart*. We intend to provide some background to the theory of modernisation before education itself is considered.

We all know roughly what the terms 'modern' and 'traditional' mean. Modernity is often pictured as good and desirable, and words such as 'progressive', 'efficient', 'innovative' and 'technologically advanced' are sometimes associated with modernity. Tradition, on the other hand, suffers from negative associations: outdated, conservative, fatalistic. Traditions can be seen in a positive light, however, such as when we speak of preserving traditions to keep a society's identity.

Some sociologists have attempted to make the terms 'modern' and 'traditional' more precise or scientific than the way they are commonly understood. Lerner (1958), Kahl (1968) and Inkeles and Smith (1974), for example, have attempted to build a scientific theory of change around the idea of a gradual shift from traditional to modern attitudes among people.

Most of their research has tested representative samples of people in various countries (although Lerner had very small samples) to find out how traditional or modern they are in outlook. Inkeles and Smith (1974) draw conclusions from studies of thousands of interviews conducted in Nigeria, Chile, Argentina, Israel, India and East Pakistan (now Bangladesh). Different writers in the field of modernisation studies have used slightly different tests of attitudes, and so the following list has been drawn up to include most of the attitudes studied. None of those studying modernisation believes that every individual falls neatly into either the traditional or modern category, and it should be remembered that each column of attitudes represents the essence of tradition or modernity: very few individuals are wholly traditional or modern in their attitudes.

MODERN ATTITUDES	TRADITIONAL ATTITUDES
(a) Innovative – seeks change	Conservative – prefers tradition
(b) Individualistic	Family and group come before the individual
(c) Rational – seeks scientific explanations	Irrational – believes magical and religious explanations
(d) Optimistic – believes in planning and controlling the future	Fatalistic – believes man is the victim of chance
(e) Has need for personal achievement	Personal ambition or mobility is secondary to habit or custom
(f) Punctual – activities are arranged according to the clock	Activities, work and social interaction not regulated by time
(g) Tolerant – has liberal attitudes towards equality of the sexes, for example	Intolerant – believes roles should be carried out according to traditional values
(h) Favours urban living and working for large organisations	Favours rural living and distrusts large organisations
(i) Occupation is the determinant of status and life's purpose	Traditional or religious positions and aims may be more important than work for determining life's purpose
(j) Well informed and receptive to mass media; favourable attitudes towards Western education	Parochial attitudes: makes little use of mass media and has unfavourable attitudes towards Western education

Modernisation theorists suggest that change towards a modern out-look results from being involved in certain social institutions – for example, schools, factories and the mass media – which carry messages of modernity. Thus listening to the radio, attending school, living in town or working in a modern factory are believed to be good predictors of modern attitudes. Parents' level of education, socio-economic status and ethnic background are also supposed to have a crucial effect on whether an individual is socialised into a modern way of life. Therefore modern individuals do not appear from nowhere, or from out of the blue; they appear because of social changes – the development of modern social institutions.

Despite the supposed link between the growth of modern institu-tions and individual change, however, modernisation theory stresses study of the individual rather than the society around him. Social influences such as factories or schools are mentioned, but the focus of the studies is on describing the modern or traditional *individual*. It is not actually explained how the school, factory or mass media teach modernity – they are just assumed to have this effect. This weakness in modernisation studies is not surprising if we remember that all the research findings are from individual interviews, not from observation of what goes on in schools, factories or supposedly modern cities.

The bias of modernisation theory towards the individual is shown quite clearly by the work of McClelland (1961) and others who have examined the psychological element in change. According to the social-psychological approach, the failure of a society to develop is largely due to its not having enough individuals of a particular person-ality type – that is, modern individuals who are predisposed to change. McClelland suggests that some individuals do not just seek rewards for their own sake (for example, wealth or social prestige), but also seek the satisfaction of success itself.

The individual who has a high personal need for achievement is willing to take risks and begin new forms of enterprise, trade or industry (entrepreneurial behaviour). This type of person has a mind open to change and the latest inventions, takes decisions rapidly, assumes responsibility, and has a determination to achieve change. McClelland has tried to show that societies differ in their proportions of individuals with a high need for achievement, and that the same society may have a high proportion of such people at one stage of its history, but fewer at another stage. For example, European societies in the first half of the eighteenth century are supposed to have encour-aged a high need for achievement. McClelland supposes that this was brought about by significant changes in child-rearing methods and in religious changes which encouraged individualism and hard work. It is when McClelland explains the origin of the achieving individual that he is thrown back to social factors (child-rearing customs, religion).

But the emphasis of McClelland's work is still on the individual – he does not actually explain why societies themselves change – why child-rearing methods change, for example, or why religious changes occur.

Criticisms

The above descriptions of Inkeles and Smith's and McClelland's ideas have already hinted at some of their shortcomings. Such a brief summary cannot do justice to them or to the work of other modernisation theorists, so before we turn to education and modernisation some criticisms of the 'tradition to modernity' model of change will be developed a little further.

Perhaps the greatest weakness of the modernisation approach – particularly as far as Africa is concerned – is its neglect of the importance of colonial rule. Modernisation theory explains lack of change by the failure of African societies to produce modern individuals with a high need for achievement, or by the strength of traditional values in Africa. But this argument does not take account of the conservative effects of colonialism on society – for example, the maintenance of traditional rulers, or even the invention of artificial offices of chief in areas which had never had such traditions. Of course colonial rule also brought significant changes as well (the subsequent discrediting of chieftaincy and the distortion of traditional rule, for example); the point is that modernisation theory has ignored history and the specific causes of present-day attitudes. By failing to look at the consequences of colonial rule, modernisation theory therefore tends to put the blame for lack of development on supposed inadequacies and faults in less developed societies themselves.

Modernisation studies also encourage the idea that all societies must follow a single path of development, and pass through set stages of traditional, intermediate and advanced development; this is what might be called a unilinear view of change. It is assumed that Europe and America represent the desirable goal of modernity that all less developed societies aim for. In most modernisation studies, modern man has become some sort of idealised American man. The research in these studies is basically looking for individuals in less developed societies who seem closest in attitudes and life-style to the idealised picture of a white American living in a pleasant suburb of Los Angeles or New York.

In fact, when we look closely at ways of life in industrial nations, strong elements of tradition are still to be found. In Japan, for example, traditional customs of paternalistic treatment of employees and of loyalty to the business firm are still strong. In Britain, long-lasting respect for the monarchy and nobility illustrate the strength of traditional attitudes. These examples show that it is difficult to distinguish societies which are supposed to have wholly modern customs, values and ways of life from those which are supposed to be more traditional (although we can make distinctions according to countries' technological development or levels of wealth).

Within African societies it is also difficult to distinguish between modern and traditional phenomena. A rapid growth of traditional fetish houses and shrines, for example, may be a sign of the stress of modern life and of rapid social change. Cohen (1969) has shown that apparently traditional tribalism among Hausa migrants to Ibadan is in fact a modern phenomenon. He discovered that the Ibadan Hausa have recently exaggerated their exclusive cultural identity and way of life in order to safeguard their strong economic interests in the cattle, kola and transport businesses.

What at first appears to be traditional may therefore turn out to be a recent or modern phenomenon. This means that the modernisation model of change, devised by Western social scientists with an image of their own industrial societies in mind, may be inappropriate to an understanding of change in Africa. In terms of the realities of change, this model probably obscures much more than it illuminates, and we should bear this in mind when considering whether education modernises a society.

Inkeles and Smith believe that 'the school in developing countries, for all its presumed defects, is surely one of the most powerful means of inculcating modern attitudes, values and behaviour'. They found that education is highly correlated with modernism – in other words, educated people are likely to have personal characteristics such as individualism, optimism about the future, and so on, as described above.

Inkeles and Smith are also anxious to point out that teachers sometimes create social change unconsciously rather than consciously: for example, by transmitting certain attitudes such as a preference for urban living or a belief in rational, scientific explanations, they change their pupils' outlook on the world. Thus teachers are not portrayed as deliberate agents of change who set out to disrupt accepted norms and social conventions, but as unwitting agents of change. Their statement about the presumed defects of schools shows that they are also aware of some of the non-modern influences of education.

For example, the school curriculum may not contain particularly modern or progressive ideas. They argue that it is the hidden curriculum of the school – timekeeping, being treated impersonally as a member of a group, being rewarded according to merit rather than traditional status – which encourages modernity among the educated. In this section we will therefore examine some of the suggestions Inkeles and Smith make about how education modernises people, together with a study of personal change among some northern

Nigerian primary pupils (Peshkin, 1972). The assumption that the hidden curriculum of the school and teachers' attitudes bring a modern outlook to students will be questioned. It will be suggested that, in some ways, the school is a very traditional institution.

Inkeles and Smith argue that the process of classroom learning has a strongly modernising effect on the personality. They suggest that schoolchildren, unlike the uneducated, are encouraged to explore the whole range of their talents. Learning in a disciplined way, absorbing new knowledge and opening up their minds, students – it is supposed – obtain an optimistic sense of being able to control their futures and their environment. This is called a sense of efficacy, a key characteristic of the modern personality.

However, if our discussion of social interaction in classrooms is recalled (see Chapter 4) the idea that schools create such a sense of efficacy can be doubted. Children are often bewildered about what is being taught and what is expected of them. Such confusion is by no means restricted to the primary level, and may be present in higher education if the quality of teaching is not very good. School classrooms are also marked by an authoritarian atmosphere, mainly because teaching methods are often of the 'chalk and talk' variety. Children are usually expected to sit passively and to learn by accepting the teacher's word.

We must also question whether students are really encouraged to explore all their abilities. Peshkin gives the example of a primary schoolgirl who discovers a hidden talent for drawing, and he argues that but for school this aspect of her abilities would have remained hidden. This is true as far as this single example is concerned, but one wonders how frequently African schools sustain a diversity of talents among children or discover hidden abilities. Pressure to pass examinations may limit learning to mastering set techniques in reading, writing and numbers. More general abilities such as expression, whether in writing, drawing or speech, may be neglected. Of course, children do learn a great deal in school, but what we are questioning is Inkles and Smith's assumption that this learning shapes what they term a 'modern' personality.

Inkeles and Smith also assume that schooling is an inherently superior form of socialisation to the learning patterns of those who do not attend. While ignorance and illiteracy should not be defended, we should be careful not to devalue the informal kinds of training experienced by some of the non-schooled. Inkeles and Smith, for example, suggest:

> Before coming to school, children have already enjoyed mastering certain skills. . . . If school did not intervene, however, there would usually be a lull until adolescence provided them with new oppor-

tunities for mastery in hunting or farming, sex or combat. (1974, p. 141)

Anthropological evidence (see, for example, Oppong, 1973) suggests that Inkeles and Smith are probably wrong in holding this view. Non-schooled children who learn traditional occupations such as farming, weaving, drumming, blacksmithing and so on have often mastered quite complicated skills before the onset of adolescence. In fact the hallmark of traditional socialisation practices seems to be the giving of gradually more complicated and responsible tasks to children (see Chapter 1). Inkeles and Smith have rather odd ideas about what unschooled adolescents do and, by stressing apparently primitive activities such as hunting and combat, they neglect vital occupations which are often competently learned by those who have never been to school.

Punctuality and learning to plan activities, it will be remembered, are important characteristics of the modern individual. Inkeles and Smith contend that the school, like the factory, gives this modern sense of time. It is certainly true that the school, particularly in a rural setting, seems to stand out from the rest of the community because its activities are timetabled. The idea of dividing each day into set periods must have some effect on those who have been to school, although Inkeles and Smith do not demonstrate that educated people transfer their training in school timekeeping to their daily lives. Attitudes to time and punctuality vary a great deal from society to society, and education does not have a uniform effect on these attitudes. In some cultures it is impolite to arrive punctually or to act in obvious haste. This does not mean that such cultures are less modern than others with different customs.

It is also doubtful whether non-schooled, apparently traditional people lack a sense of time in the way suggested. In farming, for example, during certain times of the year daily activities have to be performed quickly and with some forward planning to make the best use of limited time. While farmwork, like other traditional occupa-tions, is often performed according to alternating rhythms of hard work and leisurely socialising, rather than by the clock, so is apparently modern work in offices, factories and schools. Although schoolwork is timetabled one suspects that teachers' and students' attention and concentration vary because of boredom, hunger or tiredness. And by arriving late or finishing classes early, teachers are hardly inculcating a modern outlook, according to Inkeles and Smith's definition, but acting as many teachers are known and almost expected to do from time to time (see Chapter 4).

Are teachers the exemplars of modern attitudes which Inkeles and Smith suppose them to be? They state, for example, that 'when a teacher listens attentively to, and takes seriously, the suggestions of the children, he serves as a model of sensitivity to the feelings of subordinates and of openness to new ideas' (1974, p. 141). This is a striking example of how far Inkeles and Smith are removed from the reality of school classrooms and teachers' interpretations of their roles. We are not suggesting that all teachers are callous or do not wish to assist their students as much as possible; but what we do argue is that most teachers do not view their work in the way Inkeles and Smith suggest. The major impression teachers give of their work is one of helping their students by passing on accepted knowledge and truths. Teachers expect to provide answers rather than listen to questions or suggestions (see Chapter 4), and are often forced by the expectations of their own students to keep to the syllabus rather than experiment with new ideas. It does not follow that teachers will provide an example of modern man or woman for children to copy. The teacher's function is usually a conservative one, and he is more likely to teach accepted behaviour patterns than new ones.

To be fair to Inkeles and Smith, we should remember that part of their argument is that, by living a certain way of life, by preferring town to village life and by having a white-collar job, the teacher unwittingly spreads modern aspirations and standards. In this argument, however, there is a logical flaw and a failure to consider teachers' social status and income. If teachers posted to rural areas are often dissatisfied and wish to work in town, this tells us more about the low status of teaching (at the primary level) than the modernity of teachers. Despite their education and professional training, in some cases, teachers are about the only white-collar workers expected to work in villages. Preference for urban life among educated and non-educated alike is more to do with incentives of better living conditions than the spread of modern attitudes.

It is also difficult to see how teachers' public role in the community reflects modernity. In some places, government teachers are treated by students and their parents much the same as traditional Koranic teachers, as Peshkin notes. Thus the supposedly modern impact of the government teacher's role is outweighed by traditional definitions or expectations. Another factor detracting from the teacher's modern image is his relatively low income and, in some areas, the irregular payment of salaries (see Chapter 5). A distinction must be made here between the secondary schoolteacher who might live in a Western-style house, travel from time to time, and enjoy a professional level of income and status, and the poorer, usually untrained village schoolteacher who is not able to buy the symbols of modernity – the latest styles of clothes, a modern type of wristwatch, radio or motor car. In fact, apparently more traditional people with less education, such as successful traders, are more likely to have these modern things.

Having considered Inkeles and Smith's ideas about the supposed effects of school environment and teachers on modernity, we should also look briefly at another aspect of education – the curriculum. As we have already mentioned, modernisation theorists are willing to admit that school curricula contain non-modern, conservative characteristics, but they still make the assumption that some elements of school knowledge – particularly mathematics and science – will challenge traditional ideas.

Peshkin, for example, believes that education brings changes in ideas about medicine and health. Hygiene and biology lessons have some effect on the educated, who are apparently more sceptical than the non-educated about the power of supernatural charms to ward off ill health. Some of this change in attitude could result from receiving compulsory medical treatment such as inoculation against diseases, and not from the educational content of school. One also wonders whether the educated person would willingly abandon all traditional medical practices or herbal remedies, particularly if Western medical treatment were expensive or difficult to obtain. Use of traditional remedies, if they are the best or only treatments available, can be seen as rational rather than non-modern behaviour. We should also remember that a great deal of scientific school knowledge is learned for examination purposes but is not always accepted as fact in the students' minds, as Peshkin admits (1972, p. 135).

If school knowledge is supposed to be the key which unlocks the door to rationality and scientific beliefs, then perhaps we might expect religious beliefs and supernatural explanations to be uncommon in the mind of the educated person. Peshkin's study, however, revealed 'no apparent erosion of religious sentiment among the children'. This is partly because most school curricula include some religious teaching. In Islamic-influenced societies such as the district studied by Peshkin religious teaching in state schools is frequent and is followed with great interest by the students. In Christian or semi-Christian areas, religion is also a set part of the curriculum. Although one might expect subjects such as physics or chemistry to increase scepticism and what Inkeles defines as a secular, modern view of the world, little evidence of such scepticism exists in Africa. In any case the notions that science and religion are always incompatible, and that modern people are not religious, are to be doubted and are in fact contradicted by the evidence of a modern, secular, science-influenced yet highly religious country, the United States of America.

The modernisation argument also rests on the idea that school knowledge leads to openness to new ideas and, by implication, to a desire for individual and social change. There is some truth in this argument, although it cannot always be assumed that the knowledge contained in school curricula is being used for these modern purposes.

As was pointed out in Chapter 4, the school can be thought of as a training ground for society as it is – for example, by obtaining qualifications to become an unquestioning bureaucratic employee – rather than for learning to be individualistic or to become an entrepreneur. (See Chapter 9 for further discussion of the conformist influences of schooling.)

Masemann (1974), through study of a West African girls' boarding school, discovered a group of students who wanted education for traditional purposes. They wanted enough knowledge to be able to converse with educated people, to know rules of etiquette among well-off social groups, and to be able to manage a house. They did not want education for modern career purposes, but just a smattering of knowledge to be able to attract suitable husbands with qualifications and career prospects higher than their own. Although these students described their aim in attending secondary school as 'learning to live a modern life', theirs is not a modern goal according to Inkeles and Smith's definition. In fact, the aspirations and social roles of these educated women are in some ways more traditional than those of less educated women who have a source of income independent of their husbands.

Masemann's study shows that exposure to school knowledge does not necessarily encourage a modern outlook. However, it could be argued that her example is rather unusual, and that gradual expansion of the number of educated women will modernise society by increasing competition between men and women for jobs traditionally considered to be the preserve of males.

The experience of other societies, however, such as the USSR and Poland, suggests that deliberate attempts to raise the educational levels of women do not easily bring sexual equality in work opportunities. The modernisation of women's roles cannot be brought about by the education system alone, particularly if women are traditionally expected to spend more time rearing families and looking after children than men are.

With regard to the role of African women in family life, Clignet (1967) found that clerical workers in the Ivory Coast tend to live in polygamous families more often than manual workers. This finding may not be replicated in other West African countries, and we must be cautious in applying it generally, but Clignet's study is important because it shows that a higher than average education and supposedly modern occupations can be associated with a traditional family type. The husbands in Clignet's sample of clerical workers found that their educational qualifications give them a secure, relatively stable income which allows them to live a generally preferred life-style with two or more wives.

We should also remember that school curricula themselves contain as many traditional as modern ideas, as Inkeles and Smith admit. A glance at any primary or secondary school textbook often reveals a considerable amount of sex stereotyping of roles: that is, males are pictured as active, resourceful and intelligent, while females appear passive and intuitive. Conservative elements in the school curriculum are not restricted to teaching about male and female roles, but also include traditional views of politics and religion.

Obtaining educational qualifications can bring personal change, especially for men, if work at an appropriate level can be found. But achieving qualifications and upward social mobility are not the same as becoming modern in attitudes, as Inkeles and Smith define modernity. Attitudes to religion or the role of women in society may remain relatively unaffected by education (except, perhaps, as far as higher education is concerned), and it is not certain that the scientific information learned in school necessarily changes the fundamental outlook of the educated.

The aim of this section has been to balance the ideas of those such as Inkeles and Smith or Peshkin who claim that the school is a modernising institution. Although Inkeles and Smith are aware of some non-modern elements in education, they see these as defects in an institution which is certain to bring about modernisation. It is more likely, however, that the school will continue to be a traditional, conservative social institution. Schools teach conformity rather than innovation, and there is not much evidence that they change accepted values concerning the role of women in society, religion or the political structure. The teacher occupies a rather lowly, conventional position in society. Societies do change, but as we shall try to show in the concluding section of this chapter, the source of change is rarely the school.

These conclusions do not mean that Inkeles and Smith or other writers subscribing to the modernisation thesis are completely wrong. The school as an institution does have certain common effects on the individual, whether examples are taken from African or non-African cultures. However, the way in which the school is perceived varies from society to society: there are widely different patterns of discipline, teaching and curriculum, and differences in the status of teachers. The school is therefore unlikely to bring uniform changes like modernity in the way that has been suggested.

Much of the difficulty with the idea that schools bring modern ways of life lies in the artificial distinction between tradition and modernity implied by Inkeles and Smith, and others. As we have pointed out, it is questionable whether learning by the illiterate young outside school is always less progressive or more traditional than school learning, for example. Are those who seek a secure life in bureaucratic employment, or with a husband more educated than themselves, modern or traditional in outlook? Such problems of definition illustrate the fact that tradition and modernity are not clearly separate categories, but can only be understood with reference to the society or education system being considered.

Literacy and Social Change

In the previous section we examined the supposed relation between education and modernisation. This section will concentrate on the particular impact of adult literacy on social change, mainly because it is often supposed that widespread literacy among a population leads to social change, whether or not most of those who can read and write have ever been to school. Thus it is suggested that the existence of literacy among about half the British population in the eighteenth century was an important factor in the technical and commercial changes of the Industrial Revolution. This theory about the effectiveness of literacy (see, for example, Cipolla, 1969) has yet to be demonstrated convincingly, but it has attracted the support of the leaders of some developing countries and of others concerned with innovating change. Cuba, for example, has virtually eradicated illiteracy in an astonishingly short time (Jolly, 1969b) by means of a comprehensive adult literacy campaign. President Nyerere of Tanzania, launching an adult literacy programme, spoke of the need to teach reading and writing to as many as possible 'because we cannot afford to wait for the children': in other words, conventional schooling for the young represents a long-term investment in literacy which does not give results as quickly as a mass literacy programme for adults.

What is Literacy?

Any adult population includes those who cannot read and write at all, those with a rudimentary knowledge of reading or writing, or perhaps both, and those with various levels of schooling and of competence in reading and writing. It is quite possible to be literate without ever having attended school, either by learning to read and write oneself, or by receiving help from an official literacy programme. Levels of literacy (fully literate, semi-literate, basically literate) are very hard to determine, whether a particular individual or a whole society's level is being discussed. This difficulty of determining levels of literacy is compounded because of the existence of literacy in local as well as official, national languages.

Literacy and education should be distinguished from one another. Instruction in literacy does not necessarily mean providing a full education, as children in school might receive. Admittedly, reading is bound to provide the newly literate person with a key to fresh ideas and knowledge, but this is not quite the same as deliberately educating in a range of subjects such as history and geography, mathematics or science. If a literacy programme is designed with a specific end in view – for example, to provide tobacco farmers with scientific information about their crop and to change their attitudes to work (see Durojaiye, 1971) – then the receivers of the programme are introduced to only a narrow range of ideas. Being literate for such specific purposes is termed functional literacy. Some argue that it is unethical to teach people to read and write for specific purposes only. Freire (1970), for example, criticises the idea that literacy is just a technical skill, like ploughing or building a house, to be passed on in a neutral way to those who do not have the skill. He argues that literacy teaching is bound to have some political content and to inculcate certain social values, even when a literacy programme pretends to be neutral or technical in its aims. We will return to this argument, and to Freire's suggestions, below. For the time being the distinction between education and simply learning to read and write should be noted.

As well as functional literacy – putting literacy to specific uses – there is a more limited form described as restricted literacy by Goody (1968). Restricted literacy exists when most people cannot read more than a few words, and the dominant attitude towards the written word is that it is a sacred thing, not to be put to practical use but to act as a charm or be used as part of religious worship. This attitude is in evidence when we observe people with amulets or leather pouches containing prayers from the Koran or some other source. Those who can read and write well are regarded by people with restricted literacy as high-status intermediaries who translate sacred words to the ordinary man and woman. Such traditional beliefs about literacy abound in traditional societies, not just in Africa but in many parts of the world. There is some evidence that alphabets and skills of writing were deliberately made very complex in certain parts of the ancient world (for example, Egypt, Mesopotamia) so that scribes and high priests could maintain their jealously guarded monopolies over the skills of literacy. Thus for many centuries the written word has represented traditional authority, either in the form of religion or of a ruler of a state or kingdom, and has not been deemed suitable for understanding by ordinary folk. It is not surprising that the advent of schooling and literacy programmes has been seen as an advance which spreads not just a new skill and a source of knowledge, but a potential source of social change in terms of beliefs about authority and democracy.

Does Literacy Cause Change?
Some writers (for example, Cipolla, 1969) believe that literacy was a tremendously important invention which paved the way for fundamental social changes all over the world. Cipolla speaks of the effects of

literacy on a society. However, it is not at all clear that the introduction of literacy can cause change by itself; in fact, literacy may be a consequence of other changes rather than a cause of them. As Williams points out (1971, p. 49), literacy *appears* to be a very useful skill, even in jobs outside the so-called modern sector of African economies, but there is as yet little hard evidence of exactly how useful it is, and whether literacy brings about any further social or economic changes.

We must also be careful to distinguish between the supposed effects of literacy and the effects of literates. It is possible to have a society in which only a small minority are fully literate, but in which this minority has a great impact on the population by changing farming methods, commerce, social values or politics. This kind of change is rather different from the idea of changing everyone's outlook and knowledge through literacy.

Why do Goody and Watt (1968), and Cipolla, believe literacy plays such an important part in social change if others are rather more sceptical? In the first place, Goody and Watt believe that literacy allowed the past to be recorded accurately for the first time. Written records cannot be changed, and therefore the history of a society is no longer a matter of myths and human memory. Goody and Watt argue that the breakthrough to keeping accurate records, histories, written laws and ideas, led to a new kind of outlook or attitude among the people who could read: they define this as 'logical-empirical thought'.

Goody and Watt are therefore suggesting that illiterates lack not only knowledge but also a literate way of thinking – they have few opportunities to compare ideas logically, and are unaccustomed to classifying information on paper in the way that a literate person can. Goody and Watt do not go so far as to say that pre-literate (traditional) peoples are non-logical, but they do make a fairly clear distinction between societies where illiteracy is common and societies where people have become accustomed to literate, logical ways of thought and discussion.

There is little doubt that in the modern world those who cannot read and write are at a disadvantage. Governmental communications are nearly always in writing, and to make use of many services (for example, changing a postal order or requesting a bank loan) it is necessary to be able to read, or run the risk of being cheated. Sources of enjoyment and information, such as newspapers and popular literature, are also closed to illiterates. But it should also be remembered that people with little or no literacy may manage business affairs quite successfully. Illiteracy can be compensated for by the use of educated relatives who can read documents or write letters; there are also letter writers who, for a small fee, act as effective gatekeepers to the world of literacy.

We must also be careful not to accept entirely the arguments that literates and non-literates think in different ways, or that the spread of literacy will automatically solve all development problems. It is doubtful whether some of the cultural changes which Goody and Watt describe as being initiated by literacy – for example, tendencies towards logical thought, scepticism, self-consciousness and individualism – are solely the result of long traditions of literacy in a society. The Ibo of Nigeria, for example, are renowned for their individualistic nature and high motivation to achieve, but it is likely that these cultural traits predate the spread of literacy in the nineteenth and twentieth centuries. Therefore the introduction and spreading of literacy are not necessarily the main factors in generating new attitudes and ideas favourable to development; such attitudes may already be well established in Africa.

Literacy in an African country is often in an official rather than a local language. This may weaken some of the impact of literacy on social values and the individual's outlook. Learning to read and write in English or French rather than a mother tongue presents the student with the additional difficulties of mastering foreign words, meanings and pronunciations. In some respects this parallels the situation in Europe when Latin was the main language for writing and reading; the impact of literacy on attitudes and knowledge was dependent on mastery of this alien language.

The use of an official language in literature classes does not help people to discuss everyday matters in English or French. English teachers often find that students use flowery, complicated language copied from some of the books they have read. In letters, for example, an everyday chop bar may become a 'restaurant', or an ordinary house a 'cottage'. A vocabulary derived from foreign literature does not supply the student with down-to-earth expressions in which to describe the world as he sees it; this suggests that literacy does not have a straightforward effect on the mentality of literates, nor is it necessarily seen as something to be used practically in farming, metalwork or commerce. In a society in which many cannot read it is easy for literates to keep separate the things learned in books from the practical world.

Not all literacy is in the official language, however, and the practice of teaching reading and writing in local languages has been successfully adopted in many adult literacy schemes. This way, the literate person can make a direct translation from the printed word to his own everyday expressions and vocabulary. While this undoubtedly facilitates learning and increases the impact of literacy on ideas about farming, hygiene, birth control or voting, there is often a lack of sufficient reading material in local languages. Therefore it may be difficult for the newly literate to broaden their reading beyond technical information about farming, exhortations to use birth control, or religious pamphlets. At the same time, most of the important government documents and newspapers and the best supply of books may be in the official language which those literate only in a local language might find it difficult to progress to. Use of a local language may therefore lead to a fairly high impact of literacy in a district or group of villages, but not lead to any widespread social change.

Nowadays technical and scientific information is much more advanced than it was. To compete with the productivity of more industrialised countries, it is argued that African workers and farmers must be literate to put into practice the latest technical processes and devices. Therefore it is often suggested that although a literacy programme might have only a limited, local impact such a programme is worth it if local living standards are significantly raised. Many experiments with functional literacy programmes have been attempted, including the one with tobacco farmers mentioned by Durojaiye (1971).

As we have mentioned above, Freire (1970) has criticised the aims of such projects to educate in technical skills and teach only limited literacy. Freire's point is that literacy is not just a skill but also a form of consciousness. Therefore literacy can be taught in a way that could lead to social change – by bringing out a revolutionary consciousness or social awareness – but literacy can also be used to repress consciousness or prevent social change. Freire is concerned that literacy programmes, often designed by Westerners, aim to teach ordinary people how to obey technical instructions rather than develop their own questioning attitude towards authority and knowledge. If passive acceptance of knowledge is taught Freire concludes that literacy projects – while passing on skills of reading and writing and possibly helping a few farmers or craftsmen financially – are at the same time shaping literate consciousness in the interests of the dominant political order.

Freire is right to point out that adult literacy schemes are often designed by foreigners, and that local teachers employed in such projects are more likely to stick to the practical aims of literacy than attempt to radicalise the adults they are teaching. But even in a technical project which is aimed to teach work-oriented literacy, some general training is unavoidable; the adult learners will be taught general words and phrases which can be applied to reading fiction, newspapers and magazines as well as non-technical books and pamphlets. Durojaiye found that almost half the tobacco farmers he studied had broadened their reading habits from farming instruction manuals to religious books, pamphlets and other items. The success of literate tobacco farmers had also inspired positive attitudes towards literacy and education among illiterate neighbours, so that it would probably be wrong to view this project as completely limited to the technical changes and farming developments it brought about.

Literacy may *help to bring about* all kinds of knowledge changes and alterations in ways of life, even if literacy itself does not *cause* such changes. Popular literature in Nigeria of the sort described by Obiechina (1971), for example, relieves a widespread thirst for knowledge, stories of adventure, success and romance. While pamphlets and magazines provide entertainment they also answer a need for knowledge of how to behave in new, untried situations, how to manage relations with parents or with the opposite sex and how to pass examinations. Popular literature could therefore be described as an agent, if not a primary cause, of social change in that it encourages new kinds of behaviour or sets new social standards or norms. However, much of the content of short stories, magazines and pamphlets reflects the taste of the audience rather than an attempt to change public attitudes or behaviour. As Obiechina describes, much popular fiction adapts traditional stories and proverbs. The stories and advice given are popular because they respond to tradition as well as trying to help readers with modern problems. Thus popular literature is hardly a pioneer of social change, although it may help to facilitate changes that are already happening.

There is a strong link between the idea that education brings modernisation and that literacy also does this. It will be recalled that one of the main predictors of modernity, according to Inkeles, is literacy. Thus it is a small step from the belief that literacy inevitably brings modern ideas, knowledge and values to thinking that illiteracy means tradition and conservatism. As was pointed out in the section on education and modernisation, however, things may not be as simple as this. It is wrong to draw clear-cut distinctions between tradition and modernity and then equate literacy with modernity.

The fact that literacy in Africa is often in a foreign language such as English or French may mean that reading and writing are not seen as having much use in ordinary life; literacy may be a valuable skill for passing examinations but not for applying to work or to practical experience. It must also be remembered that adult literacy programmes, while avoiding this problem by teaching in a local language, suffer the other problem of shortage of suitable reading materials. Popular fiction, available in both official and local languages, may be as traditional as it is modern in its impact on the reader.

For all these reasons, therefore, we ought to be very careful before attributing to literacy the power to transform society. Whether literacy has any effects depends on the kind of society into which it is introduced. The example of Europe in the eighteenth century has shown us that literacy may have been one important factor among many in the birth of the Industrial Revolution; but literacy actually declined in England during the nineteenth century when machines requiring unskilled labour replaced skilled craftsmen (Cipolla, 1969). Literacy has spread widely in parts of contemporary India, but basic social and economic problems remain, and from the point of view of religion and social custom society retains many traditional elements. As far as Africa is concerned, the lesson to be drawn from these examples is that literacy facilitates social changes which are occurring anyway but by itself seems unlikely to change ideas, social norms or values.

Education and Progress

Those who believe education to be a modernising influence also tend to say that it is progressive. In this final section we wish to question the idea that education is entirely progressive, partly because the notion of progress itself is a somewhat overoptimistic view of social change (see introduction to Part Three), and also because formal education has been the subject of radical criticism by those such as Ivan Illich, who suggests that schooling can even obstruct progress.

The previous two sections might have given the impression that education is a neutral force in social change – that is, it neither holds back nor pushes forward the march of progress. It was concluded, for example, that values are not significantly changed by education; rather, traditional social values are reflected in the schooling process itself. Even knowledge gained from schooling or literacy may have little impact on society.

Perhaps this view of education as a more or less neutral factor in social change ought to be qualified by considering different levels of education. Possession of secondary or higher education may make a considerable difference or have a noticeable effect in certain areas of social life – choice of occupation, chance of upward social mobility, political values, attitudes to marriage – while having only primary education may make little difference as far as these things are concerned.

To illustrate further this important distinction between levels of education, let us consider several vital issues which affect human progress:

(a) *Population growth*

It has been found that education makes little or no difference to the fertility of a population or attitudes to birth control unless we consider those with higher education, or industrial countries where secondary education is compulsory (Bjork, 1971). Other factors, such as level of economic development or urbanisation, seem much more closely related to population growth than level of educational development.

To show this, Bjork gives the example of the Philippines, a country where basic education is fairly widespread (75 per cent are literate) but where the birth rate is higher than in Singapore, a highly urbanised and crowded state which has fewer educated (55 per cent are illiterate). Thus basic education seems to have little or no effect on social values concerning birth control or on social norms of desired family size; only extended or higher education seems to affect these values in some societies.

(b) *The role of women*
The reduction of inequality between men and women, and the willingness of women to work outside the household or family, are often taken as signs of social progress. Peil (1979), in a study of West African towns, including Aba, Abeokuta, Lagos and Kaduna, found that the likelihood of women taking jobs outside the home increases dramatically if secondary education has been obtained. Otherwise education to a lower level makes little difference; in towns where women are generally expected to work outside the home, illiterates are found in the labour force as often as educated women, while in Muslim-influenced areas women are discouraged from working outside the household even if they have primary education. Peil found, however, that Muslim women significantly improve their chances of taking jobs if they go beyond the primary school level. As with progressive attitudes towards birth control, therefore, education only seems to make a difference to the role of women if it has been obtained in relatively large doses. There is a parallel here between awareness of inequality between the sexes and general political awareness. Again, education beyond primary school level seems to be the significant threshold over which beliefs and attitudes begin to change. Research into political attitudes in Nigeria (see Chapter 9) shows that people with primary education differ little from those with none.

(c) *Social mobility*
The possible impact of education is not restricted to changes in values and knowledge, as with (a) and (b), but could include social structural changes through social mobility. If formal education brings greater equality of opportunity than before and enhances social mobility we might conclude that education is a progressive force. As we discussed in Chapter 3, African school systems do seem to have initiated certain progressive social changes in this respect. As most jobs, and certainly top-level or elite posts, require educational qualifications the spread of formal education has brought such opportunities within the grasp of a very few of the most talented young. Unlike more class-ridden societies such as England or the United States, a certain amount of social mobility has been introduced in Africa through education. We must remember, however, that the opportunities for upward social

mobility are limited, and it is likely that, as elite groups establish themselves in positions of privilege, they will monopolise most of these opportunities for their own children. At present African societies are relatively open in terms of social mobility, but it is doubtful that the education system alone will be able to prevent the emergence of class societies with considerably less mobility than now; indeed it may well speed up the process (see Chapter 3).

In important areas of progress – family planning, equality between the sexes, political development and social equality – education therefore has a limited effect. It could be described as having a neutral effect if primary education alone were considered, but this would disregard the important influence of secondary and higher education on minorities in African societies. Critics of formal education, observing its limited effects on social change and the enormous expense of schooling, have asked the questions, 'Is it worth it?' and 'Is education really a progressive influence on society?'

Deschooling Society
One of the foremost social critics of conventional education is Ivan Illich, who has written many books attacking taken-for-granted assumptions about education, the professions and the general direction of change in the West and in developing countries. His ideas are only one set of criticisms of schooling, but are considered worthy of a separate discussion because they bring together many other non-Marxist criticisms. Marxists, who have their own misgivings about the role of education in capitalist societies, have criticised Illich's ideas.

Illich's view of modern society is one in which the individual's life is becoming increasingly dominated by all-powerful bureaucracies and private corporations. Various services – for example, education, health and defence – have gradually been taken over by these organisations, or institutionalised, to such an extent that they no longer serve the real needs of the individual. In fact Illich believes that modern education or health services are preventing the emergence of more progressive, small-scale services tailored to individual needs. Illich's main criticism of schooling is therefore that it has become a major service industry, absorbing vast sums of money and creating an insatiable demand for more and more qualifications. Rather than learning useful skills or gaining knowledge, students have been dazzled by the apparent need to obtain paper qualifications. Illich sees this as an enormous waste because only a few of the students who work hard will gain the qualifications and employment that pay for an affluent life-style. Illich believes that the modern world is experiencing a crisis in values, and that people will increasingly question the conventional assumption that economic growth is certain to improve living standards for everyone. Our social status and well-being are expressed by what we own, or can show off to others, and not in what we do to occupy ourselves or work for others. Illich's conclusion is that such a love of consumer goods and materialism is a fundamentally wrong path for humanity, because ultimately it is self-defeating and is earned by exploiting the majority of the world's population, the poor.

Illich has not only put forward radical critiques of education and modern society, but also made his own suggestions for putting things right. Illich's answer, in a nutshell, is to 'deinstitutionalise' society or, with regard to education, to 'deschool'. Making a distinction between true education and schooling, Illich argues that we need to free ourselves from the notion that all learning must be certificated or guaranteed by qualifications. He suggests that we abandon schools, teachers and formal qualifications in favour of direct learning between individuals. If a person wished to study accountancy, bricklaying or a foreign language, for example, Illich suggests that he could contact another, more experienced or learned person through an informal system rather like a labour exchange. Having learned, this person could then pass on skills to someone else. This process, described in the abstract by Illich, is what takes place in many occupations which are traditional or outside the wage sector of the economy, in Africa today. Thus through the apprenticeship system or from father to son, skills such as farming, fishing, weaving, metalworking, pottery and motor car fitting are usually taught and learned without the benefit of formal education. Illich is really suggesting that this informal kind of education is spread to include training for all the work done in modern society.

It is not surprising that many view Illich's proposals as retrogressive or a romantic attempt to return society to a folk or tribal stage. While some of Illich's criticisms of formal education are valid, his prescriptions for the future are regarded with scepticism, especially by Marxist writers.

The main weakness of Illich's critique of formal education seems to lie in his analysis of the problems of modern society. He sees most of these problems stemming from a contemporary crisis in values, so that his way of removing problems is to re-educate people, to give them new goals, and to destroy the beliefs that to own a car or obtain three Advanced level certificates are essential for personal success. It is not made clear, however, how this conversion process could be practically achieved. And, as Marxists such as Gintis (1972) point out, a fundamental problem of modern society is social inequality in the distribution and exchange of goods and services; this inequality is reflected in education, so that one cannot blame individuals for wanting to take as much advantage as they can of scarce opportunities and qualifications. Society's values, the Marxists argue, are affected by its economic realities, so that deschooling society would not achieve very much if basic economic inequalities and concentrations of power were left untouched.

It is quite likely, therefore, that deinstitutionalising education as Illich suggests would not diminish social inequality. In fact it is quite possible that social inequality would increase if no one went to school, because children of literate or privileged parents would have even more of an advantage than they do at present over those from illiterate backgrounds; at least a proportion of children from humble backgrounds attain some education and literacy in the school system.

Illich also seems to have underestimated some of the positive aspects of schooling in providing for training in complicated tasks and skills. Perhaps it is feasible to train blacksmiths, weavers or farmers in an informal, small-scale way, but is this true of engineers, scientists or accountants? Illich does not convincingly show us how we could entrust the training of such people to the small-scale, person-to-person system which he envisages. So Illich's suggestions may well be appropriate to slowly changing rural economies, but not to developing countries (such as Nigeria) which need not only rural skills and crafts, but also middle-level managers and well-educated scientists.

Illich's criticism of examinations – the fact that these seem to have become an end in themselves – is a good one, but we should also remind ourselves that qualifications serve the purpose of guaranteeing a certain level of capability. One wonders whether Illich, if given the choice between a conventionally trained surgeon and another who picked up the skill informally from a friend, would choose to be operated on by the latter?

To conclude, it can be said that Illich has overestimated the negative effects of institutional education on society. As a general recipe for society, Illich's theories about deschooling are impractical and probably based on a faulty analysis of the source of social problems. This does not mean that everything to do with formal education is progressive and beneficial – in fact, some of Illich's criticisms are extremely telling – but that Illich, in seeking to deschool completely, has neglected some of the positive aspects of formal education.

While Illich's suggestions for the future of education as a whole are suspect, we should remember that some of his specific suggestions may be useful in certain training tasks. It may be better to use Illich methods than a formal course of classroom teaching to train a builder or health worker. Or at least it may be educationally effective to blend informal learning with institutional education (see 'Skill acquisition in the informal sector of the economy', by King, 1974). We therefore suggest that it is worth reading Illich's *Deschooling Society* to gain insights into educational problems and possibilities in developing countries, if not to adopt his wider social goals.

Conclusion

This chapter has been concerned with social change and the role of education in it. We hope to have challenged some commonly held assumptions: for example, that all change is basically from a traditional to a modern stage, or that progress can be taken for granted. This chapter should also have raised some doubts in your mind about the part education plays in affecting social values, norms and relationships. Does it really make the educated individual more modern than the uneducated? Does the spread of education really bring about discernible social changes? And finally, critics such as Illich have raised the doubt that schooling is a progressive influence on society.

Whatever conclusions the reader reaches about these questions will depend upon an evaluation of our preceding discussion, but we suggest that, on balance, education is a potentially progressive force but is rarely, if ever, a primary source of progressive change. For education to become an enlightening and progressive influence there must first be a great many other progressive changes in the social structure – changes towards increasing democracy, social equality and economic development.

Questions and Discussion Topics: Chapter 7

1 Make a list of the most important social and political changes that have occurred in your country in the last twenty years. Is it useful to see these as changes from tradition to modernity?
2 *Group or individual project.* Interview two or three elderly people who are not known to you from previous acquaintance. Ask them to tell you the most important changes that have taken place in their lives since childhood. Compare your findings with others in your group. In what ways is education related to any of the examples of change given?
3 Is formal education more likely to encourage attitudes of conservatism and tradition than of change and modernity?
4 Find a short story or piece of fiction from a magazine or book. Underline the parts which seem to be giving social messages or telling moral stories about how we should behave in modern society. Are the messages of popular fiction basically modern or traditional?
5 Which is the more effective policy for spreading literacy?
    (a) Rapid expansion of schooling and only a limited literacy scheme for adults.
    (b) Slow expansion of education and investment of the money saved in a mass literacy scheme.
    Discuss the consequences of both these schemes.
6 What value do Illich's ideas on deschooling society have for Africa and, in particular, how would you relate them to Nigeria's policy of introducing universal primary education?

Chapter 8

Education and Economic Development

Introduction

A sociology of education must include some discussion of economic development, even though the latter is a subject in its own right. In practice it is difficult to separate economic theories about education from the social values and political climate of a society.

The way in which economics is mixed up with the social aspects of education is seen very clearly by the effect of education on school-leavers' aspirations. This shows us that the decision of most young people to leave home is an economic one. The search for work in the towns and cities has several economic consequences: for example, the departure of the talented and literate can have an adverse effect on rural development, although this is partly compensated for by migrants sending money home. The arrival of so many educated young people in the urban areas has some economic effects which are beneficial to society and others, such as underemployment, which are not. But the migration of educated young people also has social consequences: the age and sex structure of the villages can become unbalanced because the older and female members of rural society tend not to migrate as often as the younger and male members. The presence of educated unemployed people in urban areas might also have social and political effects on the established order. This single example – the relation between education and aspirations – shows us, therefore, that education, economics and sociology are closely bound together.

In this chapter we begin by looking at some key economic ideas about the relation between education and development: first, the theory that education is an economic investment in people, or an attempt to build up human capital; secondly, the idea of manpower planning, or making calculated estimates of future demands in the labour force for people with various skills and qualifications; and thirdly, the theory that education gives economic payoffs to individuals and society which can be calculated as rates of return for investment in different types and levels of schooling.

After discussing some criticisms of these economic ideas we will look at some of the alternatives in education that have been put forward as solutions to problems of underdevelopment. These alternatives are (a) that of making education more efficient than it is at present and (b) that of redesigning the education system to make it more related to work and production – that is, the introduction of technical and vocational education on a large scale.

Schooling and Economic Growth

At independence, African countries were left with seriously underdeveloped economies and severe shortages of skilled and professional manpower. The former Belgian Congo, for example, had only thirty or so university graduates out of a total population of twenty million (D'Aeth, 1975, p. 5). Countries such as Nigeria and Ghana had higher proportions of graduates than this but far fewer educated people than today. It is not surprising that education was seen as a bright light leading the way out of the tunnel of economic underdevelopment. Industrial nations have compulsory secondary schooling and a well-educated labour force; the political leaders and professional people from developing countries were mostly educated to international standards; so, the solution appeared to be obvious – educate on a mass scale as soon as possible.

Enthusiasm for mass expansion of education was fuelled by a series of UNESCO and pan-African conferences in the 1950s and 1960s. At the Addis Ababa conference (1961) African countries took a decision to try to provide universal primary schooling by 1980 and secondary education for 30 per cent of the relevant age-group by this date. Unfortunately only one country, Nigeria, has begun to approach these targets.

Economic opinion encouraged the ambitious plans of the early 1960s because a causal relationship was thought to exist between high levels of schooling and economic growth. Rostow, for example, suggested that developing countries could take shortcuts in the long process of economic development experienced by industrialised countries, and that widespread provision of education can raise the level of scientific knowledge in the population – an essential factor in economic takeoff, according to Rostow. Harbison and Myers (1964) found significant statistical correlations between school enrolment and economic development in a large sample of countries. McClelland, whose theory of achievement motivation was discussed in the previous chapter, made calculations of economic development (on the basis of consumption of electricity, among other things) and put forward the suggestion that there is a causal connection between education, the development of a high need for achievement and, thirty to forty years after educational expansion, economic growth. Peaslee (1967), who studied primary enrolments in a wide variety of countries, also reached the conclusion that 'no country has achieved significant economic growth within the last hundred years without first attaining the 10% level' – that is, a primary school enrolment level of at least 10 per cent of the total population (not the school-age population).*

Peaslee, like the other writers mentioned, firmly believes that education is a sound investment that will repay later in terms of economic growth. There may be some argument about which level of education should be given priority, but the general thesis that education causes growth is not questioned. This is the view of education as an investment in human capital. By investing in education, by developing skills and capabilities, we are as likely to speed up growth as if we had built a hydro-electrical power station or new factories. It is argued that investment in capital equipment or machinery will be wasted unless people are prepared to work in newer, more productive ways.

Unfortunately the causal link between expanding education and economic growth has never been spelled out. McClelland, for example, never makes clear how scientific knowledge (a supposed prerequisite for development) is actually applied, or by whom, in the process of development. Most of those who support the idea that education causes economic growth are really resting their arguments on correlations between high levels of development and school enrolment. Education, it is assumed, modernises the population, makes them receptive to new technical developments, thrifty and hard-working.

Correlations, however, are not the same as demonstrations or proof of an argument. It was assumed that education, just by being present in certain amounts, would have a magical effect on the rate of economic growth. But, to use a simple analogy, there is a high correlation between serious accidents and the appearance of ambulances; we would not conclude from this correlation that ambulances cause accidents. Ambulances are a consequence of other unknown variables which cause accidents. It is possible that education is a dependent factor – that is, a consequence of economic growth rather than a cause of it. Just as the consumption of tinned milk and motor cars rises during times of growth, we might find that the consumption of education rises in the same way. If, however, we have to look outside education for the causes of economic development this does not mean that education itself is an undesirable thing. Education can be regarded as an essential human right or as something which must be expanded as a result of political pressure, whatever its relation may be to economic development.

*Peaslee explains that the indicator of percentage of total population in primary school is used because it is difficult to obtain statistics of proportions of primary-age children in school for every country. The former indicator is almost as good as the latter, except in low birth rate countries such as Sweden which have less than 10 per cent of the total population in primary school but are nevertheless economically developed.

Should education be regarded as a human investment vital for economic development or as something which has no direct effect on growth? We do not have to take this all-or-nothing approach. On one hand, African countries have invested enormous sums of money in education since independence but the anticipated economic growth has not occurred. On the other hand, some argue that it is still too early to conclude that mass schooling will not have a beneficial effect on economic growth. Others point out that some, if not all, types of education (for example, technical training) have a positive effect. So it is not easy to give a simple answer to the question about the role of education in economic development. Education can be seen as an important background factor in economic growth, if not a key causal factor. This is a different approach from the beliefs of the early 1960s, when the mass consumption of education by rich, industrial countries was taken as a sign that education brings wealth in the first place. As Sato (quoted in Dore, 1976, p. 88) points out, the beliefs of educational policy-makers and political leaders at the time can be summarised by the following saying: 'Rich men have Cadillacs; therefore we should get some Cadillacs in order to be rich.'

Manpower Planning

The above ideas of investing in human capital carry the assumption that a general increase in educational and health provision will make people economically productive. Manpower planning, like this theory, concentrates on the economic value of education. But manpower planning also attempts to be very precise about the particular numbers of educated people that will be needed in different occupations or sectors of the economy in the future. Manpower planners assume that, by working out the future rate of growth of the economy, they can anticipate demand for just the right number of civil servants, engineers, doctors, teachers and skilled workers. The justification for this forecasting, in the words of Parnes (1968, p. 263), is that 'it is useless to build a factory unless there are skilled people to man it'.

Manpower planning has often been criticised because forecasts can go wrong. The growth rates of developing countries, which are often dependent on selling two or three major products, are subject to the wild fluctuations of world prices. Budgets and development plans have to be revised, sometimes making manpower forecasts of five or ten years before quite inaccurate.

Parnes (1968, p. 269) admits that it would be foolish for manpower forecasters to predict exactly how many will be needed in certain occupational groups in ten to fifteen years' time. This is not only because of economic uncertainties, but also occupational mobility: individuals can upset forecasts by moving from one occupation to another after their training is completed. However, many political leaders and civil servants have continued to believe manpower forecasters who confidently predict manpower needs to within a few people for each occupation; there is now a need for scepticism about their efforts.

Another major reason for disillusionment with manpower planning is the realisation that it is not objective. Calculating the needs of an economy begs the question, 'Whose needs?' Ultimately such questions can only be resolved politically, as well as economically, by the rival interest groups of which every society is composed.

The subjective, political element in manpower planning is illustrated very well by educational development in ex-French countries during the late colonial period. According to Berg (1965), there was a serious shortage of middle-level and professional manpower in these countries at the time of independence; the Africanisation of many government posts was therefore delayed. Before independence, French manpower planners had been convinced of a need for greater numbers of primary school-leavers and for secondary leavers with technical and vocational qualifications. They diverted funds from academic secondary and higher education to the former kinds of schooling. As Berg points out, 'as late as 1954–58, French planners made exactly the wrong decisions'. A cynical observer would suggest that this supposedly neutral decision, based on development needs, was a device to ensure francophone countries' dependence on high-level French experts and technicians.

Today there are still political disagreements about which economic policy should be followed: should priority be given to rural or industrial development, to manufacturing industries or to agriculture? Should development be controlled by a large, centralised civil service, or should it be decentralised as much as possible to local people with less education? All these options would require different numbers of educated people and different kinds of skills. Forecasting manpower demands according to a single rational objective is therefore impossible. Policies change from time to time because of changes in government and in such factors as parental demand for schooling or unforeseen external economic influences.

Although manpower planning can give the illusion of scientific objectivity to decisions which are really political, this difficulty should not lead us to reject the idea of planning altogether. The alternative to manpower planning is simply to let the invisible hand of the market – supply and demand – control how many people receive education and jobs afterwards. Relying on market forces to solve problems of manpower supply and shortages can be highly inefficient because of the waste involved: students undertake long periods of education, sometimes at high personal cost and certainly at high social cost, only to be made painfully aware that they cannot eventually find employment of the kind they expected. This problem of producing a surplus of educated people is shown very clearly by the current five-year development plan of Cameroun. In Cameroun it is envisaged that 89,000 new jobs will be created at all levels in the period 1977–82, but at the same time 1,928,700 people will leave school (*Guardian*, 18 May 1977). Of the total of new jobs expected, 38,000 will be of the unskilled or semi-skilled kind – many fewer than desired by school-leavers. However, at the top of the job pyramid there are, still, more vacancies for highly qualified people than the number of candidates available in Cameroun.

Cameroun's manpower problems are illustrative of a general African problem: a shortage of adequately trained, highly skilled personnel – managers, engineers, technicians and so on – combined with growing numbers of school-leavers with general academic backgrounds who are not particularly skilled and who must drift into manual work or self-employment in greater numbers than before.

While it is impossible to forecast exactly how many school-leavers will be needed in any year in a given occupation there is none the less an argument for making approximate estimates of how many university graduates and school-leavers are likely to be produced to supply the professional, skilled and unskilled levels of the job market; only with such estimates can it ever be possible to try to balance the supply of general education for the many against the supply of specialist, high-level education. Planning is also important to make sure that the supply of teachers is reasonably predictable.

In some societies the state has attempted to control the market forces which affect the supply and demand of education. In Tanzania, for example, the number of students allowed into secondary school and university is strictly controlled. Thus Tanzanian estimates of how many will be needed in a particular occupation are not so much forecasts as statements of intent: if so many doctors or engineers are trained in a given year they will be employed by the state in posts created for them. In planned economies of this sort the disadvantages and waste of market forces are reduced, but inefficiencies may result if government planners miscalculate the needs of the economy for certain levels of manpower (there is a lack of professional manpower in Tanzania) or advise educational institutions to train wrong numbers of students. University students may also resent being directed into certain courses rather than others, when they prefer a free choice. In Tanzania students rioted in the 1960s to protest against controls over choice of subject. This case illustrates a moral problem which is present in every African country: should students accept that they are privileged members of society and that they should, in return, accept direction into occupations and training courses which fit the economy's needs or manpower plans?

Rates of Return

These can be calculated according to the individual's or society's payoffs or rewards from education. A rate of return is an assumption that education, like any other investment, will repay outlay in so many years. It is a kind of cost-benefit analysis of education. It can be applied to education in socialist or planned economies as well as in capitalist free market economies such as the Nigerian. In either kind of society the anticipated economic benefits from a new agricultural college, for example, might be carefully considered before building is approved.

From the individual's point of view, the private rate of return from a particular course of education – say, a university degree – involves a number of factors. First, the individual has to calculate approximately how much he might gain in future income from having a degree. This is done by looking at the income levels of recent graduates and comparing them with the income levels of others of the same age-group who left school without going to university. The comparison can be made over a period of ten, twenty or thirty years. Having estimated the probable gain in income from attaining a degree, he then has to consider the costs of continuing to study at university: there are fees (unless university education is free or almost wholly subsidised), books and other educational items, and the income and career advancement the individual *would have earned* if he had not become a university student (this is called 'opportunity loss'). The costs of continuing in education can now be subtracted from whatever gains in future income the graduate can expect, and this gives the private return for university education.

The procedure just described can be adapted to any level of education: for example, whether it is worth going to secondary school, teachers training college, or whether private rates of return justify going to school at all. Hinchcliffe (1970) provides an interesting illustration of rate of return analysis in his study of the unprofitability of secondary modern schooling in Nigeria. Between 1955 and 1963 the number enrolled in secondary modern schools rose from 3,531 to 73,839, but by 1968 the number had fallen to 22,372. Secondary modern education (a three-year non-academic education for primary-leavers) was originally seen as desirable and profitable, but it was soon realised that secondary modern leaving certificates were little better than primary school qualifications for obtaining employment.

Rate of return qualifications also have to take into account the individual's abilities. The intending student may have to work out whether the expense of time and fees is justified if there is a good chance that he or she will fail the course. Average individual rates of return for university education have been estimated for Nigeria (37 per cent higher income than those without degrees) and Ghana (35 per cent). These indicate such high rewards that for those with a chance to go to university there is no choice to be made – the opportunity must be seized and the risk of not being academically able to complete the course must be taken. Dore (1976, p. 91) mentions that for university graduates, '30% rates of return are common in African countries'. These rates are high by international standards. In Japan, for example, the rate of return for university education is 9 per cent and in Israel only 8 per cent.

The idea of a *social* rather than an *individual* rate of return will now be considered. A social rate of return is similar to the 'investment in human capital' theory: both ideas suggest that financial investment in education yields tangible economic rewards. But social rates of return calculations imply that it is possible to make choices about which kind of education is most likely to give the most economic rewards, whereas investment in human capital suggests that it is desirable to expand all levels and types of education to improve the general educational level of a whole population.

It should also be noted that applying social rates of return does not end with education but also includes other kinds of government spending. If the economic payoff of education can be valued in units of currency, it follows that this can be compared with payoffs expected from other investments, such as agricultural machinery or a new power station. If funds are scarce and a new school promises a higher social rate of return than an improved road or irrigation dam some economists would argue that in such cases the school should take precedence. The social costs to be taken into account would include building the school and providing teachers and equipment; rewards would be calculated in terms of the improved economic efficiency or productivity of the educated, together with their higher tax contributions to the state.

Criticisms

What are the shortcomings of the economics of education? We have already mentioned the flaws in the argument that an expansion of education always leads to economic growth. A general level of basic education may be conducive to economic development but it is probably not the prime cause of it. There is also the question of what kind of education is most useful as a background factor in development? Dore, who thinks that the effect of economics on the study of education has been 'deplorable' (1976, p. 84), argues that many economic studies have ignored the content of schooling in developing countries. The schooling process often does the opposite of what economists think it does: it often does not teach useful skills, it encourages conformity rather than innovativeness and an unthinking acceptance of the need for qualifications rather than the application of useful knowledge.

The question 'What kind of education makes a difference to economic development?' is discussed by Zymelman (1971). From a detailed study of education, occupations and economic productivity in a large number of countries, Zymelman shows that productivity – output per worker, a factor which directly affects economic growth – is related to the level of skills in a country's labour force, not the level of formal education. Economic growth really depends on skill levels in various occupations (and skill levels are not necessarily related to the number of years workers have spent in school), coupled with good modern equipment in industry and agriculture.

Zymelman's study reveals the importance of informal and part-time ways of improving skills and productivity in the workforce: these are on-the-job training, apprenticeship schemes and in-service courses. How widespread formal education has become is not a very good indicator of labour productivity, and neither is the official school-leaving age of a country. Zymelman's criticism of the 'investment in human capital' idea is that it tends to assume that schools teach productive skills when in fact these seem to be learned in different ways.

As sociologists have pointed out (see Collins, 1971, and Part One), the major purpose of education in society is to justify social inequality between those with qualifications and those without; this function may be much more significant than any contribution towards improving work skills or raising productivity. However, it would be wrong to disregard completely the economic functions of education. While much education is certificate-hunting which gives little reward to the economy, it does improve the productivity of some occupations, particularly those in which technological change is rapid and in which certain types of academic knowledge are valuable. There is also general agreement that economic development cannot proceed beyond a certain level unless about half or more of the population can read and write.

However, it is hard to believe that economics can be precise enough to compare the economic payoffs of education with the rate of return from investment in machinery, equipment or development projects. Shaffer (1968) argues that investment in man is different from investment in equipment or capital goods; with regard to the latter, definite rates of interest or improvements in productivity can be expected. Loans to farmers to buy tractors, for example, can be expected to be repaid at a certain rate of interest, and the tractors will probably enable farming to be done more productively than before. This is not really the case with education, the economic benefits of which are less tangible and more difficult to calculate. It has been doubted for a long time whether investment can ever be as productive in education as in capital equipment – it may be better, as far as economic growth is concerned, to invest in machines rather than men.

We ought to be cautious about the optimistic claims of economists that they can measure the future payoffs of education. First, economic forecasts of manpower needs or rates of return can go badly awry because of economic uncertainties: for example, education may become more expensive to provide than initially expected, or parents and students may decide to invest in certain types of education in greater or lesser numbers than anticipated, or school-leavers may not be able to obtain the kind of productive work that planners had expected them to. This latter problem is clearly shown by the over-supply of school-leavers in Cameroun, mentioned above.

Secondly, manpower planning and rates of return analyses usually do not take into account the drift of school-leavers into the so-called 'hidden' or informal sector of the economy. This kind of employment (either self-employment or work in small businesses) is not known to government planners and statisticians, but many school-leavers take it because of lack of jobs in the formal wage sector of the economy. No economists really know the manpower needs of the informal sector (which is a vital part of every African economy), or whether the educated who work in this sector gain a return from their schooling or training. Neither is it known whether formal education improves the efficiency of small-scale businesses or craft industries, although what little evidence there is of the effects of literacy (see Chapter 7) is not very encouraging. Conventional education is not likely to be much use in the informal sector, where jobs are done with the minimum of paperwork and formal qualifications are not required.

A third problem with many studies of the economic payoffs of education lies in the use of previous income experience to predict the future. Estimates of rates of return from primary education, for example, may be far too high because they are based on the earnings of primary-leavers of previous years when lower qualifications were needed to obtain work. Economists often forecast from such earnings in previous times without considering how unemployment and the devaluation of qualifications are going to affect school-leavers. As Rado (1971) has pointed out, the flooding of the job market with unemployed school-leavers results in an ever greater demand for more qualifications by those who wish to obtain work at any cost. There is a danger that the demand for education becomes explosive and com-pletely unrelated to the needs of the economy.

Qualifications and the social prestige attached to them can therefore assume an importance of their own. Economists often suggest that the educated earn more than the less educated because their qualifications represent skills and capabilities which the latter do not have; the educated deserve more because they contribute more to the economy. If Rado is correct, however, the level of education reached by many will be unrelated to the work obtained. Thus O or A level certificates become qualifications for menial jobs. In such cases education is not really improving the productivity of the workforce. It is being used as a rationing device to select people for work rather than as a test of skills or potential productivity.

At the higher end of the social scale, the salaries of professionals and civil servants are supplemented with all sorts of perquisites from car allowances to subsidised accommodation. It could be argued that economists are mistaken in assuming that these high financial rewards really match improved productivity and efficiency resulting from the higher education of professional people. A much more credible explanation lies in the tradition of paying such groups high salaries that was established during the colonial period. Such high levels of pay continue because elite groups have successfully maintained their privileges and power.

Many in professional and administrative groups are therefore paid according to the high status of their qualifications, not necessarily for the content of their education or the skills they have picked up in training. This may not be as true of doctors and lawyers (who have taken vocational courses) as of graduates who have taken non-vocational courses, but even in the former kind of work probably as many practical skills are learned on the job as in educational institutions. Professional and managerial workers may be efficient, but let us not delude ourselves that their efficiency or productivity depends entirely on their formal education and qualifications.

A further point should be noted about individual rates of return from higher education. In Africa economic payoffs to the individual graduate are so high only because the initial cost of the degree course is usually subsidised. Far from sacrificing lost opportunities and large sums of money in order to study, most of those lucky or able enough to gain entry to higher education are cushioned from having to bear the cost themselves. High salaries after graduation can hardly be justified, therefore, on the grounds that they compensate for heavy losses to the individual while studying. Some people have suggested that in the interests of social equality students should take loans to pay for their higher education. To minimise financial hardship, loans could be repaid over a long period. There is also a suggestion (Foster, 1975) that the amount paid should not be a fixed loan, but a payment which is a percentage of a graduate's income; this kind of education tax would not penalise graduates who take up relatively low-paid occupations or who become unemployed.

Whether you agree or disagree that the highly educated should repay society for the financial rewards they enjoy from their qualifications, the point being made here is that economists' discussions of individual rates of return often obscure the heavy cost of education to the general public. Needless to say, the proposal to introduce loans for study is always unpopular among students themselves, although it is not a bad idea for those who become the privileged members of society to remember their debts to society. Those who oppose loans argue that a progressive tax system should suffice to make the better off pay their full share of the cost of all social services, including education, and that the procedure of taking loans might inhibit students from poorer backgrounds from continuing their studies.

So far we have considered some of the problems of the human capital approach to education, manpower planning and rates of return. All these approaches can be criticised for some common failings: an assumption by economists that people think entirely in economic terms, or that economics should be the dominant perspective on education.

Economists tend to assume that people make very sophisticated economic calculations about the costs of education and its payoffs. But are people informed well enough to make such judgements and, assuming that they are, do they normally wish to take a purely investor's view of education? Education in Africa is certainly seen as a means to attaining a good job, and accurate knowledge of school quality and payoffs from education is plentiful (see Chapter 4). But at the same time educational aspirations are often unrealistic. Large sums of money may be spent on private education, for example, with little hope of passing any examinations. Sometimes mediocre students waste time persisting with examinations or state education courses when they would be better off trying to find work. Another point is that the purposes for which education is sought are not always of the kind envisaged by economists. This is illustrated by Masemann's study of a girls' boarding school, discussed in the previous chapter. The students of this school expect a social payoff from their education in the form of prestige, learning how to behave in elite company and a smattering of general knowledge. They do not expect a permanent career in an occupation attained as a result of educational qualifications.

The author's research (Blakemore, 1975) shows that parents do not take a wholly economic view of their children's education. The decision to send children to school is not just shaped by economic forces, or anticipation of payoffs, but also by social norms, traditional views of Western education and simple lack of knowledge about the school system.

Economic studies of education can therefore be criticised for suggesting that individuals are, or should try to be, economically rational. As we know, individuals' decisions reflect social and political influences and ethical choices as well as economic costs and benefits.

Just as it would be wrong for an individual to take a purely investor's view of education, it would also be a mistake for a society to make educational policy solely according to economic criteria. To begin with, it is doubtful whether a single rational course of action ever exists. As we have already mentioned, economists themselves are often in disagreement about which kinds of education assist economic development or provide payoffs or whether education causes any growth at all. Assessing the needs of the economy is a matter of continual argument, so that it is never clear which is the most rational economical policy. A society may spend on education in a particular way (for example, by providing universal primary education in Nigeria) to try to meet a fundamental human right, or because the political climate encourages such a plan. Thus economic costs are sometimes subservient to political and social goals. No country can afford all the goals its political leaders dream of, but this does not prevent countries from at least trying to achieve some of them, in some cases putting politics and social standards before economics.

The economics of education, by focusing on rates of return, manpower needs and the idea of investment in human capital, has tended to divorce economic subject matter (statistics of costs and payoffs, for example) from political and social realities. Economists have tempted us to view ordinary people as objects, research statistics or a form of capital. This kind of mystification has permeated many decisions concerning education and development. It feeds the myth that decisions about the size or purpose of the education system can be reached in a scientific way by a few technical experts.

Taking the economic investor's view of education to its logical conclusion, it could be argued that higher education for men is a better investment than for women, so that men should be given priority in the allocation of university places and no attempt should be made to equalise opportunities. Or it might be argued that primary education in one region is more cost-effective than in another where, because of local reluctance to send children to school, there are fewer children per school. But should this economic criterion be the basis for deciding not to try to expand formal education in the second region? We ought also to ask whether economic criteria should be allowed to decide educational issues when so many planners and economists make mistakes in their calculations anyway.

To sum up, economics can be an extremely useful insight into the financial costs of education, its contribution to the quality and skills of the labour force and the effects of education on economic growth. But economics, if it becomes the dominant way of thinking about education, distorts the reality that education is also influenced by social and political forces.

Alternatives in Education

The costs of education rise rapidly, yet one result of this ever-increasing investment seems to be a rise in the number of educated unemployed. Foster (1975) suggests that the problem of school-leaver unemployment is not as serious as some have claimed, and argues that the educated who cannot find jobs in the wage sector of the economy should turn their hands to productive work in the informal sector. It may be true that this does happen, and that school-leavers are employed (or underemployed) in such jobs as car mechanics and fitting, welding, carpentry, small workshop crafts or in one of the many service occupations (transport, buying and selling) of the large towns and cities. But this raises a question: is it worth expanding conventional education, with its emphasis on academic study and preparation for further education, when increasing numbers of school-leavers never use their academic learning in the kind of work they are forced to accept? Many educationists and economists suggest that now is the time to provide useful and productive forms of training directly related to work.

Alternatives to education and their possible benefits to economic development are the subject of this section. One alternative is to provide special schemes for technical and vocational education. Another is to introduce practical, work-oriented study into the ordinary school classroom. There are also further possibilities such as apprenticeship schemes, or training at work, or in-service courses.

It is not always agreed, however, that any of these alternatives is desirable. Similar adaptations to work-oriented education were tried in colonial times (see Chapter 6) and met with resistance because they were seen as attempts to impose inferior education on ordinary people and reduce their chances of attaining high-status academic education. Foster (1966 and 1975) makes a further point – that conventional academic education is just as likely to improve labour productivity (through teaching basic literacy and numeracy) as special schemes of technical education. Before we turn to these arguments, however, another alternative should be considered – that of improving the efficiency of existing educational provision.

Efficiency in Education

One reason why education has proved to be disappointing as an engine of economic development may be that it is inefficient. Perhaps if the education system could teach more students with fewer resources, then literacy could be spread widely and money normally spent on education could also be invested in agriculture or industry.

It is possible to look at education as if it were a business: how much money is spent on each student, school and teacher? Is value for money being maintained and is the system being run efficiently? One example of this way of thinking about social services such as education and medicine can be found in Tanzania. It has been decided in Tanzania that health services can be dispensed more effectively through local health centres and health workers than by trying to expand hospitals or train many more doctors.

As with health services, there are several ways in which the cost of schooling could be reduced. One of the commonest problems of African education is student dropout, or wastage. For every four children who complete primary school, another one or two may drop out (the exact proportions vary from country to country). This raises the overall cost of each completing student because educational and teaching resources have been wasted on others who leave school before completing the course and quickly forget most of the literacy and numeracy they have learned.

As dropout mostly occurs during the first three years of school, the source of the difficulty seems to lie in failure to develop an early commitment to attendance at school among young children and their parents. Exactly how this attitude might be encouraged will depend on the social conditions in the areas in which dropout is a serious problem. Resources devoted to training teachers how to cope with dropout and counsel parents, waiving school fees or uniforms in certain schools, or scheduling school terms or classes according to the agricultural year, might all be worthwhile costs if economic losses caused by dropout can be reduced.

Repeating classes is also economically wasteful because extra teacher time, school places and books are devoted to students (some not very able) who overcrowd classrooms and may hold back the progress of others. Repeating should not be seen as just the fault of individual students, but also as a reflection of teaching effectiveness and the academic selection system. Poor teaching or inadequate facilities may hinder the educational progress of some children, causing them to repeat classes before they can proceed to the appropriate level. Anxiety to enter secondary school also leads children to repeat the final form of primary school year after year in the hope of passing the secondary entrance examination. Sometimes this anxiety stems from the fear that secondary entrance examinations are unfair. Those who fail may believe that they are bright pupils or at least as capable as others who have passed. Such beliefs encourage repeating the final year of primary school and the secondary entrance examination. Only when the children, their parents and teachers are assured that the examinations are a reasonably fair and accurate test of ability will the anxiety disappear. Accurate testing also weeds out the less able students who might otherwise enter secondary school and waste a place by dropping out before they complete the secondary stage.

Teachers' salaries are a very large item in educational budgets (in some African countries, they amount to 95–97 per cent of the education budget, according to Kouyaté, 1978, p. 38). Teacher efficiency is therefore a prime concern if we are concerned with reducing waste. Since the 1960s African countries have had to face spiralling salary costs because the large numbers of teachers recruited earlier have been advancing, year by year, up the salary scales. Just keeping the number of teachers constant and not expanding the education system at all would cost more every year.

Better-trained and more experienced teachers are more expensive to maintain than inexperienced teachers, and it is difficult to work out whether it is preferable to employ an army of not very good pupil teachers, or fewer good teachers. Only research into the effectiveness of teaching (for example, by looking at school-leavers' literacy levels or examination results) would show which is the better policy. Another alternative – trying to hold down teachers' salaries – is politically difficult and would be regarded as unjust (see Chapter 5). Among university students there is certainly a considerable amount of concern for primary teachers' pay and working conditions, both of which are seen as poor (Beckett and O'Connell, 1977). But primary teachers are in fact better off than urban manual workers and most farmers in terms of income and accommodation. Teachers' salaries, being higher than average, boost the cost of primary schooling. In Mali, for example, state primary education costs the government 16,000 Mali francs per pupil per year, yet the average income there is only 40,000 francs per annum (D'Aeth, 1975). So a year of primary schooling costs the Mali government the equivalent of 40 per cent of the average person's income. In developed countries such as France or the United Kingdom a year of primary schooling represents only 6 per cent and 9 per cent respectively of the average person's income. Therefore most of the relatively high cost of schooling in Africa is caused by teachers' salaries being higher than average.

Perhaps one way to minimise the cost of training and employing teachers is to opt for a plan similar to the one Tanzania has worked out for its health service: that is, to train a relatively small number of experts and increase the number of auxiliary workers with less training and low salaries. In educational terms, it would mean using pupil or 'peer' teachers as assistants to professional teachers, although this might be strongly resisted by teachers' unions. However, as Kouyaté suggests,

> peer teaching could make it possible, if necessary, for one teacher to teach and supervise a hundred pupils, which represents a two-thirds saving in salaries. This does not mean that two-thirds of the teaching force should be dismissed, but that with the existing number of

teachers it would be possible to have three times the number of pupils. In other words, without increasing expenditure on salaries, it would be possible to achieve universal schooling immediately. (1978, p. 45)

It is easy to see that Kouyaté's suggestion could become a political weapon in the hands of a government wishing to cut costs rather than increase school enrolment. But Kouyaté insists that his plan should not be seen just as a cost-cutting exercise, but as a way to revolutionise the provision of education. The poor quality of teaching by peers can be compensated for by the use of educational broadcasting and specially prepared texts and learning programmes. Such innovations have been implemented quite successfully in the Ivory Coast and elsewhere. Teaching at a distance can provide high-quality education at a much cheaper rate than the labour-intensive method of deploying one teacher to every class of students. However, the extra costs of training teachers and their assistants to use educational broadcasts effectively and the costs of providing special instruction texts have to be considered.

In addition to teachers, another major item of educational expenditure and potential waste is the cost of providing and maintaining schoolbuildings. Some communities provide part or all the cost of schoolbuildings but, whether the state is entirely responsible or not, it is important to ensure that schools are used in the most effective way. This may not be easy in many parts of Africa where rural populations are thinly scattered. A school may have to be kept open for a handful of students, and governments sometimes have to face difficult decisions about whether to keep such schools open or whether to merge them in order to benefit from economies of scale.

In urban and densely populated rural areas there is sometimes a reverse situation because of pressures on school facilities: shift systems may have to be introduced to cope with extra classes. But at least this is an intensive economic use of school buildings. Secondary boarding schools, common in Africa, also represent a sensible centralisation of school resources and teachers, although costs of accommodation and food are incurred. Generally, school quality improves with increasing size (see Chapter 4) because of economies of scale – students in a large school can benefit from a better library, more science laboratories and sports facilities and a wider range of teachers than is available in a small school. Nor is there much educational evidence to suggest that small classes benefit a student, while larger classes of thirty to forty are certainly more economical.

Efficient use of schoolbuildings, facilities and teachers can be further enhanced by the introduction of continuous, year-round teaching. At present most schools lie empty for up to four months a year.

This waste can be reduced by students taking shorter, more intensive courses with fewer holidays. Teachers would not take seasonal holidays, as they do now, but would take leave at any time while colleagues continued working. There are difficulties with this idea – namely, the timing of examinations and the tradition of long holidays – but these problems might be regarded as acceptable if year-round teaching meant that more education was available at less cost per pupil than before. The costs of the existing arrangements of long seasonal holidays are particularly high as far as colleges and universities are concerned. These institutions represent a great deal more public investment (per student) than schoolbuildings or equipment, so the cost of their standing idle is proportionately more.

To conclude, there are three major ways in which education systems can be made more efficient than they are at present: reduction of student dropout and repeating; using teachers more effectively, perhaps by using assistants or supplementing their work with peer teaching and educational broadcasting; and by making the most effective use of schoolbuildings and facilities.

At some point these alternatives of trying to make the existing system of education more efficient must begin to affect the basic aims and philosophy of the system itself. In other words, cutting costs or making schools efficient can only go so far before the quality and purpose of education is affected. Changing from a conventional teacher-classroom model of schooling to a system based on fewer teachers, educational television and peer teaching might mean change for the better or worse, but it will certainly affect the curriculum and educational standards in some way. Therefore such innovations, if they are to be introduced on a large scale, should not just be debated on grounds of economics, but also according to educational criteria and implications for development.

Technical and Vocational Training

These terms refer to a whole range of alternatives to conventional education. They overlap in meaning because both refer to training which is directed in some way towards work or production. Vocational training is more specifically concerned with a particular occupation than technical education. Teacher training, learning to be a doctor or a bricklayer are all examples of vocational education. Technical education implies training in skills and the scientific knowledge relevant to such skills, but this training may be applied to more than one occupation. A training in electronics, for example, might lead a student into a number of occupations. Both technical and vocational education may be provided in different ways: for example, special vocational schemes may be created for school-leavers; or technical instruction may be given to workers at their place of work; and both types of education may be available in special colleges or institutes.

For a number of reasons, the progress of work-related education in Africa has been disappointing. It is not certain that these alternatives actually promote economic development any more than conventional schooling does. However, this does not yet mean that the alternatives should be ruled out, or that experiments with them should be regarded as useless.

The main reason for failure lies in the naïvety of educational planners who thought that work-related education could be developed in isolation from the attractions of conventional academic education. As social selection for the better jobs and higher-status positions is carried out mainly by secondary and higher education, it is foolish to expect above-average or even average-ability students to want to attend technical schools. Unfortunately technical education is perceived as second best, to which less able students and teachers are allocated. This view of technical and vocational education stems partly from British and French influences. Work-related education has never been well regarded or given adequate resources, least of all in Britain. The colonial elites, with their general and classical education and lack of technical knowledge, became a powerful reference group for aspiring Africans (see Chapter 6).

The strength of aspirations to attain academic secondary education is shown by the attitudes of students in technical or vocational colleges, many of whom intend to re-enter the mainstream of education if at all possible. Thus investment in technical schools or vocational institutes can turn out to be an expensive way of providing technical students with an alternative route into academic education, or of cooling out academic failures (few of whom are really motivated to attain technical skills). As Dore points out (1976, p. 103), some technical schools cater primarily for academic study and spend less than 20 per cent of their time teaching vocational or technical subjects.

Another flaw in the movement to establish work-related education is the lack of jobs for technicians or those with practical skills. As Foster (1966) points out, building vocational schools does not create jobs for the students who graduate from them. However desirable it may be to raise the skill levels of the labour force, educational changes will not make the economy grow faster to provide extra employment.

The content of many vocational and technical education schemes has also been criticised. First, the quality of instruction is often poor because it is difficult to find good technical teachers; most of those with suitable qualifications obtain better-paid work in the industrial or commercial sector of the economy. Secondly, the training given is often inappropriate to the job in view and unlikely to improve productivity. It may be too specialised for jobs in the informal sector, where work is often done with crude or second-hand equipment and requires unorthodox skills to adapt materials and machines to a variety of uses. Or the training given may be regarded as unsuitable by employers in the formal sector, who usually prefer to recruit from academic schools (because students with academic qualifications are thought of as brighter than technical students) and train to suit their specific requirements.

Technical schools can therefore in many cases be regarded as centres of inappropriate technology and considerable investment in technical equipment (technical schools are more expensive to equip and maintain than academic schools) is largely wasted. Foster (1966 and 1975) argues that it would be better to scrap most vocational and technical education schemes and to concentrate on training adults who are already in employment.

He also suggests that education of the academic kind is in fact vocational because it prepares a minority of the population for a certain range of occupations. According to Foster, conventional education has the added advantage of performing the task of social selection relatively cheaply, as well as passing on literacy and numeracy and general knowledge that is useful in employment. Foster (1965) dispels the myth that academic education encourages disdain for manual work, and shows that school-leavers opt for skilled manual jobs and commercial farming if the financial and social rewards equal those of white-collar work. Thus he concludes that academic education does not necessarily divert manpower away from productive sectors of the economy in the way portrayed by political leaders and some economists.

The main ingredients in Foster's recipe for economic development are market forces and free enterprise. He distrusts the idea of an expansion of technical and vocational education because it smacks of the state attempting to give people what they do not want. If academic education is in demand, let the people compete for it from a limited number of state schools, or from private schools if they are willing to pay.

There are two major problems with Foster's line of reasoning. First, can modern societies develop without widespread, efficient and well-regarded systems of technical and vocational education? Is it enough to rely on training at work for adults already employed, as Foster suggests? Developed nations such as Germany and Japan are renowned for the high quality of their technical schools. Although the economic growth of these countries results from a great many factors other than quality of technical training, it is perhaps significant that a country such as Britain, which has never given much priority to technical education on a large scale, is experiencing little or no growth. The experience of developing nations such as Singapore and South Korea also suggests that large amounts of technical education are conducive to economic growth; although unemployment among those with technical and vocational training has been very high in both countries, it has been shown that these skills are eventually put to good use in all sorts of occupations.

African societies do not lack technical skills. Traditional skills and crafts, such as pot-making, metalwork and weaving, together with modern workshops and small-scale businesses, all show that such talents exist. But these talents can be supplemented by formal training, either at work, by apprenticeship or day-release schemes, or by inculcating scientific and technical knowledge before students leave school.

According to Zymelman (1971), it is the richness and variety of technical skills that cause economic development, not the level of formal education in a country. Zymelman argues that 'the inclusion of vocational curricula in the general [academic] school is no panacea for the problem' of spreading technical skills, but suggests that other ways must be found if economic development is to be assisted. Unlike Foster, Zymelman believes that the only way to make education contribute to development is to abandon academic types of education inherited from the colonial era, as well as models of technical education which are often unsuitable because they have been copied from other developed countries. Like Foster, however, Zymelman thinks that training adults in employment or relating education to practical work is more effective than schooling wholly within an institution. This is particularly important as far as informal sector jobs are concerned. Too much vocational education starts from the assumption that sophisticated trouble-free equipment will be used, when really students need to be given ideas about how to substitute one piece of equipment for another.

A second problem with Foster's market economy approach to education is his assumption that academic schooling is usually cheaper and less wasteful than work-related training. While running costs of academic schools are usually lower, what is the eventual economic value of the content of academic education? It may be relatively cheap to provide but it is in many ways little more than a useless process of gaining qualifications. Students gain skills of literacy and numeracy, but they could gain these equally from work-related education which might be more economically useful as well. Students of academically oriented schools develop attitudes and gain knowledge which are hardly conducive to development: innovativeness and independence of thought are discouraged (see Chapter 4), and school knowledge is rarely applied to the real world of agriculture, commerce or industrial work. Conventional education, in its role as a selective device for employers, weeds out the majority who are regarded as failures. The fact that most African education is designed around the needs of an academic elite, rather than the majority of ordinary workers, the waste of talent involved in this, and the tendency for many educated people to become unemployed until they can find wage sector work, are all hidden social costs of the existing school system which we think Foster does not take fully into account.

Whether work-related education can avoid the institutional problems and the waste of talent by conventional schools depends, however, on continuing experiments with vocational and technical education. Foster is quite right when he points to higher rates of unemployment among graduates of technical schools than among graduates of academic schools, and to the fact that work-related education is often unpopular, expensive and unrelated to the economy's real manpower needs. But it might be wrong to conclude from Africa's experience so far of work-related education that the case has been proved for continuing with traditional academic curricula and qualifications. As there is little or no evidence to suggest that conventional education (beyond a general level of basic education in the population) aids economic growth, is there not an alternative case for continually trying new types of education related to work and economic production?

Perhaps training methods and curricula designed according to local conditions will succeed where previous attempts in work-related education have failed. Hutton (1971) describes one vocational training scheme for young farmers which was successfully adapted to local requirements. This scheme involved school-leavers who had already reached the conclusion that agriculture was their best economic opportunity, and gave them a sense of being scientific rather than traditional farmers.

We therefore agree with Foster that there is not much point providing work-related education unless the realities of society's existing academic education system and job market are borne in mind. Where we disagree with Foster is in his conclusion that because many work-related educational schemes have not fully succeeded, the established system of academic schools and job allocation should be left untouched.

Education for Self-Reliance

Tanzania is often discussed as a leading African example of a radical attempt to reform conventional education and to introduce a new type of work-related schooling. Tanzania's experience is not entirely appropriate to arguments about the role of vocational education in other African countries, as her economy supports a relatively small number of people in administration, the professions or industry compared with richer countries such as Nigeria. Nevertheless Tanzania's experiments with education for self-reliance, begun by President

Nyerere in 1967, are of great interest to anyone concerned with economic development. In Tanzania there have been attempts to boost vocational and technical education and to encourage a new work-related spirit in the general academic schools. Tanzania has attempted to make many economic, social and political changes all at once, so that changes in education are not isolated from other developments.

The aims of Tanzania's education policy are to change students' attitudes to work as well as to teach skills. Service to the surrounding community (for example, by leading adult literacy classes) and doing practical work and farming are valued at school (although there have been problems with assessing students' efforts in these directions). The educated are exhorted not think of themselves as privileged by right, but as servants of the community which pays for their education.

Along with attempts to reform attitudes, changes in the curriculum have been made towards work-related themes and practical subjects. Examinations have been downgraded in importance, so that promotion from one level of schooling to another partly depends on teachers' assessments of attitudes and service to others, as well as examination marks. The education system is therefore designed to provide a basic and practically oriented type of schooling. Selection for secondary education is extremely restricted (see the following chapter).

As the education system has remained so selective, and as examinations retain much of their former importance, secondary schooling is still the key to the most important jobs in Tanzania. The education for self-reliance policy has only partly realised its objectives. No amount of teaching practical skills or the virtues of manual work will prevent primary schoolchildren from concentrating their efforts on selective secondary entrance examinations, even though chances for selection remain low. Academic competition has led to the building of private secondary schools in Tanzania, a phenomenon which does not fit well with Nyerere's socialist policy but which has taken place because certain groups of parents (particularly from such occupations as clerical work, the police force and teaching) have been able to disguise their private schools as self-help or self-reliance institutions (Mbilinyi, 1976b).

Many of the values incorporated in Tanzania's education for self-reliance policy have been enthusiastically adopted by teachers, students and parents, although there is some argument about whether this policy is really providing a stimulus to the economy in the form of important technical skills. Some of the bookish, theoretical aspects of the traditional education system remain, and Nyerere's ideas have been watered down in the more academic schools. And, as Dore (1976) points out, there is still a shortage in Tanzania of highly educated technical manpower and of middle-level managers and administrators. To gear education to basic skills in a country where most people work on the land is an understandable and laudable policy but this does not mean that higher levels of skill should be neglected.

The object of this brief examination of Tanzania's alternative path in education is not to throw cold water on education for self-reliance, nor on the emphasis on work-related education. The Tanzanian experiment shows that some reform of the conventional education system can take place and, although it is not yet clear whether the changes will enhance economic development, we should remember that the policy has political and social goals as well.

Conclusion

There is now less optimism than before about the ability of formal education to bring about economic development. Economic studies carried out in the 1960s or earlier established that there are correlations between rising school enrolments and economic growth, but this is probably a reflection of education being an item of consumption rather than a stimulus to production. Doubts have also been expressed about the validity of the detailed planning of student numbers according to manpower needs. The dominance of economics in educational thinking has been questioned, and while general education is accepted as an important background factor in economic development it is doubtful whether economists can engineer growth by expanding primary enrolment here, or tinkering with secondary enrolment there. Perhaps the most effective contribution to development that can be made by the education system is in terms of increased efficiency, thus freeing resources to be invested elsewhere in the economy. It is not yet certain that the other alternative, that of adapting education to technical or vocational requirements, will provide a more productive stimulus to the economy than the existing system of conventional academic education. Tanzania has achieved only limited success with her experiments in work-related education and changes in the goals of schooling, mainly because the fundamental basis for allocating employment according to academic qualifications has remained largely unchanged.

Questions and Discussion Topics: Chapter 8

1 Discuss the proposition that students should be directed by government into the educational courses most appropriate to national economic and manpower needs.
2 Estimate the economic rewards you hope to gain from the educational course you are now taking, or hope to take. Use the method

for calculating individual rates of return described in this chapter. Now answer:

(a) Is it going to be economically worth while for you to have taken the course on which you are now enrolled/hope to be enrolled?

(b) Are economic and financial considerations the most important in deciding your educational career?

3 *Group discussion.* Thinking back to your schooldays, try to remember a classmate who dropped out of school. Write a couple of paragraphs on why you think this particular case of dropout occurred. Now compare notes with others in your group. Are the reasons for dropout economic in nature?

4 What are the arguments for and against the idea that students in higher education and teacher training should be given loans to pay for their education?

5 Do you think something similar to Tanzania's experiments in education for self-reliance could be introduced in your own country? Would it be (a) economically and (b) socially desirable to introduce such work-related education in every school?

6 Write an essay summing up what you think should be the place of economics in the study of education.

Chapter 9

Education and Politics in Africa

Introduction

Since colonial times schooling has had distinct political overtones. The fears of the colonial authorities that too much of the wrong kind of education would lead to political unrest are a case in point (see Chapters 2 and 6). Some people think that politics and education should be kept apart, that politicians should not try to use the education system for political ends. This ideology is not widespread in Africa, and it is naïve to suppose that education can ever be separated from political questions, interests and conflicts. Nowhere is this more obvious than in contemporary Africa.

Since independence the political importance of education has intensified. The supposed role of education in furthering national integration and development, together with intense popular pressure for more schooling, underline the political importance of education. To a significant degree the popularity and legitimacy of political leaders depend on their willingness and ability to satisfy the demand for schooling. All the major parties contesting the 1979 Nigerian elections put rapid educational expansion high on their list of policy priorities. A generally high degree of intervention in education has characterised post-independence governments.

This does not mean that political intervention is simply a process of setting goals and adjusting the education system in order to achieve them. In practice there are strict limits to what politicians can hope to achieve by intervention in educational affairs. These limits partly reflect the low general capacity of the political system to satisfy the demands of the public for more and better welfare services. They also reflect conflicts of ideology and interest between various groups of political actors: politicians and those they represent, civil servants, parents and students, headmasters and teachers, private educators (missions and businessmen) and international bodies such as UNESCO, International Labour Organisation (ILO) and the World Bank. The ways in which these groups interact in the political arena affect the size, shape and character of the educational pyramid. In the first section we will examine some of the main aspects of this interaction.

Politicians are anxious to generate support for themselves and the machinery of state through which they exercise their power. To varying degrees politicians have tried to manipulate syllabuses and curricula in order to increase their popular support. This is one aspect of what modernisation theorists call 'nation-building'. In the second section we consider the ways in which governments have tried to use education for political socialisation and the limits to this process.

Whatever governments do, the experience of education is likely to affect political knowledge and values in various ways. In the last section we will look at this hidden curriculum effect in relation to the political opinions and activities of students. Students sometimes get involved in political activities of one kind or another and we will be looking at the reasons for this as well as at the factors which tend to limit the degree of student politicisation.

The Politics of Education

Despite the failure of African governments to achieve the optimistic educational growth targets set at the 1961 Addis Ababa conference, rapid growth is still the major characteristic of African education systems and the one most frequently commented on. The post-independence optimism concerning the likelihood of rapid social and economic progress is more or less a thing of the past, as is the uncritical belief in education as the key to development. The heavy burden of education on national budgets, low levels of economic growth and high levels of unemployment help explain this change in attitude. Many African governments have returned to the old colonial policies of containing growth and stressing vocational and relevant rather than academic curricula (see previous chapter).

In spite of official misgivings education systems continue to grow, and this growth reflects the decisions and choices of individuals and groups within society. In this section we are concerned with the decision-making process and the question of who benefits from educational expansion. This is a political question to the extent that schools and teachers are scarce and often highly valued resources and are consequently competed for by individuals and groups. We will be looking at some of the processes which bring together the political actors listed in the introduction and which determine who benefits from educational expansion. These processes are complex and inadequately treated in the literature, and for the sake of brevity we will limit the discussion to certain major questions. These are:

(1) Which sectors of education are expanding most rapidly?
(2) What types of education are expanding most rapidly (academic or technical, vocational and agricultural)?

(3) Who benefits most from educational expansion (everybody, the underprivileged, the already privileged, certain classes or ethnic groups)?

Some of these questions have already been discussed in relation to social inequalities and educational opportunities (Chapter 3) and colonial reforms in education (Chapters 2 and 6). In Chapter 3 we showed how the wealthy, the educated and high-status occupational groups benefit disproportionately from the education system. Do political advantages also ensure that the elite and their children benefit from educational expansion in similar ways? What benefits does control of educational provision afford governments?

The question of who gets how much of which kind of education frequently involves conflicts of interest which are articulated at government level. Governments collect taxes to pay for schoolbuilding and maintenance, teachers' salaries and teaching materials, school supervision and inspection, and must justify to parents (who are the taxpayers) the ways in which they carry out their responsibilities. Although not all the important decisions affecting education are taken at government level, we may conveniently begin our discussion there.

For political leaders it is important that the education system should satisfy as far as possible the demands put upon it by the population. This is because education is the major social service provided by governments and the one to which the general population attach the most importance. Up to a point, popular opinions of central and local governments reflect their performance in the educational field. Put another way, governments gain or lose legitimacy to the extent that they satisfy or fail to satisfy popular demands for education.

In practice, the selection function of education – which ensures that the majority of children are eliminated from the school system at its lower levels – means that most parents and pupils will not be satisfied with the system. Criticism of the authorities is muted to the extent that parents and students accept success and failure as reflections of themselves rather than of the system. But high failure rates can also be turned against governments as proof that they are not providing enough school places, and this kind of discontent sometimes takes violent forms.

Governments habitually stress their efforts in the educational field, and often talk as if they were making personal sacrifices or spending their own money rather than public funds. Schooling is nowhere free, of course, and the sacrifices and spending of parents and relatives are, in the final analysis, the main sources of educational provision and expansion, not the efforts of politicians and civil servants. The sacrifices of poorer parents are generally greater than the benefits they receive in return, since their children make proportionately much less use of subsidised education than those of the privileged. Also, the outlay of a given sum represents a relatively greater sacrifice for a poor than for a wealthy parent or kinsman.

It is certainly true that educational spending soaks up a relatively high proportion of government revenue. Many governments would gladly reduce the burden of educational spending if they thought it feasible, but political factors usually prevent this, as we will see. Education continues to feature highly in overall development strategies and it would be wrong to think that political leaders are invariably intent on limiting educational growth. But this does not solve the problem of financing expansion and choosing between alternative demands on government resources.

Governments are faced with three broad problems concerning educational expansion:

(1) How much to spend on education as opposed to alternative services such as health and rural development.
(2) How to allocate funds between levels of education (primary, secondary, teacher training, higher) and between kinds of education (academic, technical, adult).
(3) Which groups of the population to give priority to in terms of social class, ethnicity, region, religion, sex and race.

We may look at each of these points in turn.

(1) *Education versus Alternative Spending*

By any standards African governments spend a substantial proportion of their total revenue on education. In the early 1960s 10 to 15 per cent was about the norm for Third World countries, and by the end of the decade up to a quarter of government revenues was taken by education (Dore, 1976, p. 4). Between 1955 and 1966 the Eastern and Western Regions of Nigeria spent no less than 40 per cent of their recurrent budget on education (Abernethy, 1969) and Kenya currently spends about one-third of its budget in the same way (Court, 1976). A combination of popular pressure and other political considerations account for these high levels of spending. The southern Nigerian case studied by Abernethy is a good example.

During the 1950s both regional governments of southern Nigeria attempted to introduce universal primary education; the Western Region 1955 and the Eastern Region two years later. From 1954 to 1955 primary enrolment in the Western Region increased from 457,000 to 811,000, the number of primary schoolteachers rose from 17,000 to 27,000 and the number of primary schools increased by nearly a third. Spending on education rose from £2,200,000 in 1954 to £5,400,000 the following year (from a third to almost a half of total expenditure). In the Eastern Region between 1956 and 1957 enrolment increased from 775,000 to 1,209,000, the number of schools from 5,060 to 6,986, the number of teachers from 30,000 to 41,000 and spending on education rose from £3,600,000 to £6,000,000 (Abernethy, 1969, pp. 128–9). Abernethy gives three reasons for these extraordinary increases: popular demand; competition between the regions, between voluntary agencies (Catholic and Protestant), between ethnic groups, political parties and between villages; and the new regional governments' need to establish their legitimacy with the local population.

Popular demand. Education in the Western sense was introduced in Nigeria over a century ago and soon became very popular, for reasons discussed in Chapters 1 and 2. The high level of popular demand gave the regional governments an incentive to expand education and exerted pressure on the governments, voluntary agencies and local authorities to bring about expansion.

Competition. Competition between the two regional governments was a factor contributing to educational expansion which was unique to Nigeria. Competition between other groups – ethnic, religious, local communities – is a common feature of educational politics in many African countries. Many African governments try to reduce regional inequalities in enrolment levels in the interest of national unity, but these attempts are generally frustrated by the types of competition mentioned above. In Nigeria, primary enrolment levels in the north were 20 per cent of those in the south in 1950 but only 10 per cent in 1960.

Competition between the two southern governments reflected rivalry between the Ibo and the Yoruba and between the two major political parties in the south, the National Council of Nigeria and the Cameroons (NCNC) and the Action Group. The introduction of a UPE programme in the Western Region reflected an awareness of the educational advance of the Eastern Region. Moreover, 'once the Western Region had introduced free primary education for all, the Eastern Region was under considerable political pressure to follow suit' (Abernethy, p. 142), even though the financial position of the region was not strong.

Competition between Protestant and Catholic missions was an important factor in the expansion of primary education, especially in the Eastern Region where NCNC leaders came into serious conflict with the missions over the waste of resources and social divisiveness caused by such competition. Unfortunately,

the government's commitment to educational expansion doubtless contributed to religious rivalry, since it led to further competition among voluntary agencies for liberally dispensed grants-in-aid and acted as an incentive to immediate expansion while the grants were still available. During 1956 more voluntary agency primary schools were constructed than in any previous year, for parents and church members 'knew that the Church that had the greatest number of children also had the surest hope of survival'. (Ibid., p. 169)

The search for legitimacy. Popular pressure and competition between various groups formed the background to the UPE programmes in the two regions. The third major factor was the crisis of legitimacy which followed the establishment of the two governments in 1951. The political leaders in the two regions were concerned to solidify their links with the mass of the population by showing that they could provide services that the British and the traditional authorities could not. What they required was

a dramatic, far-reaching welfare scheme to win popular support. . . . The career of the Southern Nigerian politician . . . depended on his ability to popularise a vision of a far better future, to mobilise the population, and to channel newly aroused energies into specific projects with quickly realised and visible benefits. (Ibid., p. 133)

UPE was thus seen as the best way of enhancing legitimacy.

Supplementary factors which affected the overconcentration of government spending on education were the large number of teachers in the two houses of assembly and the convictions of politicians concerning the importance of education in fostering development. About a quarter of the members of the Western Assembly and a third of the Eastern were ex-teachers. These 'teacher-politicians [helped] to give legislative priority to their own field of professional competence' (ibid., p. 137), helped on by their consciousness of the strength of popular demand for more education and their special competence and confidence in matters of educational planning. Both Ministers of Education, Awokoya (West) and Akpabio (East), were former teachers and 'tended to assert themselves more readily and self-confidently than other Nigerian ministers when confronted with the objections of British civil servants' (Ibid., p. 138).

Lastly, southern Nigerian politicians were convinced that UPE would have beneficial economic, social and political consequences. These included greater mass political participation and integration, greater work efficiency and a widening of the pool of human capital from which high-level manpower would be selected, a reduction in levels of social inequality and the mass mobilisation of the human resources and energies of the population.

Thus the popular thirst for mass education coincided with the convictions of the politicians and their need to prove themselves to the public. Competition between regional governments and other groups reinforced the pressure for expansion. With the exception of inter-governmental competition all the other factors are found in many other African countries and are sufficiently powerful to explain the high concentration of public spending in education. Without these strong pressures for expansion planned educational growth would certainly be considerably lower than the recent African average.

Opposition to rapid educational expansion from various sources (cautious civil servants, other ministries requiring funds, foreign advisors) may not be sufficiently powerful to alter significantly government spending. For example, the rapid increase in spending on education in the Western Region led to rising opposition within the government to Minister Awokoya's requests for more money.

> Because of the government's commitment to universal primary education, Awokoya's requests were inevitably granted, but by 1954 approval was given so begrudgingly that at one point the Minister threatened to resign if he did not receive greater support from his colleagues. (Ibid., p. 159)

(2) *Competition within the Educational System*

Given the political pressures for educational expansion, what factors determine the relative rates of expansion of the various educational levels? The answer depends partly on the existing level of educational provision. Where levels of primary enrolment are low, popular pressures for educational expansion (if these develop) will be concentrated on primary expansion. In areas and among groups of high primary enrolment pressure for secondary school expansion will be more in evidence. For example, in southern Nigeria increased popular demand for greater secondary provision followed soon after the attempted introduction of UPE, and during the early 1960s enrolment in public and private grammar and secondary modern schools expanded rapidly.

Frequently demand for expansion at all levels overstrains government resources, so that extremely difficult decisions have to be made concerning sectoral expansion. Governments are forced to choose between what, broadly speaking, we may call populist and elitist alternative policies. Elitist policies are based on the argument that educational spending should be concentrated in the sectors where the economic return will be greatest and which will help achieve high-level manpower targets most rapidly. As we pointed out in the previous chapter, the provision of limited, high-quality secondary and higher education has sometimes been considered a sounder investment than general primary educational expansion. Mass primary, vocational and adult education, aimed at spreading literacy and numeracy as widely as possible throughout the population, constitute the populist policy. The strain between the populist and elitist alternatives is a common phenomenon in educational politics, and not just in Africa. The example of UPE policies in southern Nigeria during the 1950s is clearly one where a populist ideology was dominant.

> UPE was perfectly adapted to the populist goals of Southern Nigerian leaders, for it benefited large numbers of people and enabled previously disadvantaged groups – the poor, females, Muslims, inhabitants of areas neglected by the voluntary agencies, and others – to reach the level of more privileged groups. (Ibid., p. 132)

Nigeria is not a typical example, however, because higher education was a federal rather than a regional responsibility, so that the southern regional governments did not have to worry about post-secondary expansion. Morrison's Tanzanian study (1976) provides a more typical example of the populist/elitist dilemma in relation to educational expansion.

Tanzanian education policy immediately after independence was markedly elitist. Following the advice of the Ford Foundation and UNESCO, the government adopted a policy of training high-level manpower to replace all expatriate personnel by 1980 and to divert funds from primary education (which had been expanding rapidly) to secondary and higher levels. The 1961–4 plan stressed secondary and higher educational expansion 'because of the "obvious economic benefits" that would accrue'. The plan stated that there would 'not be an increase in the number of places available for children entering Standard I'. The introduction of UPE 'would have to await the closure of the manpower gap and the production of sufficient wealth to pay for it' (Morrison 1976, p. 110). Essentially the same policy was followed in the 1964–9 plan.

In practice this elitist policy was a failure, largely because pressures for primary level expansion were too powerful for the government to resist. We may look at the reasons for this failure in some detail as an example of the way in which popular demand can frustrate the implementation of government policy.

Between 1956 and 1961 (the year of independence) enrolments in aided primary schools increased from 382,000 to 484,000 (an increase of 26 per cent), and from 1961 to 1966 they increased to nearly 741,000 (54 per cent above the 1961 figure). It is true that secondary enrolments increased by 125 and 100 per cent during the same period, but these increases were from a much smaller base and show a falling rate of expansion, unlike the primary figures. In accordance with its policy the government did succeed in modifying its spending pattern: the amount of the education budget spent on primary provision fell from 53 to 41 per cent between 1962 and 1966, whereas the corresponding amounts for secondary technical and higher education increased from 40 to 51 per cent (ibid., pp. 113–18). But again, the 1966 budget was considerably larger than that of 1962 and in absolute terms spending on primary education rose by 27 per cent. Given that the government allocates its own funds, why was it incapable of effectively putting its elitist policy into practice?

The short answer to this question is that there was little or no support for the government policy among MPs and district councils, parents and their educational associations (Tanganyika African Parents Association, TAPA, and East African Muslim Welfare Society, EAMWS), the rank and file of Tanganyika African National Union (TANU, the national party) and the mission societies. The pressure from these sources led to a rapid expansion in primary schools run by the government, the voluntary agencies and TAPA, which ran a large number of self-help schools. Expansion in these three types of primary school reflected popular enthusiasm in all urban and most rural areas. At both the national and local levels politicians brought pressure to bear on the government to lengthen the primary course throughout the country, to abolish fees and to recognise bush schools. Also, 'several members [of the Legislative Council] made strong pleas for special consideration for their own "underprivileged" constituencies and districts' (ibid., p. 131). TANU and TAPA leaders had been active in encouraging the building of self-help schools, 'but once they were established a cry soon arose for local education authorities to assume financial responsibility for them'. The party leaders were unwilling or unable to discourage local activists from opening schools, even when these merely duplicated existing facilities in the name of abandoning 'the institutions of the "imperialists" for those of the "people"' (ibid.).

Similar expansion (often equally unjustified) took place as a result of continued competition between Christian voluntary agencies in areas where no single agency dominated. 'Once bush schools were established, Education Secretaries, priests and clergymen reinforced local demands for government registration and aid' (ibid.). Lack of funds prevented the government from taking over voluntary agency schools completely, although certain measures were taken to increase government control over such matters as student selection, discipline, inspection, in-service training, recruitment, salaries, postings and working conditions. Throughout Africa lack of central control of private schooling has constituted a major constraint on effective policy implementation and planning.

In the case of schools run by EAMWS a similar trend was evident. The government could not oppose new school building for Muslim pupils, given the strong influence of the Muslim community on the government and the low level of educational provision for Muslim children.

A final source of pressure for primary school expansion was inter-village and other kinds of local competition.

> The school had tended to become an important status symbol for a community because of the growing prestige of education. Talk of building a new school or extending an existing one often led to conflicts over siting among leaders of nearby villages. District coun-cillors, members of Parliament, and other TANU activists who depended on local power bases also intervened because of the importance of educational expansion to their political careers. Many times disputes of this sort were settled by a decision to proceed with two or more projects rather than one. (Ibid., p. 132)

The Tanzanian government did not reverse its elitist policy in the light of its obvious failure but rather continued to try to control the expansion of primary schooling throughout the early 1960s. For example, pressures towards UPE in Pare area (Kilimanjaro region) were opposed by the Ministry of Education which banned the opening of new Standard Is. Opposition to the ministry's move was mobilised through the local TANU branches and a delegation of TANU officials was sent to Dar es Salaam. The minister eventually backed down.

The Tanzanian government lacked the resources, the collective will and the coercive powers to realise its policy goal of containing primary school expansion. Similar factors explain the high failure rate of educa-tional plans, policies and reforms throughout post-independence Africa. The uncontrolled expansion of primary enrolments invariably brought about a rapid rise in the number of unemployed school-leavers, and this led many African governments to introduce reforms similar to those which the colonial governments had attemp-ted previously.

In the Tanzanian case, by the time primary expansion showed signs of declining government policy underwent a complete reversal and a populist era in education began. The immediate cause of this change was the growing primary school-leaver crisis and increasing failure rates in the secondary General Entrance Examination. In 1965, 46,700 pupils sat this exam and only 7,000 were admitted. This rep-resented a threefold increase in the failure rate over the previous year. Immediately the results were published disappointed parents and pupils began to besiege local TANU and education department offices throughout the country. The situation was made worse by a new regulation preventing unsuccessful candidates from repeating their final year. The government response was to relax its restrictions on the building of private secondary schools and to begin planning the reintroduction of agricultural curricula to vocationalise primary education. This policy was justified on the grounds that Tanzania was an agricultural country and that those who failed to get secondary school places had no real alternative to going back to the land.

The publication of President Nyerere's booklet *Education for Self-Reliance* followed closely the Arusha Declaration of 1967. The former contains proposals for reforming education in order to achieve the socialist goals contained in the latter. Thus primary education was to become terminal, schools were to produce their own food, examinations were to be downgraded and pupils were to be taught co-operation, egalitarian values and knowledge relevant to agriculture. The fact that UNESCO and the World Bank have sponsored and helped finance large numbers of ruralisation reforms of primary education in Africa during the 1970s shows that these reforms are less connected with socialism than with the need to keep the rural population on the soil and reduce rural–urban migration and unemployment among primary-leavers. Mbilinyi (1976a, p. 233) goes so far as to say that 'every major education "innovation" in adult education, primary school and secondary school is wholly or in part dependent on foreign aid. Indeed, sixty percent of the 1973/74 Development Expenditure on education in Tanzania was funded by foreign aid.' Ultimately the aid agencies are interested in functional or basic education in so far as they help stabilise the rural population and increase the production of cash crops for export.

Since the Arusha Declaration primary enrolments have continued to expand rapidly. The proportion of primary-leavers entering secondary school has declined from 36 per cent in 1962 to 12 per cent in 1968 and 7 per cent in 1974 (Ministry of National Education, figures for public schools only). Central planning for the attainment of manpower self-sufficiency has continued at the secondary and higher levels, although many of the targets have not been met. According to Court (1976, p. 669): 'Since 1967, the government has attempted to relate secondary school enrolments to tight manpower projections, and to prevent the kind of uncontrolled expansion which has taken place in Kenya.' Nevertheless the government has accepted the opening of substantial numbers of secondary schools. Private secondary schools accounted for 14 per cent of all secondary schools in 1966 and 28 per cent in 1975 (Tanzanian Ministry of National Education, 1977, p. 180).

Recent primary enrolment expansion has been phenomenal compared with the 1966–71 period of relatively slow growth. If the post-1967 period was strongly marked by Nyerere's thinking and ideology, more recently the party itself (TANU, now Chama cha Mapinduzi, CCM) has taken up the populist, anti-elitist initiative in education. Thus at the 1974 meeting of the national executive committee the Musoma Resolution was issued, announcing a crash programme for the achievement of UPE by 1977 and reinforcing the anti-elitist tendencies of official policy by making work experience the basic qualification for university entrance rather than the successful completion of secondary schooling. Total primary enrolments increased from 1,874,000 in 1975 to 3,414,000 two years later. By 1979 there were no less than 600,000 pupils in Standard I alone (*Daily News*, 5 July 1979). The strength of the populist tendency can also be judged from the adult education budget, which accounted for 4 per cent of educational spending in 1971 and 8 per cent in 1973 and 1975. The five-year literacy campaign is said to have reached some 5 million adults.

The post-1967 populist policy has been more successful in changing the shape of the educational pyramid (broadening its base) than the elitist policy which preceded it, although the elitist ethos has been by no means eliminated. The Tanzanian example shows us that the ability of the government to change the shape of the educational pyramid is limited by popular preferences, the small means at the disposal of the government and the lack of common purpose or consensus over policy goals within the administration.

The tensions between elitist and populist educational policies are also evident in Nigeria, but in this case huge revenues from oil production facilitated the introduction of both a crash national UPE programme and a rapid expansion of higher-level enrolments. However, inadequate planning, over-hasty implementation, budgetary cuts, administrative complexity and unequal commitment to the policy between the states have made the realisation of UPE problematic.

(3) Who Benefits from Educational Expansion?

If the government cannot always impose its will regarding the expansion of education it seems probable that it will be similarly limited in ensuring that expansion benefits certain groups rather than others. We might expect that those who are already educationally privileged will be well placed to reinforce their privileges, even when government policy is aimed at reducing educational inequalities.

All governments are concerned not to appear to be favouring particular individuals or groups when initiating or pursuing policies; invariably they claim to be acting in the national interest. This is particularly true in the provision of welfare services such as education, where discrimination in favour of certain classes or ethnic groups is likely to cause considerable hostility towards the authorities among excluded groups.

But the reverse is also true: privileged groups often resist positive discrimination policies designed to favour the educationally backward regions and sections of the population. Consider, for example, the effect of introducing a quota system based on regional or ethnic origin for secondary school or university entrance. Such a policy will be defended by the government on the grounds that reducing educational inequalities between regions and ethnic groups fosters national integration and is thus in the national interest. But those from the educationally advanced areas who fail to obtain places will blame their failure on the policy which accepts less qualified candidates from educationally backward areas. Fear of such consequences may lead governments to stop short of all-out reverse discrimination policies. As a compromise they may concentrate the construction of new facilities in the backward areas but not introduce a quota system for places. As a result most of the extra places provided may be filled by students from advanced areas. The Nigerian government follows such a compromise policy. The siting of new university construction reflects demands for regional equity rather than the distribution of primary and secondary facilities. Also, a joint admissions and matriculation board (JAMB) has been set up to control university selection throughout the nation. 'The criteria for selection were merit, the number of places available . . . in the universities and the Federal Government policy of reflecting the federal character of the nation in our universities, (*Daily Times*, 9 March 1979). In response to allegations of favouring the advanced states (see the following section which discusses student politics in Africa), JAMB published figures demonstrating the extent of reverse discrimination. Thus the ten northern states accounted for only 14 per cent of candidates for degree and remedial courses but 29 per cent of admissions (ibid., figures for 1978). On the other hand students from Bendel, Imo and Anambra States accounted for 46 per cent of all candidates but only 35 per cent of new entrants. Selection patterns are discussed in Chapter 2.

The issue of positive discrimination can, in the short run, be more politically divisive than the continued preferential treatment of the already privileged. This is because privileged groups (for example, urban or elite parents, those from areas or ethnic groups of traditionally high enrolment) are more vocal in defending their interests than are the underprivileged in trying to advance theirs. Of course, the underprivileged may or may not desire more educational opportunities, a point discussed in Chapter 2. Also, those who control the state and its institutions must be counted among the most privileged, which makes it highly unlikely that any policy aimed at radically redistributing educational rewards will ever see the light of day.

African governments use education policy to generate support for themselves and to extend their own legitimacy in the eyes of the population. Education policy itself is justified in terms of overall government ideology. To illustrate these points we may look at the contrasting examples of Kenya and Tanzania. The political ideologies and development strategies of these two countries are often contrasted. Both governments claim to be dedicated to the building of a socialist society. In practice, Kenyan policies have been oriented towards encouraging private enterprise, foreign capital investment and rapid class differentiation, whereas Tanzanian policies have stressed self-reliance and the reduction of income and class inequalities as a major development goal. As regards education, Kenyan policy stresses meritocracy (see Chapter 3) and equality of opportunity, whereas Tanzanian policy stresses equality of outcomes, meaning that the educated should not form an elite enjoying special privileges as a result of their education. One result of this policy has been a reduction of income differentials in the public sector, which are approximately twice as high in Kenya as in Tanzania. Let us look at who benefits from the two contrasting education policies.

Kenya
Educational expansion in Kenya since independence has been remarkable both in quantity and in the degree to which the central government has followed rather than led local initiatives. A tradition of self-help (*harambee*) has existed in Kenyan education since colonial times, and this tradition has been extended from the primary to the secondary (academic and technical) and more recently to the post-secondary technical levels. Between 1965 and 1968 the proportion of unaided secondary schools rose from 45 to 61 per cent of the total (Anderson, 1970, p. 150).

After independence the government stressed the need to expand secondary schooling in order to satisfy manpower needs. 'However, as the harambee impetus gathered steam, more and more schools were built with local finance on a self-help basis, were filled with students, and were presented for government support . . . these institutions developed a growth momentum of their own' (Court, 1974, p. 680). Consequently manpower needs were no longer used to justify further expansion and the ideology of equality of opportunity took its place.

Popular pressure for educational expansion and political pressure to launch self-help projects help explain the *harambee* phenomenon. As elsewhere, rapid primary expansion (an 80 per cent increase in enrolments between 1960 and 1970) led to the familiar unemployed school-leaver problem and pressure for secondary school expansion. Rapid secondary expansion meant that

by the early seventies the problem of secondary leaver unemployment was recognised to be acute. The new self-help movement started at the next level: politicians from each major area of the country launched subscription lists for polytechnics to absorb the secondary school graduates who could neither get jobs nor get into the single state university. The government had no politically feasible alternative but to announce its support. (Dore, 1976, p. 68)

The sponsorship of *harambee* schemes is an important source of support for local politicians and for the civil servants, businessmen and academics seeking to replace them in parliament.

Government attempts to reduce enrolment inequalities include (1) abolishing fees in the first four years of primary school; (2) partially allocating educational spending on a regional basis; and (3) building extra schools in the most deprived areas. But the predominance of self-help activities has counteracted government efforts in this field. For example, Central and Nairobi Provinces, with one-fifth of the total Kenyan population, had 29 per cent of the national primary and 42 per cent of secondary enrolments in 1970 (Court and Prewitt, 1973, p. 110). Variations in *harambee* activities reflect existing levels of social inequality and make the redistribution of educational opportunities problematic. Regional variations in political influence and high levels of inequality in income and land ownership explain enrolment inequalities and their perpetuation through time.

Meritocratic ideology is reflected in the secondary school entrance examination which contains no element of preferential treatment for ethnic or regional groups which are educationally backward. This means that many of the new school places created in the backward areas are taken by students from the more advanced areas. Every attempt is made to ensure the fairness of the exam: background and schooling inequalities are not regarded as sources of unfairness. Only the wealthiest parents are able to afford the fees of the best schools, from nursery level upwards, which now guarantee for the children of the elite a high-quality education which was once reserved for the children of white settlers. Thus although political leaders may be formally committed to widening educational opportunities, in practice, 'education is particularly vulnerable to the interests of the new elite' (Anderson, 1970, p. 155). Even *harambee* projects, especially those at the post-secondary level, may help elite children more than any others. Local contribution to self-help schemes may be made compulsory for all adults. To the extent that poor parents are unlikely to have children who qualify to enter the higher-level *harambee* schools this practice represents a form of regressive taxation.

Throughout Africa attempts to increase equality of educational opportunity have frequently failed because the social inequalities responsible for educational inequalities in the first place were left untouched (see Chapters 2 and 7 for further discussion). Kenya's capitalist development strategy sanctions growing socio-economic inequalities and these are inevitably reflected in the education system. The expansion of the latter does not result in reduced social or ethnic/ regional inequalities but in their perpetuation and deepening through time.

Tanzania. How has Tanzanian educational policy affected the level of educational inequalities? We would expect the introduction of a socialist education policy to reduce inequalities of access to education, at least at the primary level where, as already pointed out, recent expansion has been phenomenal. The abolition of primary school fees in 1973 was aimed at reducing enrolment inequalities, but as Mbilinyi (1976a, p. 184) points out: 'Parents must pay for school uniforms, school notebooks and contribute to a "building fund" which requires resources greater than the former school fees.' The need for child labour is also an important factor militating against greater equality of primary enrolment.

The government's inability to control the expansion of primary education before the mid-1960s meant that inequalities in enrolment between regions and ethnic groups, urban and rural areas and social classes remained high. Moreover: 'The Development Plan for 1964–9 actually abandoned the formal commitment to regional parity by emphasising the need for consolidation of earlier expansion and by placing the onus for further development on local authorities; both provisions favoured the richer, more well-endowed areas' (Morrison, 1976, p. 171). Self-help schools added to the overall level of inequality as they were concentrated in the areas with the highest enrolment in aided schools. 'Kilimanjaro Region . . . led all other regions in the percentage [67] of school-age children enrolled: only three of the other sixteen regions had a proportion even two-thirds as great, and five had less than half' (ibid., p. 172, figures for 1965).

By 1975 Standard I enrolments of 7-year-olds showed a somewhat different picture. Although six regions had achieved enrolment levels of 73 per cent or more, five regions still had 49 per cent or less, and these were essentially the regions with the lowest enrolments in 1965. Also, the range of enrolment inequalities increased from 43 to 48 percentage points between the two years. However, nine regions were within two-thirds of the enrolment level of the top region and only one region had less than half that level. Thus there was some sign of a narrowing of enrolment inequalities if not of their elimination. With the recent drive to UPE enrolment inequalities will inevitably fall as certain regions achieve more or less total school attendance and the less advanced regions continue to expand enrolments.

At the crucial secondary level, however, enrolment inequalities have remained high, mainly as a result of the government's decision to allow private secondary school expansion after the school-leavers crisis of 1966. Private secondary schools accounted for 14 per cent of total enrolment in 1966 and 28 per cent in 1975. Between 1973 and 1974 private secondary school enrolments increased by 14 per cent compared with only 3 per cent in state schools. In 1976 Kilimanjaro Region had one-ninth (nine out of eighty-one) of all public secondary schools and one-third (twenty-eight out of 139) of private secondary schools. The five most backward regions had over a quarter of the national population but only 10 per cent of the total number of schools, both public and private (Mbilinyi, 1976a, p. 183).

One factor tending to reduce regional inequalities is the secondary school selection procedure, which is based on regional rather than national recruitment. This means that competition for secondary school places in areas of high primary enrolment serves to force up the minimum pass mark in those areas, whereas candidates from less competitive areas obtain places which they would not have obtained in a national competition. This contrasts markedly with the Kenyan system discussed above; the element of positive discrimination involved meant that the Tanzanian government could resist demands for the introduction of a quota system of reserved places for backward areas.

We cannot document changes in urban/rural and class inequalities, but from the above discussion we would expect that these have not declined significantly. Private secondary schools have been widely used by elite children as a means of eventual back door entry into the state system. The elite want primary education to be terminal for the mass of the population but not for their own children.

Selection to secondary school is now, theoretically, only partly dependent on examination performance but, in practice, the element of continuous assessment based on attitudes to work makes little or no difference to selection procedures. Productive activities in primary school are still only a marginal element in the curriculum rather than an integral part of it serving to prepare the mass of primary-leavers for a life in agriculture. Primary level expansion is not designed, as in Kenya, to widen opportunities for secondary schooling but, in practice, the primary curriculum continues to prepare children for a secondary education which over 90 per cent of them will never enjoy. In Tanzania post-primary education still serves to improve the individual's chances of finding a good job with a reasonable salary. Consequently competition for the limited number of secondary school places is fierce, which inevitably favours the urban, middle-class children. Without eliminating both income differentials and competitive selection completely it is difficult to see how the Tanzanian government can solve the contradiction between educational inequalities and the building of a socialist society. We will come back to the attempt to mould socialist attitudes in the school in the following section.

Conclusion

One of the points we have stressed in previous chapters is that it is difficult to change the structure or function of education simply by introducing piecemeal reforms and policy changes. In the long run major structural changes occur in both education and the wider society, but in the short term educational systems cannot be manipulated at will unless accompanied by revolutionary changes in the social structure.

In the above discussion we have tried to show the difficulties involved in increasing educational opportunities (Kenya) and reducing educational inequalities of outcome (Tanzania). In both cases existing patterns of social stratification tend to reproduce educational inequalities even though both education systems have expanded rapidly in recent years. Morrison sums up the problem of equality and educational provision as follows:

> Although it is true that schooling can be a great equaliser by heightening social and economic mobility and hastening effective integration of disparate groups and strata, the distribution of educational opportunities can also be such that vertical social cleavages are widened and sharpened and that the gulf separating the privileged few from the underprivileged many is deepening. (1976, p. 307)

African governments, like all others, are not as free to determine the course of events as they would like to appear. But in Africa the ambitious goals which governments set themselves, the often extremely limited resources which they have at their disposal and the deep social cleavages which inhibit unified action all serve to highlight the vast gap which exists between objectives and achievements. Nowhere is this more evident than in the politics of education. Government has been defined as the art of the possible, but in education African governments frequently attempt the impossible.

In this section we have only looked at some of the major issues concerning who gets how much of which kind of education. We have not dealt with such important issues as the political role of teachers, the influence of foreign aid, advisors, experts and agencies, and the importance of conflicts within the political leadership in determining educational policy. We hope, however, to have shown that political processes impose strict limits on the freedom of action of governments in determining educational policies and practice. This being the case, we should not take too seriously governments' claims to act simply in the national interest in educational matters or expect their achievements to match their ambitions.

Western educational systems were introduced in Africa to serve the purposes of colonialism, and these systems have not been radically transformed in structure or function since independence. During colonial times educational ideology and policy were quite clearly related to the problem of social control. Many would argue that, after the brief honeymoon following independence, African governments, partly through their inability to control educational expansion or provide adequate employment possibilities for school-leavers, have increasingly come to resemble the colonialists in this respect.

Education and Political Socialisation

According to Coleman (1965, p. 18), 'the concept of political socialization . . . refers to that process by which individuals acquire attitudes and feelings toward the political system and toward their role in it'. This process includes (1) learning how the political system works; (2) the growth of feelings (positive or negative) about the system; and (3) the development or non-development of a sense of competence to participate actively in politics. Like all learning processes political socialisation begins early in life, and it continues into adulthood.

In Chapter 1 we showed how the coming of Western education had the effect of removing part of the socialising function from the family and local community to the school, particularly as regards the acquisition of relevant skills such as literacy in an official, second language. In a similar way schooling takes over some of the functions of family and community concerning the understanding of, and participation in, the polity.

In Africa there is considerable variation in the extent to which governments attempt to inculcate political values through the school. This is partially a reflection of different colonial experiences. For example, in many francophone countries the French system of using the school for purposes of civic training has been followed. In these countries school authorities attempt, through civics classes and other means, to produce good citizens with positive feelings about their nation and its institutions. In countries following the British tradition such direct methods of civic training have been exceptional, although they are becoming less rare.

In all countries political values are developed in the individual irrespective of the use made of the school as an instrument of political socialisation. In many important and subtle ways the school is an indirect source of political values. These may include a positive evaluation of the political institutions of the nation but they may equally involve alienation from, and a rejection of, all or part of the political system. In Africa, levels of identification with the nation state, the government and the other institutions of state are generally rather low. Many parts of the modern world suffer from serious problems of poorly integrated racial, regional, class and cultural or religious minorities, and it is hardly surprising that the same phenomenon is to be found in the new nations of Africa, most of which lack common cultural, linguistic and political traditions.

Modernisation theorists have been concerned with the problem of the transformation of the recently independent states into nation states, that is, to polities in which the great majority of citizens identify positively with the nation and its institutions and participate in some way in the political process. In their concern with political modernisation these theorists have pointed out the use to which formal education may be put by politicians seeking to build the nation. Modernisation theorists have tended to stress the importance of developing a political culture and common nationalist feelings in ensuring political stability. Marxist theorists, on the other hand, stress the essentially conservative nature of nationalist ideology and its manipulation by politicians who are more concerned to disguise social conflicts than to eliminate their causes. We may begin this section by looking at the formal attempts to use education as a means of political socialisation and the difficulties which such attempts are likely to encounter.

Schooling and Citizenship

Education in Kenya must foster a sense of nationhood and promote national unity. Kenya's people belong to different tribes, races and religions, but these differences need not divide them. They must be able to live and interact as Kenyans. It is a paramount duty of education to help the youth acquire this sense of nationhood by removing conflicts and by promoting positive attitudes of mutual respect which will enable people of different tribes, races and religions to live together in harmony and to make a positive contribution to the national life. (Kenya Ministry of National Education, quoted by Court and Prewitt, 1973, p. 111)

Many millions of African children spend a significant part of their lives as the captives of formal education. They have no say in what they learn and are more exposed to attempts at manipulation by the political authorities than any other group of the population. It is understandable, therefore, that governments should turn to the school as a means of developing feelings of national identity. Also, as the school-going population is quite young it is reasonable to suppose that pupils and students are likely to be relatively open to attempts to mould their political attitudes. The teacher and headmaster constitute figures of authority, particularly to the younger pupils, which may increase the likelihood of successful political manipulation. We may briefly consider three forms of government intervention in schooling which relate to the question of political socialisation.

First, governments have taken over many privately run schools and colleges, particularly those established by mission bodies. Despite the high cost involved in the nationalisation of education it was politically unacceptable to post-independence governments to leave large sections of national education in private, often foreign, hands. The sectarian beliefs and practices propagated by the various Christian churches conflicted somewhat with the political ideology of secular nationalism and development. European history shows that the religious authority of the church and the temporal authority of the state frequently come into conflict, and in the modern world numerous examples of similar conflicts can be observed. As was shown in the previous section, missionary bodies have frequently been involved in political conflicts in Africa, but in general they have submitted with a good grace to the encroachment of the political authorities on their sacred preserves.

This does not mean that the churches have lost all influence in political affairs, in the schools or outside. Many schools and colleges are still run by mission bodies, particularly at the secondary level, and nationalist sentiments do not prevent political leaders from sending their children to these (often high-quality) institutions. It is at the primary level that the takeover of private schools has been most extensive since independence, with the consequence that the evangelical content of primary schooling has been greatly reduced. This does not mean that a persuasive secular ideology has been introduced to replace this religious content, as will be shown below.

Secondly, since independence there have been widespread efforts to indigenise curriculum content, to replace colonial teaching materials by something more African and locally relevant in inspiration and content. This was particularly necessary in such subjects as history and geography, which sometimes ignored Africa completely or (in the case of history) interpreted the past in such a way as to downgrade African achievements and paint a flattering picture of the colonial period. However, the Africanisation of curriculum content and the extension of local control over textbook writing and distribution still have a long way to go. Questions of curriculum reform have already been dealt with (see Chapter 6) and the student is referred to the discussion of the effectiveness of curriculum reform, which is also relevant in the present context. Lastly, and closely related to the Africanisation of curriculum is the introduction of specific courses in civics and other forms of citizenship training, such as singing the national anthem before classes, raising the national flag, distributing pictures of national leaders, political slogans and maps and parading on independence day. This form of political training has been attempted to varying degrees in Africa. As we have already pointed out, English-speaking countries have generally been slow to introduce civics into the school curriculum, although nowadays social studies courses are increasingly popular at both primary and secondary levels. To a certain extent such courses are designed to produce good citizens. The French tradition is evident in the ex-French colonies, where civics classes (*instruction civique*) were common during the colonial period. Here content has been generally changed to satisfy national instead of colonial goals.

In these three ways – by eliminating much religious indoctrination, by introducing African topics into school curricula and by the use of civics courses and related means – African governments have attempted to develop national consciousness and train good citizens. What is the likelihood that such attempts will have the desired effect?

Difficulties in Citizenship Training

There are serious practical limitations to the use of curriculum manipulation for citizenship training. First, civics teaching is generally peripheral to the main syllabus, and the priority which it is given in terms of hours per week is usually low compared with, say, language teaching or mathematics. Even when civics is an examinable subject and may affect promotion to the next class there is no guarantee that the patriotic message will get through to pupils. They may well treat it as any other subject – detached from the real world and merely to be memorised and regurgitated in examinations. In Tanzania, for example, a country where citizenship training through schooling is taken very seriously,

> the atmosphere in which political education is imparted becomes an artificial one in which ... critical thought is unceremoniously banished. Not infrequently it turns into a tug of war between the pupils and the teacher as to who can praise the government most. It is no wonder that neither the pupils nor the teacher care to understand what they say or remember it outside the classroom. ... Political education has been relegated to the level of a compulsory examinable subject, a pass in which is essential if one is to proceed to the next stage of education. (Hirji, 1973, p. 21, quoted by Court, 1976, p. 676)

Secondly, teaching civics in a convincing way requires teachers who are highly motivated, well informed in current affairs and supplied with adequate books and other teaching materials. These conditions are frequently lacking. Few primary or secondary schoolteachers have any formal training in civics teaching and frequently civics do not figure in teacher training college syllabuses. More important, many teachers exhibit the kind of particularistic values which (among other things) the civics course is intended to counter. Teachers may neither see the use of citizenship training in school nor accept that school is the right place for such training to be undertaken. A teacher who does not practise ethnic tolerance will not convince the class of the importance of such tolerance. A headmaster who uses manual labour as a punishment will not convince pupils of the high esteem which should be accorded to farmers and farming. Even when teachers are conscientious they may be forced to rely on their own resources through the absence of suitable textbooks and manuals. In some places pupils have few or no textbooks at all, and buying a civics textbook (should one exist) is unlikely to have high priority for them. In countries like Nigeria, with greatly differing cultures and histories between regions, it is difficult to produce a civics manual equally acceptable to all parts of the country. There are few or no common national heroes who can be referred to; in fact, one region's hero may be another region's arch villain. In other words, the kinds of ethnic/regional tensions found in many parts of Africa make the writing of history, civics and social studies texts politically problematic and as likely to intensify conflicts as to reduce them.

These considerations lead us to a major problem of political socialisation, that of the congruence between the theory of citizenship and the everyday practice of public affairs. One of the major political socialisers is, of course, the polity itself, and political events and practices have a far greater effect on the political cognitions and values of students (or anyone else) than the exhortations of a civics primer. The old command 'Do as I say, not as I do' does not carry much weight in the real world. We wonder, for example, how many Nigerian schoolchildren would be able to relate the following statement to their own country: 'Enlightened leadership is given to a country by its educated elites – in such a country there will be no chaos, no tension or rebellion; development is rapid' (National Educational Research Council (Nigeria), 1977, p. 246). When political leaders and civil servants are seen to be particularistic, tribalistic and corrupt, rather than universalistic, nationalistic and honest, it is unlikely that citizenship training will have much impact as regards forming positive attitudes towards the polity. Table 9.1 (overleaf) shows how attitudes are affected by exposure to politics. It is most unlikely that any of the students in Abernethy's sample had been exposed to any citizenship training at school. The sevenfold increase in negative responses between primary and sixth-form students is, however, a substantial index of the effect of exposure to politics on political attitudes.

On the other hand, a study of Tanzanian primary schoolchildren concluded that the introduction of political education and agriculture into the curriculum did little to instil in pupils the values of self-reliance, co-operative activities and socialism, which are the basis of official ideology. Pupils were inclined to see agricultural activities more as an attempt by the government to save money than as a useful

A Sociology of Education for Africa

Table 9.1 **Southern Nigerian Students' Attitudes towards Politicians**
(Percentages)

Attitude	Primary	Secondary modern	Secondary grammar	Sixth form
Positive	15	13	14·4	17
Neutral	26	46	50·6	47
Negative	5	9	25·2	35
Don't know/ no answer	54	32	9·6	1
Total	100	100	100·0	100

Source: Abernethy (1969, p. 217).

learning process, and the lack of special agricultural knowledge among teachers reinforced this attitude. Court concludes that

> didactic styles of teaching, authoritarian and hierarchical relation-ships, and bureaucratic styles of work provide a standing contrast to the ideals of co-operation, participation, and democracy which the students know are the ideals for decision-making and organisation within the schools. (1976, p. 678)

Variations in attitudes between students in different African coun-tries seem to indicate that the national political context of each country (for example, state of calm or crisis, degree of ethnic rivalry, popularity of political leaders) strongly conditions political attitudes and values (Koff and Muhll, 1967; Klineberg and Zavalloni, 1969; Hanna, 1975). We would expect this to be more or less true for students and non-students alike.

Court and Prewitt (1973) found that the attitudes of Kenyan secon-dary students towards the central government varied between privileged and underprivileged regions, showing that awareness of regional inequalities has a stronger socialising effect than common educational experience. Asked whether the government were doing many things for their families, nearly a third of Central Province (privileged) students replied in the affirmative compared with only 14 per cent in Nyanza Province (underprivileged). Also, 34 per cent of Central and 14 per cent of Nyanza Province students said that it was not a good thing for people to criticise the government. The Kenyan government's policy of reducing ethnic and regional feelings through education (see the quotation on p. 236) clearly has a long way to go.

From an early age children are unconsciously learning political values from parents, village elders, older siblings and others, so that if and when they enter primary school they are no longer *tabula rasa* for learning correct political attitudes. If the image of politics which parents and other adults communicate to the young are hostile, critical or negative, then it is unlikely that the experience of schooling will, either directly or indirectly, have much impact on the values already internalised (and probably constantly reinforced).

There is evidence that primary schooling alone has little or no effect, directly or indirectly, on political values. Peil (1976) found that there was little difference between the political attitudes of southern Nigerian illiterates and those with only primary education. A study by Beckett and O'Connell (1977) found that only 6 to 12 per cent of university students interviewed thought that they had begun to think in national terms during primary school and only up to 20 per cent at the university level. We may conclude that primary education alone, with or without attempts at political socialisation, is unlikely to alter the political values which are learned from family, community and the polity itself. This does not mean that primary (or post-primary) education has no socialising effect: it means that the values (political or other) learned at primary school are congruent with those learned outside. There is evidence to suggest that remaining in formal education at the secondary and higher levels exerts its own independent socialising pressures, and we will come back to this point shortly.

The two studies quoted above are both concerned with southern Nigeria, where primary schooling for the majority of children has come to be accepted as a normal and desirable thing. In such a context politically relevant lessons learned at school are not likely to differ drastically from those learned at home. For example, deference to elders, the likelihood of physical punishment for misbehaviour, the need to protect one's own interests in a hard and frequently unfair world, ideas of hierarchy and competition, may all be internalised both at home and in the school. Where parents are reluctant to send their children to school it is sometimes because they fear that schooling will in some way reduce their own authority over their children. A study by Hake (1970) of Western education in Kano, northern Nigeria, showed that parents considered non-Islamic education to be responsible for the rejection of traditional authority, especially among girls.

This brings us to a final point. As primary enrolment levels vary widely within most African countries it is perhaps fortunate that political socialisation is relatively unaffected by primary schooling. Were this not the case, it would mean that students in high enrolment areas would develop an allegiance to the state and the political leadership, whereas those in the low enrolment areas would retain their parochial attachments to locality, ethnic group, region and clan. In other words, education would serve to widen rather than reduce regional and other inequalities. Politicians continue to believe in the power of education as an aid to nation-building, however, and this is one of the main forces behind the current UPE movements in such widely different countries as Nigeria and Tanzania.

Summary and Conclusions
There is little indication from available data that education for citizenship contributes to nation-building in the way that both modernisation theorists and African politicians would like it to. Few African governments have the necessary human and financial capacity to undertake large-scale political socialisation campaigns in the schools, and there is no reason to believe that they would be effective even if they were feasible. There is no reason to believe that changes in curriculum, the introduction of civics and the nationalisation of primary schooling have had any significant effect on political attitudes. Even in Tanzania, where these policies have been supplemented by attempts to restructure the whole education system in order to achieve the goals of self-reliance and socialism and to combat elitism and the growth of social inequalities, there are few signs that the desired attitudinal changes are taking place. It is perhaps early days to judge the Tanzanian experiment a complete failure, however, and further research is needed before a sound assessment can be made.

In Chapter 6 we criticised the proposition that curriculum reform can change values and orientations. As regards changing levels of political consciousness we would argue that political change itself is the major causal factor involved. Conscious attempts to mould the minds of schoolgoers or anyone else are doomed to failure as long as they are not linked to real changes in the polity. The school should not be expected to lead the way in nation-building. If people feel that the state is an oppressive imposition from outside, an exploitive and alien force or, simply, irrelevant to their lives, then no amount of citizenship training will convince them of the contrary. Ideological manipulation is no substitute for attacking the social, economic and political problems which are the real obstacles to nation-building.

Students and Politics

Students are frequently a thorn in the flesh of governments. The US involvement in Vietnam sparked off widespread student protest during the 1960s; in May 1968 student protest in France and elsewhere brought about a near revolutionary situation; in 1976 secondary school students in Soweto (Johannesburg) started a popular revolt against the authorities which led to violent confrontation and many deaths; student protest helped dislodge Haile Selassie in Ethiopia and Bokassa in the Central African Republic. African governments are generally intolerant of criticism, so that student protest may result in serious government sanctions, ranging from the withdrawal of grants and dismissal from the university, to physical violence and even death. Given the high price of activism, students have been remarkably courageous in risking imprisonment or worse throughout the continent. We may begin this section by delineating the types of protest with which we are primarily concerned.

The most common form of student protest is that directed against school, college or university authorities. Students protest about such things as poor food and living conditions, maladministration and inadequate teaching; and these protests can become violent. It is not uncommon for teachers to be manhandled and for property to be destroyed. Often the apparent cause of unrest (that which the newspapers report) is simply the last of a long line of issues on which students and the authorities have come into conflict. Compared with the well-ordered, semi-monastic atmosphere of the older mission establishments modern post-primary education often seems to be chaotic in the extreme. The level of unrest and indiscipline seems to be on the increase in Africa (and elsewhere) and educational authorities and public figures frequently express their concern with this problem. For students, of course, it is the authorities who constitute the problem, especially as regards their failure to provide education of a satisfactory standard.

Protests against the national educational authorities constitute a second and wider level of student activity. Such protests are concerned with issues of interest to parts of the student body or to students as a whole. Admissions procedures or students' grants frequently constitute bones of contention between students and the authorities. The Ministry of Education is, of course, part of the central government machinery, and many decisions concerning education are taken at the highest level. Protests aimed at the education authorities, therefore, often constitute attacks on the government itself.

An example of an educational issue involving political protest by students (in this case only a minority of students) is the question of university admissions in Nigeria. A joint admissions and matriculation board (JAMB) was set up in 1977 to co-ordinate university entry in the light of the federal military government's policy of reducing regional enrolment inequalities through a number of 'affirmative programmes', including the 'establishment of Schools of Basic Studies in each of the disadvantaged states . . . and the establishment of remedial programmes in all the seven new universities as an integral part of their programmes' (*Daily Times*, 9 March 1979, p. 7). Early in 1979 newspaper reports purporting to show that enrolments from the disadvantaged states were declining as a result of JAMB led to protests among teacher training college and university students from those states and a number of institutions were temporarily closed. In fact the number of student protesters was low, and JAMB was quick to deny the accuracy of the reports, publishing its own statistics which showed an improvement in the overall representation of the disadvantaged states. Newspaper editorials were critical of the protesting students for not checking the accuracy of the newspaper reports. This example demonstrates the politically sensitive nature of admissions procedures, especially when they involve questions of reverse discrimination or 'affirmative programmes'.

We can quote a more serious example of student protest over educational affairs from Tanzania. In 1966 it was announced that all university students would be liable to two years' compulsory national service on graduating, and this was seen 'as a method to cleanse students of the elitist attitudes which they might have acquired during their final years of schooling' (Barkan, 1975, p. 14). Students reacted strongly to the proposals, feeling 'that they were being singled out for unfair treatment, and that the government was guilty of discriminating against intellectuals' (ibid.). Finally:

> On 22 October 1966, an angry crowd of university students confronted the President . . . at the State House in Dar es Salaam. Shouting slogans and waving placards – 'Colonialism Was Better' read one sign . . . – they demanded that the President reconsider the relatively spartan terms of the compulsory National Service programme. . . . Passive resistance was threatened should he fail to comply. (Von der Muhll in Prewitt, 1971, p. 25)

Over 300 demonstrators were formally expelled from the university as a result of the demonstration, although most of them were eventually reinstated.

A youth corps on the Tanzanian model was introduced in Nigeria in 1973, and led to similar unsuccessful protest. Many other examples of this kind of protest could be quoted in which students, acting like any other pressure group, attempt to defend their interests as they see them.

Students and academic staff may combine to protest against what they see as undue political interference in academic affairs. Attempts to politicise higher education in Ghana during the Nkrumah regime were strongly resisted by the university authorities in the name of academic freedom, a notion inherited from the British along with the elitist, boarding-school-based education system. This resistance led Nkrumah to declare that 'we do not intend to sit idly by and see these institutions . . . continue to be the centre of anti-government activities. We want the University College to cease being an alien institution' (quoted by Hanna, 1975, p. 94). When Nkrumah fell in 1966 university students were among the first to come out on the streets and demonstrate their support for the new regime, thanking it 'for the successful overthrow of the old, corrupt and tyrannical regime of Kwame Nkrumah' (Finlay, Ballard and Koplin, 1968, p. 84). The issue of whether universities should be free from government interference and free to criticise government policy and actions is still a sensitive one in many African countries.

A third type of student protest concerns general government policy, not just that directly related to education and students' interests. Periods of political crisis often prompt student protest. For example, in the former Western Region of Nigeria before the 1966 coup University of Ibadan students demonstrated against ballot rigging, intimidation and corruption among politicians. In 1977 University of Dar es Salaam students went on the streets to protest against proposed increases in MPs' salaries. Educational issues sometimes spark off protests which then develop a more general character. For example, in early 1978 students throughout Nigeria protested against proposed increases in fees 'and the granting of what were seen as extravagant salaries and benefits to civil servants and soldiers'. Increasing violence and the death of a number of demonstrators led to general student condemnation of the government with slogans such as 'This is Soweto in Nigeria' (*Financial Times*, 29 August 1978, p. 34). The actual Soweto confrontation took place in 1976 and was sparked off by secondary students protesting against the introduction of Afrikaans in the school syllabus. Their protest prompted a general popular uprising, leading to brutal police repression and hundreds of deaths.

Some of the most intense ideological criticism of African governments comes from student bodies abroad. This is frequently the case with French-speaking countries, when the students and permanent exiles in France often take radical positions in condemning what they see as neo-colonial regimes in their own country. These groups can afford to be more vocal in their criticism than the students back home as they do not risk direct reprisals from the government. The latter usually denounces the 'foreign inspiration' of protest from groups of students abroad and often explain local protests by branding them as inspired by exiles. More recently Liberian student politics have also begun to conform to the above description.

A final type of student protest is that which is aimed at foreign governments. Other African governments are sometimes the target, but more usually protest is against ex-colonial powers (Portugal, Britain, France) or the USA, and concerns their foreign policies and activities in Africa or other Third World countries. There are many protests concerning the politics of decolonisation in Southern Africa and what is considered unacceptable interference in African affairs by the forces of imperialism. Such protests are safe as long as they do not implicate the national government in collusion with outside interests.

In summary, student protest varies widely in its objectives, from complaining about the quality of refectory food to condemning American imperialism. The most important kinds of student protest are those aimed at the central government concerning educational and other issues. We may note that students do not always take up leftist positions against reactionary regimes in Africa. Although this is often the case, many examples can be cited of student resistance to radical politicisation by government, whether from Ghana, Guinea or (pre-1968) Mali. Student protests usually make news, but it should not be thought that student bodies throughout the continent are in a state of permanent turmoil, endlessly criticising their governments and seeking radical political change.

Students' Political Attitudes and Values
Before we turn to the question of why students do or do not get involved in political activities it will be useful to consider the kinds of attitudes and values which characterise students.

A number of surveys of African students have been made which give a good indication of their conceptions of politics and politicians, their degree of national as opposed to local or ethnic identity and their feelings of political competence and desire to participate actively in the political process. These surveys would be more interesting if they compared students with similarly aged groups of non-students, for this would give us some idea of the socialising effect of extended education. To our knowledge only Peil's survey (1976) attempts to do this. We can nevertheless learn quite a lot from students' responses without this comparative dimension.

We have already cited Abernethy's survey showing an increase in negative attitudes towards politicians between primary and secondary students. Other information suggests that students' attitudes towards political incumbents are generally negative. Barkan (1975) found that students in Tanzania, Ghana and Uganda rated MPs and ministers as basically opportunistic, wasteful and proud. The Nigerian students questioned by Beckett and O'Connell (1977, p. 145) ranked politicians very low, 'both in terms of the importance of their skills, and in terms of their actual contribution to society'. When asked who should replace the military regime 'the overwhelming majority of students ranked the old politicians ("members of the former political parties") and military officers turned politicians lowest' (ibid., p. 152).

Such negative assessments of politicians do not, however, correspond to a general alienation from political matters. Students indicate a relatively high level of interest in political affairs. Rooks's study of Ibadan students (in Hanna, 1975, p. 40) found that over a quarter of those interviewed indicated a great deal of interest in politics, whereas only 13 per cent showed no interest at all. Students also consider themselves potentially important in helping solve national problems, (see Table 9.2).

Table 9.2   Students' Beliefs about their Ability to Help Solve Nigeria's
Problems (Percentages)

Belief	Secondary modern	Secondary grammar	Sixth form
Can help	29	61	62
Cannot help now, but can help later	5	5	13
Cannot help	40	25	20
Don't know/no answer	26	9	5
Total	100	100	100

Source: Abernethy (1969, p. 219).

Fully three-quarters of sixth-formers thought they could help solve
Nigeria's problems now or in the future. In another survey (United
States Information Agency, 1966) two-thirds of Nigerian students
interviewed indicated that they expected to be moderately or very
active in public affairs by the age of 45 (in Hanna, 1975, p. 27). Over
three-fifths of Kenyan students interviewed by McKown (1975, p.
236) agreed that 'in the future people like me will have a lot of
influence on government decisions'.

On the other hand, very few students indicate a desire to enter
politics as a career. Only 5 per cent of Ibadan students interviewed by
Rooks aspired to a political career and none expected to enter such a
career. Barkan found a very similar pattern among Tanzanian, Ugandan and Ghanaian students.

We can conclude from these figures that students are both disdainful
of politicians and uninterested in political careers but generally
interested in politics and conscious of their possible contribution to
national life.

To criticise the incumbents of power is not necessarily to reject the
state and its institutions. If education directly or indirectly encourages
the growth of a national consciousness this should be most evident at
the university level. Peil (1976, p. 88) found in her Nigerian survey
that 'the well-educated . . . tend to emphasise the nation as opposed to
the locality. . . . The uneducated . . . remain more tied to local interests'. But Beckett and O'Connell found a rather low level of national
identity among students from Ahmadu Bhello University, Nsukka and
Ibadan. Students were asked to compare different levels of personal
identity as an index of their relative sense of belonging to one community or another. Comparing the relative strength of home state as
opposed to national identity, only Ibadan students (mostly Yoruba)
indicated the latter to be more powerful than the former, as the two top
lines of Table 9.3 indicate. Nsukka students (mostly Ibo) were the least

Table 9.3   Relative Strength of Different Levels of Identity among Nigerian Students (Percentages)

	ABU	Ibadan	Nsukka
Nigerian identity stronger than			
state identity: YES	48	59	36
NO	52	41	64
Total:	100	100	100
Nigerian identity stronger than			
ethnic identity: YES	48	55	39
NO	52	45	61
Total:	100	100	100
Nigerian identity stronger than			
home community: YES	43	36	35
NO	57	64	65
Total:	100	100	100

Source: Beckett and O'Connell (1977, p. 69).

nationally inclined, voting two to one in favour of state identity. As regards ethnic as opposed to national identity a similar pattern emerges, and all three groups of students expressed a higher level of attachment to home community than to the nation.

The data in Table 9.3 demonstrate an important fact: national identity, at least in Nigeria, is not automatically associated with higher education but rather reflects the Nigerian political context and recent history. It is a fact that ethnic rivalry is rife among the Nigerian academic community, as university politics demonstrate, and neither university staff nor students are exempt from the particularistic conflicts which characterise the national political scene. A comparative study of students in Senegal, Ghana, Ethiopia, Zaire, Uganda and Nigeria found ethnic identity to be higher among Nigerian students than among the others:

> Nigerian students showed the highest frequency . . . of tribal and regional membership as identity attributes; the highest frequency of friendship and . . . a greater feeling of ease with others of the same tribe; the lowest frequency of 'nation' as an identity attribute . . . ; a very large proportion agreeing that traditional authority and tribal structure may be useful to progress; an almost unanimous perception of intergroup tensions within Nigeria as constituting a serious problem. (Klineberg and Zavalloni, 1969, p. 239)

We would not expect the educational experiences of Nigerian students to vary significantly from those of students in other countries. It is generally true that university students have a greater knowledge of national politics than non-students and an above-average level of national identity. If, therefore, Nigerian students demonstrate lower levels of national identity than other African students we may conclude that this is because regional and ethnic cleavages are more serious in Nigeria than elsewhere. This reinforces our previous conclusion that political events and the nature of the polity are more powerful socialisers than the educational experience of students. The modernisation hypothesis – that a large dose of Western education will lead to the formation of modern individuals with universal rather than particularistic orientations towards their society – exaggerates the power of education to overcome political realities.

Causes of Student Action and Inaction
We will conclude by examining the various factors which account for both the fact of student political activity and its practical limits. We may first cite a number of factors predisposing students towards political activity.

Students constitute the most literate and best-informed group in society. Their ability to think for themselves should be developed by their long educational experience and exposure to a wide range of ideas and values. They may not have travelled to Europe and America, but Europe and America have travelled to them. Students have a better opportunity than most of the population of being well informed about politics and are often close to the decision-making machinery which, like most universities (outside Nigeria), is situated in the national capital. The closeness of the university to the centre of power and the relatively small size of the modern political and social system tend to draw students and politics together. This tendency is reinforced by the overwhelming importance of government service as the major occupational opening for graduates and the extent to which governments stress the role of higher education in manpower formation.

Throughout the world it is the educated, high-status groups who are the most likely to become involved in public affairs. Students are accorded more social honour in Africa than anywhere else in the world (in many countries they are generally looked down upon), and this is likely to enhance their feeling of competence and their role as leaders of opinion, mentioned above.

Common living and recreation and everyday activities and anxieties help develop feelings of group solidarity and shared interests and lead to the growth of student subcultures. Organisations such as the student union and clubs provide the base for the voicing of student opinion and the defence of common interests. In Africa only unionised workers and, up to a point, voluntary associations share all these advantages with students. In the absence of other organised interest groups, students may take it upon themselves to become opinion leaders for the rest of the community. In the heat of the 1978 student unrest the Nigerian students' union NUNS issued a statement, claiming that

> students are the conscience of any neo-colonial society. They are students because they possess a critical outlook to society. Having been equipped with the necessary apparatus of thought, they are able to make the required analysis of any government action and, more importantly, act upon it. (*Financial Times*, 29 August 1978, p. 34)

These are rather extreme claims, as the following discussion will show.

Zolberg (1966) maintains that student political activity is a reflection of generational conflict between existing and aspiring elites. There may be some truth in this, to the extent that students generally have a higher educational level than the incumbents of power and do not share the same common experiences (colonial oppression, nationalist struggle) as the older generation. Throughout the world young people, unencumbered by the responsibilities of family and the demands of work, tend to look down on their more compromised and less idealistic elders. In Africa this tendency may be compounded by the high rate of social change which can cause a great gap of culture, values and ambitions to develop between the generations.

On the other side of the balance there are a number of powerful forces at work tending to inhibit political participation and protest by students. One set of factors relates to the indirect socialising experience of extended schooling. We have discussed the hidden curriculum effect of schooling which causes students to internalise a set of values likely to influence their social attitudes and behaviour. The longer the student stays in formal education the more likely are these values to become deep-rooted. The boarding schools which many secondary students attend are a fertile ground for socialisation, as they constitute a more or less closed community, uncontaminated by the alternative influences of family and local environment. What politically relevant values does education teach the individual? Some major ones are individualism, competition, respect for hierarchy and authority, elitism and careerism. Competition and individualism are complementary values in that they both encourage the student to pursue his or her own personal interests and aims and not those of the group. (This aspect of the hidden curriculum made the introduction of Western education a considerable problem in societies where co-operation and equality were highly valued and in Tanzania, for example, makes the reintroduction of such values very problematic). In an education system where 'many are called but few are chosen' the imperative to look after one's own interests in order to survive is very powerful. In other words, the highly competitive nature of African education forces the individual student to be competitive and self-oriented rather than community-oriented. The consequences of this for group solidarity and collective political involvement are obvious.

In a number of ways extended schooling encourages respect for authority and hierarchy. The teacher is the repository of all wisdom and his word is not to be questioned, even when he is clearly out of his depth. Discipline is strict and punishment often severe for the offender. The idea that the incumbent of a position of authority should be respected uncritically may be transferred to the level of the political leadership, reinforced by the traditional respect afforded to leaders and elders. The use of force may be taken as a legitimate expression of leadership. Democratic ideas such as consultation, representation and checks on the abuse of power carry little weight in such an authoritarian context. Surveys show that students are often hostile to one-party authoritarianism, but they are often less than enthusiastic about democratic alternatives in which every man's opinion is held to be important. For example, students interviewed by Beckett and O'Connell were asked whether or not they agreed with the statement: 'The masses in African countries are not yet capable of making rational choices in elections for national political offices.' From their various samples between 73 and 82 per cent of respondents agreed with the statement (Beckett and O'Connell, 1977, p. 154).

Elitism is encouraged by the knowledge that going to secondary school and university is reserved for the fortunate few. While some of these fortunates are successful because of their advantageous social backgrounds, many students are of more than average ability and succeed in a competitive system through merit rather than privilege. The strategic importance of education for achieving high social status and well-paid jobs also leads to elitist sentiments among students. These three factors – the small percentage of any age-group who succeed, the high ability of many students and the great practical rewards attached to success – encourage elitist attitudes among students.

The feeling of social superiority may well serve to isolate students from the mass of the population and discourage identification with their fate and problems. This social distance from the man in the street will not inhibit political action to defend student interests, but may well lead to a feeling that student interests are separate from and perhaps opposed to those of the rest of the community. President Nyerere of Tanzania observed, when attempts to involve students directly (and altruistically) in development projects came up against opposition, that 'there is a temptation for students at universities to regard themselves as a group which has rights without responsibilities' (Hanna, 1975, p. 265).

Careerism results from the high correlation between educational and occupational success, the knowledge that the stakes are high (there is little alternative chance of mobility) and the commitment of much time, effort, family hopes and money on education. In these circumstances considerations of future career are likely to weigh heavily in the mind of the student. Given that political involvement often leads to government reprisals (withdrawal of grant, rustication of participants, imprisonment) students must be extremely highly motivated before putting their careers in jeopardy.

Thus concern with future careers is a major disincentive to political action. Students are likely to leave politics to the politicians as long as they feel their own futures to be guaranteed. Surveys have shown a generally high feeling of future job success and security among students. For example, 77 per cent of Ghanaian, 69 per cent of Tanzanian and 68 per cent of Ugandan students expected to get the job they desired on graduation (Barkan, 1975, p. 61). Eighty-eight per cent of ABU students interviewed declared that they were satisfied or very satisfied with their career prospects after graduation (Beckett and O'Connell, 1977, p. 93). Only a few students expressed doubts about their future occupational opportunities.

Feelings of already belonging or ultimately belonging to the elite are likely to make students identify with the existing elite and to adopt their attitudes, beliefs and values. Sociologists call this process 'anticipatory socialisation'. The existing elite are also willing to absorb some candidates for elite status in order to ward off any challenge to their privileges from unsuccessful candidates.

Thus both positive incentives (the reward of eventually entering the elite) and negative incentives (the fear of sanctions) encourage students to accept the current order of things. A social order which more or less guarantees high social honour and economic security is likely to receive positive endorsement from students.

The above factors affect all students almost equally, but not all students are equally likely to get involved in political activities. For example, male students tend to be more politically active than females. In Africa and many other parts of the world political activity is almost exclusively a male preserve, so this finding is not very surprising. Another common phenomenon is that arts and social science students are more politically active than those in pure and applied scientific disciplines. For example, over half the social science and law students interviewed by Barkan (1975, p. 160) said they discussed politics once a week or more compared with less than a third of natural science and medical students. The nature of arts and social science is more likely than science to make students sensitive to political ideas and involvements. Also, science subjects tend to be more demanding than other subjects on the time and energies of students. Again, these are common features outside Africa.

Hanna (1975) found that in both Ibadan and Makerere Christian students were more politically active than Muslims from similar social backgrounds. This may reflect the Muslim tendency to accept established authority and to be more fatalistic than Christians.

Social background does not seem to play a large part in levels of political involvement. Students from high occupational backgrounds are socialised into the elite culture, so that membership of the elite is more natural for them than for newcomers to the elite. But at the same time they may feel freer to be critical of their parents' generation in so far as they will probably not be risking their future careers to the same extent as an elite aspirant of more humble birth (both President Nyerere's and ex-Emperor Bokassa's sons have been involved in student political activities). The student from a manual or rural background may be anxious to establish his credentials for entering the elite and be less sure than the high-status student of gaining entry, but at the same time his awareness of the social distance between his own background and the elite may lead him to be critical of the privileges of the latter. Thus contradictory forces are at work in both cases and, from the information available, seem to balance each other out.

The forces inhibiting political involvement among students generally outweigh the forces facilitating such involvement. Whether African students will become more politically active in the future depends on a number of factors. For the moment good salary and career prospects are practically assured for graduates, but this situation need not continue indefinitely. The pressure to increase educational facilities and the rather slow rate of new job creation have already brought about a severe unemployment problem among primary and (to a lesser extent) secondary school-leavers. There is no guarantee that this will not eventually extend to graduates, as it has elsewhere in both the developed and the underdeveloped world (for example, Britain, the USA, India, the Philippines). It is also very likely that graduates will enjoy less rapid promotion in the future than at present and may have to accept more modest employment than they would like. These factors could lead to frustration and disaffiliation among students, which could be expressed in political terms. Government attempts to satisfy a (by definition) insatiable popular demand for education may sooner or later be translated into unemployed graduates, another breakdown in modernisation with ominous implications for those in power.

Throughout this chapter we have stressed the primacy of general political conditions in determining students' views and activities. Developments in the former will have an important effect on changes in the latter. We would not like to hazard a guess as to future trends in this respect. The one-party regimes of Africa are sensitive to, and intolerant of, criticism from whatever quarter. In some countries, for example Nigeria, a healthy freedom of speech flourishes, whereas in others no channels whatsoever exist for legitimate public opposition to government. Pessimists would argue that world economic recession, unemployment and inflation are likely to take their toll in Africa and elsewhere, leading to conditions of political siege and popular unrest and violence. The reader may like to speculate on these issues and on the possible role of students.

Summary and Conclusions
The relationship between political leaders and higher education in Africa is a tense and contradictory one. The politicians are aware of the possible challenge which the students (and academics) can pose to their legitimacy and consequently keep a close and constant watch on staff and student activities. At the same time, vast sums of public money are spent on higher education in order to train the high-level manpower needed for the national development effort, giving the politicians more leverage over higher education than they would otherwise enjoy. The saying 'He who pays the piper calls the tune' corresponds closely to the official attitude.

Students' dependence on government patronage mutes their potential for protest, but not their often low opinions of the political authorities. Both higher education staff and students are sensitive to official interference in academic affairs, whatever the motives and merits of the case, but cannot afford to overantagonise their paymaster. Given the possibility of official sanction it is remarkable that so many students do get involved in political activities, a fact which underlines the fragile nature of the student–government pact.

Students and governments are therefore forced into a reluctant and sometimes tense interdependence. As we have tried to show, the forces of mutual attraction generally outweigh the forces of hostility and rejection, but there is no reason why this should continue to be the case indefinitely. Just as too much of the wrong type of education helped dig the grave of colonialism, so political leaders could be helping to dig the grave of one-party authoritarianism by investing in the expansion of higher education, even for the most praiseworthy of national goals.

Questions and Discussion Topics: Chapter 9

1. What form does student political activity take in your country? Give examples.
2. Compare and contrast the political activities of students in any two African countries.

3 In what ways does schooling affect political socialisation? Give examples.

4 How do politics affect the size and shape of the educational pyramid in your country?

5 Who benefits from educational expansion? Refer to Chapter 2 for help with this question.

6 Governments try to manipulate the education system mainly in order to increase their own legitimacy. Discuss this statement.

7 The people rather than the government determine the nature and rate of educational expansion. Discuss this statement.

8 Many would consider it desirable for governments to eliminate educational inequalities. What factors prevent them from doing so?

9 African governments preach populism and practise elitism. Discuss this statement in relation to education.

10 Discuss the pros and cons of positive discrimination.

11 Discuss the difficulties involved in EITHER (1) the Tanzanian government's attempt to implement *Education for Self-Reliance* OR(2) attempts in Nigeria to introduce universal primary education.

12 *Project A.* Obtain as many civics and social studies textbooks for primary and secondary schools as you can. What do these try to teach students as regards (1) national identity and (2) the responsibilities of the good citizen?

13 *Project B.* From newspapers and other sources collect as many examples of student political activity as you can. Analyse these in terms of (1) the reasons for student unrest and (2) the reaction of the authorities. What patterns (if any) emerge?

14 *Project C.* Look up your government's national plan or find a recent statement of educational policy. What are the elitist/populist implications of official policy? What difficulties do you foresee regarding the successful implementation of the policy?

Glossary of Sociological Terms

Achievement motivation: the desire to succeed or gain by one's own efforts; a psychological drive to achieve for the sake of success itself.

Aspirations: hopes or ambitions; in educational studies, a distinction is often drawn between students' hopes for the future (aspirations) and what they expect to happen in the future (expectations).

Authority: the right to command or hold power. A person may not have to force another to obey him if he holds authority; the norms of society justify or give authority to the person who can command (see *Power*, *Legitimacy*).

Bureaucracy: government or administration by officials who must themselves follow written rules which are rational. Each official has particular responsibilities and has superiors and subordinates among other officials in a pyramid of authority. For further definition, see Chapter 4.

Cadre: those who play professional roles in an organisation of some kind – for example, a government bureaucracy, an army or a large company. They are often thought of as senior professionals, but we can also talk of junior cadres, those in lower or intermediate positions in an organisation (see *Elite*).

Concept: a general idea; an idea which gives an overall view of something. Concepts in science or social science help us to understand the real world. Almost all the terms in this glossary are concepts.

Correlation: a correspondence or a relationship between things. For example, if the wealth of a country rises at the same time as a rise in school enrolment, we would say that there is a correlation between these two things.

Critique: an assessment or judgement; a discussion which searches out the faults and merits of someone's ideas or arguments.

Culture: a way of life as represented by the rules, standards, religion and beliefs, symbols and rituals of a society. For example, ancestor beliefs are a strong element of most traditional African cultures. School cultures are marked by their own rules and standards and by their own rituals and symbols (for example, the ritual of a speech day or sports ceremony).

Curriculum: a course of study which covers various areas of knowledge over a given length of time.

Curriculum, core: This refers to compulsory subjects which all students must take. A core curriculum is composed of knowledge thought basic or most important to all students' learning, whereas optional subjects may be taken in less basic areas of knowledge.

Curriculum, hidden: Students learn not only what is formally prescribed by the school timetable, but also about such things as how to adapt to the atmosphere, rules and culture of the school. The hidden curriculum may also include the knowledge which is necessary to pass examinations or to succeed educationally. Sometimes teachers pass on this knowledge in the form of hints or advice, or students help each other in deciding which knowledge is essential for successful examination performance.

Development: a process of expansion or growing complexity and specialisation. Social development means the emergence of increasingly complicated social institutions (for example, law courts, schools, welfare institutions) and a complex society. Economic development refers to the emergence of sophisticated economic institutions (money, banks, insurance and so on) and a complex economy in which production and consumption increase.

Discretion: autonomy or freedom to choose, decide or take responsibility. We may draw a contrast between discretion to act professionally (for example, as a professional teacher) and being bound by rules and bureaucratic authority (see Chapters 4 and 5).

Efficacy: ability to control or change things. Modernisation theorists suggest that the modern individual has a greater sense of efficacy than the fatalistic traditional individual.

Elite: a general term to describe the top people or leaders of a society, an organisation or a particular field of activity. The term is often used in relation to those who rule – that is, the political elite. In the African context we hear a lot about the educated elite. In *elite theory* the governing elite is distinguished from the rest of the population, the *mass* or *masses*. Elite theory is used as an alternative to class theory (see *Social class*).

Ethnic group: a social group identified as such by its members and by outsiders and possessing a common name, common descent (real or imagined) and culture. This term is sometimes used in place of *tribe*.

Exemplar: a person who is expected to show an ideal or moral pattern of behaviour (see Chapter 5, in relation to the role of teachers).

Function: When we say X is a function of Y we mean that changes in Y bring about changes in X. We might say, for example, that school performance is a function of a number of things, including intelligence and home background.

Functionalism: a theory which suggests that the various institutions of a society (for example, the family, the school, economic institutions) are all interconnected and affect one another in various ways; each institution is supposed to have a purpose in society as a whole and helps to keep society together (see *Social structure*).

Goals: purposes or desired objects in life. Social goals refer to things which are generally thought to be desirable – for example, educational attainment or material wealth.

Hierarchy: a social organisation which is ranked in terms of power and authority. Hierarchies can be bureaucratic (for example, a civil service) or non-bureaucratic (for example, a traditional kingdom).

Human capital: a term used by economists to refer to the idea that a nation's wealth is comprised of *human* resources (a population's skills, health and attitudes to work) as well as natural resources (for example, oil).

Ideal type: the essence of something, or a pure, abstract example. It is possible to imagine an ideal type of criminal behaviour, for example, in order to judge to what extent real individuals or criminals match the ideal type (see Chapter 4).

Ideology: a set of ideas or beliefs which justify vested interests and the authority of those in power. Usually these ideas are put forward as expressing the interests of everyone, but they really support the interests of a dominant group. Examples of ideologies: Nationalism, African Socialism, Liberalism, Populism, Conservatism (see *Legitimacy*).

Inequality: the uneven distribution of anything, though inequality is usually discussed in terms of the uneven distribution of valued things such as power or material wealth.

Informal sector: This refers to the sector (part) of an economy in which activities or occupations are unofficial – that is, not officially known by government agencies. Little information about these activities or occupations is ever gathered. Informal economic activity includes a wide range of service, trading, manufacturing and criminal occupations which are usually (but not always) small-scale.

Innovation: a change or the process of introducing changes or new methods of doing things.

Institution: a social institution can mean specifically (a) an organisation such as a school or hospital, or more generally, (b) a cluster of social rules and norms which regularise human behaviour – for example, the family is an institution which governs and makes regular the social relations between the sexes. We may also speak of political and economic institutions.

Internalise: the process of adopting a rule, belief or attitude so that it becomes a part of one's inner mind or character.

Legitimacy: acceptance of the distribution of power, and the process by which power is transformed into authority. Traditional religious beliefs, for example, may *legitimate* the power of a chief; or beliefs in the superior knowledge of teachers may legitimate their power over students. In most modern organisations, the position one holds and the power one has are legitimated by educational qualifications.

Literacy, functional: the ability to read and write in order to perform work tasks; this term is often used to describe literacy training which is undertaken to provide farmers, for example, with the ability to read about and put into practice new farming methods. But functional literacy training does not give a full ability to read and write.

Literacy, restricted: the ability to read and write a few words only (see Chapter 7).

Manpower planning: the method of calculating the number of people working or available to work in the future in given occupations.

Modernity: having the qualities or characteristics of recent and present times. A state of modernity is supposed to be reached by those living in cities, having education and other characteristics (see Chapter 7).

Neo-colonialism: This describes the present relationship between the Western powers (including the ex-colonial countries) and most of the less developed countries. The term suggests that the influence of capitalist interests, values and exploitation continues and affects all spheres of life – technology, investment, markets, manpower planning, aid and culture. State socialist or communist countries could also be described as neo-colonial in their influence on developing countries.

Norms: social standards. Norms convey the idea of what is usually done in a society. For example, it may become the norm to send most children to school.

Occupational mobility: changing from one kind of employment to another. Note that this term means a change from one *occupation* to another; thus changing teaching jobs is not occupational mobility, but a change from teaching to hairdressing is.

Organisation: a social group or association which has a common purpose, social rules and expectations and some specialisation of duties and roles among its members (see Chapter 4).

Peer, peer group: Peers are one's equals in age and/or status. A peer group is a group of equals. Peer groups form the basis of activities of various kinds – for example, recreation and play among schoolchildren.

Power: the ability to enforce one's will on others. Examples are coercion by military and police authorities, or the power of an employer over employees. (Compare with *Authority*.)

Profession: an occupation for which long training and intellectual ability are required; a social group which has the power to restrict entry to its membership, has a certain amount of autonomy in society and is responsible for the conduct and standards of its members. (For further discussion, see Chapter 5.)

Rationality: a characteristic of individuals or societies which are influenced or governed by reasonable principles and laws. Prejudice, tradition and superstitution are thought of as irrational influences, whereas reasoned and enlightened laws are supposed to be rational.

Role: This term may be used in two ways. First, role may refer to an individual's position in society (for example, a student or teacher) and to the behaviour expected of an incumbent of that position. Secondly, role may refer to an institution's functions in society – for example, we may discuss the role (function) of education in society.

Role differentiation: a process which involves the increasing specialisation of social roles. As societies become more complex than before, different roles which in the past could be performed by one individual (for example, one man could be a part-time farmer, trader and traditional healer) tend to be performed by different individuals (full-time farmers, traders, doctors).

Social background: a general descriptive word which sums up the family and social origins of an individual. Social background is usually established by reference to parental income, occupation and education. Thus the term summarises economic, social and cultural characteristics. Similar terms: socio-economic status, class background.

Social class: a major dimension or characteristic of social stratification. Social classes are abstract categories which are defined according to differences in occupation, property ownership and/or relationship to the means of production (that is, owner or worker). This term is used differently by different authors. (See the Introduction to Part One.)

Social control: the enforcement of society's rules and norms, either by extreme means (for example, imprisonment or ostracism) or by subtler social pressures such as the expectations of friends, relatives or teachers.

Social mobility: movement within the occupational/class structure or society; movement may be up or down the hierarchy of society. Intergenerational mobility refers to movement up or down the hierarchy from the starting point of *parental* social status or position in society. For example, to rise from a small farm to professional status in one generation is considered upward social mobility (see Chapter 3).

Social status: the position occupied by a person in society. Status is reflected in a person's prestige or standing in the community, by his or her education, income, occupation and possessions.

Social structure: This is a general term referring to the way in which society is composed of institutions (political, social and economic) which are relatively permanent – they form a structure. These relatively permanent parts of society assume a reality which is longer-lasting than most individuals' lives or their participation in a particular institution. For example, the students of a college may come and go, but the social structure of the college continues (although it may change gradually over time). This is the same in society as a whole – people are born, are socialised into a society and die – but the social structure in which they have played a part continues.

Socialisation: the process whereby individuals learn the norms, values and culture of a society. We may distinguish childhood from adult socialisation. The former occurs when children learn from parents or teachers; the latter when adults enter new or unfamiliar social groups and learn how to interact with others.

Specialisation: This word may be used in various ways. It may refer to a gradual social change, whereby roles in society become increasingly specific or particular to given kinds of activity (see *Role differentiation*). But this term may also be applied to education. In some countries students are limited to intensive study of a few skills or areas of knowledge. Such examples would be described as highly specialised education systems. Other kinds (for example, the American) do not encourage so much specialisation in a few subjects at school but emphasise general education and delay specialisation until the later years of school or university.

Stratification: All human societies are unequal in some way. For example, the simplest society may have inequalities of age and sex. But in more complicated societies (for example, present-day Nigeria or Tanzania), inequality differences between different groups or *layers* of people (social strata) become established. Social stratification therefore sums up the combination of social inequalities (class, status and power) which rank people into different groups. (See the Introduction to Part One.)

Subculture: This refers to the culture and life-style of a *subgroup* of a society. Schools, for example, have a culture, but there may also be a school *subculture* among the students. Subcultures often oppose the official or dominant culture, and in the case of school subcultures students vary between those who support the official culture and conventional rules and those who, in different ways, oppose it (see *Culture*).

Theory: an idea, explanation or principle for interpreting the world as we see it. For example, we may observe conflict between teachers in a school and develop a theory to explain this.

Tradition: the beliefs, customs, norms and way of life of a people handed down from one generation to the next (see *Culture*).

Values: the ethical standards of a society; moral judgements about what are wrong and right actions. It is important to remember that values change: what was considered wrong yesterday may be acceptable today.

Variable: a factor which is taken into account as an effect on something else, but which varies quantitatively or qualitatively. Education, for example, may be taken into account as a variable when we discuss reasons for migration from village to town. Other factors or variables will also enter this discussion – age, sex and family background are other variables which affect migration. *Independent* variables are those which bring about changes in other variables, known as *dependent* variables. Some variables fall in between these two and link the independent with the dependent variables; these are called *intervening* variables. (See Chapter 3 for examples in education.)

Vocational education: training to prepare for a specific career or occupation. A vocation is a calling, a trade or an occupation.

Bibliography

Abernethy, D. B. (1969), *The Political Dilemma of Popular Education: An African Case* (Stanford, Calif.: Stanford University Press).

Achebe, C. (1958), *Things Fall Apart* (London: Heinemann).

Achebe, C. (1960), *No Longer at Ease* (London: Heinemann).

Adeyinka, A. A. (1973), 'The impact of secondary school education in the Western State of Nigeria', *Comparative Education*, vol. 9, no. 3, pp. 151–5.

Alele Williams, G. (1974), 'Dynamics of curriculum change in mathematics: Lagos State modern maths project', *West African Journal of Education*, vol. 18, pt 2, pp. 241–53.

Anderson, J. E. (1970), *The Struggle for the School* (Nairobi: Longman).

Apter, D. (1963), *Ghana in Transition*, 2nd ed. (New York: Atheneum).

Ayandele, E. A. (1966), *The Missionary Impact on Modern Nigeria 1842–1914* (London: Longman).

Ayandele, E. A. (1971), 'The coming of Western education to Africa', *West African Journal of Education*, vol. XV, no. 1, pp. 21–33.

Ayandele, E. A. (1974), *The Educated Elite in the Nigerian Society* (Ibadan: Ibadan University Press).

Azikiwe, N. (1970), *My Odyssey* (London: Hurst).

Bame, K. N. (1974), 'The application of Western social theory to the study of Ghanaian elementary teachers' work values and attitudes', *Ghana Journal of Sociology*, vol. 7, no. 2, pp. 11–29.

Banks, O. (1968), *The Sociology of Education* (London: Batsford).

Barkan, J. (1975), *An African Dilemma: University Students, Development and Politics in Ghana, Tanzania and Uganda* (Nairobi: Oxford University Press).

Barnes, D., *et al.* (1969), *Language, the Learner and the School* (Harmondsworth: Penguin).

Beckett, P., and O'Connell, J. (1977), *Education and Power in Nigeria* (London: Hodder & Stoughton).

Berg, E. J. (1965), 'Education and manpower in Senegal, Guinea and the Ivory Coast', in F. Harbison and C. A. Myers (eds), *Manpower and Education* (New York: McGraw–Hill), pp. 232–67.

Berman, E. (ed.) (1975), *African Reactions to Missionary Education* (Columbia, NY: Columbia Teachers College Press).

Bibby, J. (1973), 'The social base of Ghanaian education: is it still broadening?', *British Journal of Sociology*, vol. 24, no. 3, pp. 365–75.

Bibby, J., and Miller, J. (1968), 'Accra schoolboys', *West African Journal of Education*, vol. XII, no. 3 (October), pp. 170–4.

Bibby, J., and Peil, M. (1974), 'Secondary education in Ghana: private enterprise and social selection', *Sociology of Education*, vol. 47, pp. 399–418.

Bidwell, C. (1965), 'The school as a formal organisation', in J. G. March (ed.), *Handbook of Social Organization* (Chicago: Rand McNally).

Bjork, R. M. (1971), 'Population, education and modernisation', in D. Adams (ed.), *Education in National Development* (London: Routledge & Kegan Paul), pp. 98–117.

Blakemore, K. (1975), 'Resistance to formal education in Ghana: its implications for the status of school leavers', *Comparative Education Review*, vol. 19, no. 2 (June), pp. 237–51.

Blakemore, K. (1976), 'Resistance to education in Ghana: a sociological study of declining enrolment', unpublished PhD thesis, University of Birmingham, UK/Institute of African Studies, University of Ghana, Legon.

Blaug, M. (1968), 'The rate of return on investment in education', in M. Blaug (ed.), *Economics of Education 1 – Selected Readings* (Harmondsworth: Penguin).

Brown, G., and Hiskett, M. (eds) (1975), *Conflict and Harmony in Education in Tropical Africa* (London: Allen & Unwin).

Callaway, H. (1975), 'Indigenous education in Yoruba society', in G. Brown and M. Hiskett (eds) (1975), pp. 26–38.

Carnoy, M. (1974), *Education as Cultural Imperialism* (New York: McKay).

Castle, E. (1966), *Growing up in East Africa* (London: Oxford University Press).

Centre for the Study of Education in Changing Societies (CESO) (1969), *Primary Education in Sukumuland, Tanzania* (The Hague: Wolters-Noordhoff).

Cipolla, C. M. (1969), *Literacy and Development in the West* (Harmondsworth: Penguin).

Claiborn, W. (1969), 'Expectancy effects in the classroom: a failure to replicate', *Journal of Educational Psychology*, vol. 60, no. 5, pp. 377–83.

Clignet, R. (1967), 'Environmental change, types of descent and child rearing practices', in H. Miner (ed.), *The City in Modern Africa* (London: Pall Mall Press).

Clignet, R. (1970), 'Education and elite formation', in J. Paden and E. Soja (eds), *The African Experience* (Evanston, Ill.: Northwestern University Press), pp. 304–30.

Clignet, R. (1974), *Liberty and Equality in the Education Process* (New York: Wiley).

Clignet, R. (1976), *The Africanisation of the Labour Market* (Berkeley, Calif.: University of California Press).

Clignet, R., and Foster, P. J. (1966), *The Fortunate Few* (Evanston, Ill.: Northwestern University Press).

Cohen, A. (1969), *Custom and Politics in Urban Africa: A Study of Hausa Migrants in Yoruba Towns* (London: Routledge & Kegan Paul).

Coleman, J. S. (ed.) (1965) *Education and Political Development* (Princeton, NJ: Princeton University Press).

Collins, R. (1971), 'Functional and conflict theories of educational stratification', *American Sociological Review*, vol. 36, pp. 1002–19.

Cooksey, B. (1978), 'Education and class formation in Cameroun', unpublished PhD thesis, University of Birmingham, UK.

Corwin, R. G. (1965), *A Sociology of Education* (New York: Appleton-Century-Crofts).

Cosin, B. (ed.) (1972), *Education: Structure and Society* (Harmondsworth: Penguin).

Court, D. (1973), 'The social function of formal schooling in Tanzania', *The African Review*, vol. 3, no. 4, pp. 577–94.

Court, D. (1974), 'Village polytechnic leavers: the Maseno story', *Rural Africana*, no. 25 (Fall) pp. 91–100.

Court, D. (1976), 'The education system as a response to inequality in Tanzania and Kenya', *Journal of Modern African Studies*, vol. 14, no. 4, pp. 661–90.

Court, D., and Ghai, D. (eds) (1974), *Education, Society and Development: New Perspectives from Kenya* (Nairobi: Oxford University Press).

Court, D., and Prewitt, K. (1973), 'Nation vs region in Kenya: a note on political learning', *British Journal of Political Science*, no. 4, pp. 109–20.

Crowder, M. (1968), *West Africa under Colonial Rule* (London: Hutchinson).

Currie, J. (1974), 'Has the die been cast? A study of Ugandan secondary school recruitment patterns before and after independence', *Rural Africana*, no. 25 (Fall), pp. 47–63.

D'Aeth, R. (1975), *Education and Development in the Third World* (Farnborough: Saxon House).

Dore, R. (1976), *The Diploma Disease* (London: Allen & Unwin).

Dornbusch, S. M. (1955), 'The military academy as an assimilating institution', *Social Forces*, vol. 33, no. 4 (May), pp. 316–21.

Dubbeldam, L. (1970), *The Primary School and the Community in Mwanza District, Tanzania* (Groningen: Wolters-Noordhoff).

Dumont, R. V., and Wax, M. L. (1969), 'Cherokee school society and the intercultural classroom', *Human Organisation*, vol. 28, no. 3, pp. 217–26.

Durojaiye, M. O. A. (1971), 'Attitudes associated with functional literacy among tobacco farmers of western Nigeria', *East African Journal of Rural Development*, vol. 4, no. 1, pp. 34–50.

Elliott, C. (1975), *Patterns of Poverty in the Third World* (New York: Praeger).

Elliott, K. (1970), *An African School: A Record of Experience* (Cambridge: Cambridge University Press).

Emmerson, D. K. (1968), *Students and Politics in Developing Nations* (London: Pall Mall Press).

Ewusi, K. (1971), 'The distribution of money income in Ghana', Institute of Statistics, Social and Economic Research, University of Ghana, Legon, mimeo.

Fafunwa, A. B. (1970), 'Teacher education in Nigeria', *West African Journal of Education*, vol. 14, no. 1 (February), pp. 20–6.

Fafunwa, A. B. (1974), *History of Education in Nigeria* (London: Allen & Unwin).

Fajana, A. (1973), 'The Nigerian Union of Teachers – a decade of growth 1931–40', *West African Journal of Education*, vol. 17, no. 3, pp. 383–97.

Fallers, L. (ed.) (1964), *The King's Men* (London: Oxford University Press).

Ferron, O. (1969), 'The progressiveness of indigenous teachers in the secondary schools of Sierra Leone', *West African Journal of Education*, vol. 13, no. 1 (February), pp. 46–52.

Finlay, D., Ballard, J., and Koplin, R. (1968), 'Students and politics in Ghana', in D. K. Emmerson (1968), pp. 64–102.

Fogarty, M. P., *et al.* (1971), *Sex, Career and Family* (London: Allen & Unwin).

Forde, T. (1975), 'Indigenous education in Sierra Leone', in G. Brown and K. Hiskett (1975), pp. 65–75.

Foster, P. J. (1963), 'Secondary schooling and social mobility in a West African nation', *Sociology of Education*, vol. 37, pp. 150–71.

Foster, P. J. (1965), *Education and Social Change in Ghana* (London: Routledge & Kegan Paul).

Foster, P. J. (1966), 'Vocational school fallacy in development planning', in C. A. Anderson and M. S. Bowman, *Education and Economic Development* (New York: Aldine), pp. 142–63.

Foster, P. J. (1975), 'Dilemmas of educational development: what we might learn from the past', *Comparative Education Review*, vol. 21, no. 1, pp. 375–92.

Freire, P. (1970), 'The adult literacy process as cultural action for freedom', *Harvard Educational Review*, vol. 40, no. 3, pp. 205–25.

Freire, P. (1972), *Pedagogy of the Oppressed* (London: Sheed and Ward).

Gay, J., and Cole, M. (1967), *The New Mathematics and an Old Culture: A Study of Learning among the Kpelle of Liberia* (New York: Holt, Rinehart & Winston).

Gintis, H. (1972), 'Towards a political economy of education: a radical critique of Ivan Illich's *Deschooling Society*', *Harvard Educational Review*, vol. 42, pt 1, pp. 70–96.

Goffman, E. (1968), *Asylums: Essays on the Social Situation of Mental Patients and Other Inmates* (Harmondsworth: Penguin).

Goldthorpe, J. E. (1965), *An African Elite: Makerere College Students 1922–60* (Nairobi: Oxford University Press).

Goody, J. (1968), 'Restricted literacy in northern Ghana', in J. Goody (ed.), *Literacy in Traditional Societies* (Cambridge: Cambridge University Press).

Goody, J., and Watt, I. (1968), 'The consequences of literacy', in Goody (1968).

Graft-Johnson, K. de (1966), 'The evolution of elites in Ghana', in P. C. Lloyd (ed.) (1966).

Graham, S. (1966), *Government and Mission Education in Northern Nigeria 1900–1919* (Ibadan: Ibadan University Press).

Hake, J. (1970), *Parental Attitudes toward Primary Education in a Hausa Community of Northern Nigeria* (Kano: Government Printer).

Hanna, J. (1975), *University Students and African Politics* (New York: Africana).

Harbison, F., and Myers, C. A. (1964), *Education, Manpower and Economic Growth* (New York: McGraw-Hill).

Hawes, H. W. R. (1970), 'Primary school curriculum development in Africa – hopes and facts', *Journal of Curriculum Studies*, vol. 2, no. 2, pp. 108–17.

Herskovits, M. (1962), *The Human Factor in Changing Africa* (New York: Vintage Books).

Heynemann, S. (1976), 'A brief note on the relationship between socioeconomic status and test performance among Ugandan primary school children', *Comparative Education Review*, vol. 20, no. 1, pp. 42–7.

Higgins, P. (1976), 'The conflict of acculturation and enculturation in suburban elementary schools in Tehran', *Journal of Research and Development in Education*, vol. 9 (Summer), pp. 102–13.

Hilliard, F. (1956), *A Short History of Education in British West Africa* (London: Nelson).

Hinchcliffe, K. (1970), 'The unprofitability of secondary modern schooling in the Western Region of Nigeria', *West African Journal of Education*, vol. 14, no. 3 (October), pp. 180–7.

Hirji, K. F. (1973), 'School education and underdevelopment in Tanzania', *Maji Maji*, no. 12, pp. 12–25.

Hopkins, A. G. (1973), *An Economic History of West Africa* (London: Longman).

Howell, D. R. (1958), 'The status of teachers in Nigeria', *Overseas Education*, vol. 30, pp. 102–9.

Hubbard, J. P. (1975), 'Government and Islamic education in northern Nigeria', in G. N. Brown and M. Hiskett (eds), *Conflict and Harmony in Education in Tropical Africa* (London: Allen & Unwin), pp. 134–51.

Hurd, G., and Johnson, T. (1967), 'Education and social mobility in Ghana', *Sociology of Education* (Winter), pp. 55–79.

Hutton, C. (1971), 'The good life – attitudes of peasants and school leavers towards agriculture', paper presented to the Conference on Urban Unemployment in Africa, Institute of Development Studies, University of Sussex, UK, September.

Illich, I. (1971), *Deschooling Society* (New York: Harper & Row).

Inkeles, A., and Smith, D. H. (1974), *Becoming Modern: Individual Change in Six Developing Countries* (London: Heinemann).

International Defence and Aid Fund for Southern Africa (IDAF) (1978), *The Facts about Rhodesia* (London: IDAF).

Johnson, H. G. (1968), 'Towards a generalised capital accumulation approach to economic development', in M. Blaug (ed.), *Economics of Education 1 – Selected Readings* (Harmondsworth: Penguin).

Johnson, R. W. (1975), 'Educational progress and retrogression in Guinea (1900–43)', in G. N. Brown and M. Hiskett (eds), *Conflict and Harmony in Education in Tropical Africa* (London: Allen & Unwin), pp. 212–28.

Jolly, R. (1969a), *Education in Africa: Research and Action* (Nairobi: East African Publishing House).

Jolly, R. (1969b), *Planning Education for African Development* (Nairobi: East African Publishing House).

Kahl, J. A. (1968), *The Measurement of Modernism: A Study of Values in Brazil and Mexico* (Austin, Texas: University of Texas Press).

Kelleher, J. (1975), 'Primary and teacher education in the Kano State of Nigeria', *West African Journal of Education*, vol. 19, no. 2, pp. 247–54.

Kenyatta, J. (1959), *Facing Mount Kenya* (London: Secker & Warburg).

King, K. (1974), 'Skill acquisition in the informal sector of the economy', in D. Court and D. Ghai (eds) (1974), pp. 291–309.

King, K. (1977), *The African Artisan* (London: Heinemann).

Klineberg, O., and Zavalloni, M. (1969), *Nationalism and Tribalism among African Students* (The Hague: Mouton).

Knight, J. B. (1967), 'The determination of salaries in Uganda', *Bulletin of the Oxford University Institute of Economics and Statistics*, vol. 29, no. 3, pp. 233–64.

Koff, D., and Muhll, G. (1967), 'Political socialisation in Kenya and Tanzania', *Journal of Modern African Studies*, vol. 5, no. 1, pp. 13–51.

Kouyaté, M. (1978), 'The teaching shortage and peer teaching in Africa', *Prospects*, vol. 8, no. 1, pp. 33–46.

Labrousse, A. (1970), 'Les déperditions scolaires et leur incidence sur le coût des élèves', Cameroun Ministry of Education, Yaoundé.

Lerner, D. (1958), *The Passing of Traditional Society: Modernising the Middle East* (Glencoe, Ill.: The Free Press).

Lévi-Strauss, C. (1966), *The Savage Mind* (London: Weidenfeld & Nicholson).

Little, K. (1973), *African Women in Towns: An Aspect of Africa's Social Revolution* (Cambridge: Cambridge University Press).

Lloyd, B. (1966), 'Education and family life in the development of class identification among the Yoruba', in P. C. Lloyd (ed.) (1966), pp. 163–83.

Lloyd, P. C. (ed.) (1966), *The New Elites of Tropical Africa* (London: Oxford University Press).

Lloyd, P. C. (1974), *Power and Independence: Urban Africans' Perceptions of Inequality* (London: Routledge & Kegan Paul).

Lynn, R. (1979), 'The relation between educational achievement and school size', *British Journal of Sociology*, vol. 10, no. 2 (June), pp. 129–36.

Maas, J. (1970), 'Educational change in pre-colonial societies: the cases of Buganda and Ashanti', *Comparative Education Review*, vol. 14, no. 2 (June), pp. 174–85.

McClelland, D. C. (1961), *The Achieving Society* (Princeton, NJ: Van Nostrand).

McKown, R. E. (1975), 'Kenyan university students and politics', in J. H. and J. L. Hanna (eds), *University Students and African Politics* (New York: Africana), pp. 215–55.

McWilliam, H. (1959), *The Development of Education in Ghana* (London: Longman).

Makulu, H. F. (1971), *Education, Development and Nation-Building in Independent Africa* (London: SCM Press).

Masemann, V. (1974), 'The hidden curriculum in a West African girls' boarding school', *Canadian Journal of African Studies*, vol. 8, pp. 479–94.

Mbilinyi, M. (1973), 'Education, stratification and sexism in Tanzania', *The African Review*, vol. 3, no. 2, pp. 327–40.

Mbilinyi, M. (1976a), 'Peasant education in Tanzania', *The African Review*, vol. 6, no. 2, pp. 167–253.

Mbilinyi, M. (1976b), 'The study of education and community', paper presented to the Seminar on Education and the Community in Africa, Centre of African Studies, University of Edinburgh, UK, June.

Moeller, G. H. (1964), 'Bureaucracy and teachers' sense of power', *School Review*, vol. 72, no. 3, pp. 137–57.

Morrison, D. R. (1976), *Education and Politics in Africa – the Tanzanian Case* (London: Hurst).

Moumouni, A. (1968), *Education in Africa* (London: Deutsch).

Mutua, R. (1975), *The Development of Education in Kenya* (Kampala: East African Literature Bureau).

Nadel, S. (1942), *A Black Byzantium* (London: Oxford University Press).

National Educational Research Council (Nigeria) (1977), *Primary School Social Studies Project* (Lagos: Ministry of Education).

Nduka, O. (1964), *Western Education and the Nigerian Cultural Background* (Ibadan: Oxford University Press).

Ngugi Wa Thiong'o (1967), *A Grain of Wheat* (London: Heinemann).

Ngugi Wa Thiong'o (1977), *Petals of Blood* (London: Heinemann).

Nyerere, J. K. (1967), *Education for Self-Reliance* (Dar es Salaam: Government Printer).

Obanya, P. A. I. (1974), 'Nigerian teachers' perceptions of a new French syllabus', *Journal of Curriculum Studies*, vol. 6, no. 2, pp. 167–72.

Obiechina, E. (1971), *Literature for the Masses – an Analytical Study of Popular Pamphleteering in Nigeria* (Enugu, Nigeria: Enugu Press).

Okedara, J. J. (1971), 'The relationship between unemployment of primary and secondary school graduates and the socio-economic status of their parents in Ibadan, Nigeria', *International Review of Sociology*, vol. 1, no. 1, pp. 1–11.

Olson, J. B. (1972), 'Secondary schools and elites in Kenya: a comparative study of students in 1961 and 1968', *Comparative Education Review*, vol. 16, no. 1, pp. 44–53.

Onwuka, U. (1968), 'Teachers and teaching in Nigeria – a subjective viewpoint', *Teacher Education in New Countries*, vol. 9, pp. 27–39.

Open University (1971), *School and Society: A Sociological Reader*, ed. B. Cosin (London: Routledge & Kegan Paul/Open University).

Oppong, C. (1973), *Growing up in Dagbon* (Tema: Ghana Publishing Corporation).

Parnes, H. S. (1968), 'Manpower analysis in educational planning', in M. Blaug (ed.) (1968).

Peaslee, A. L. (1967), 'Primary school enrolments and economic growth', *Comparative Education Review*, vol. 11, no. 1 (February), pp. 57–67.

Peil, M. (1965), 'Ghanaian university students: the broadening base', *British Journal of Sociology*, vol. 16, pp. 19–28.

Peil, M. (1968), 'Aspirations and social structure', *Africa*, vol. 38, no. 1, pp. 71–8.

Peil, M. (1972), *The Ghanaian Factory Worker* (Cambridge: Cambridge University Press).

Peil, M. (1976), *Nigerian Politics: The People's View* (London: Cassell).

Peil, M. (1977), *Consensus and Conflict in African Societies* (London: Longman).

Peil, M. (1979), 'Urban women in the labor force', *Sociology of Work and Organisations*, vol. 6, no. 4 (November), pp. 482–501.

Peshkin, A. (1969), 'Education and national integration in Nigeria', *Journal of Modern African Studies*, vol. 5, no. 3, pp. 323–4.

Peshkin, A. (1972), *Kanuri Schoolchildren: Education and Social Mobilization in Nigeria* (New York: Holt, Rinehart & Winston).

Phelps-Stokes Fund (1962), *Phelps-Stokes Reports on Education in Africa*, ed. L. J. Lewis (London: Oxford University Press).

Prewitt, K. (ed.) (1971), *Education and Political Values* (Nairobi: East African Publishing House).

Price, R. (1973), 'The pattern of ethnicity in Ghana: a research note', *Journal of Modern African Studies*, vol. 11, no. 3, pp. 470–5.

Pye, L. (1966), *Aspects of Political Development* (Boston, Mass.: Little, Brown).

Rado, E. (1971), 'The explosive model', paper presented to the Conference on Urban Unemployment in Africa, Institute of Development Studies, University of Sussex, UK, September).

Raum, O. (1940), *Chagga Childhood* (London: Oxford University Press).

Richardson, E. (1973), *The Teacher, the School and the Task of Management* (London: Heinemann).

Roberts, P. (1975), 'The village schoolteacher in Ghana', in J. Goody (ed.), *Changing Social Structure in Ghana: Essays in the Comparative Sociology of a New State and an Old Tradition* (London: International African Institute), pp. 245–71.

Rodney, W. (1972), *How Europe Underdeveloped Africa* (Dar es Salaam: Tanzanian Publishing House).

Rogers, D. (1971), 'Productivity and efficiency within education', in D. Adams (ed.), *Education in National Development* (London: Routledge & Kegan Paul), pp. 47–64.

Rosenthal, R., and Jacobson, L. (1968), *Pygmalion in the Classroom* (New York: Holt, Rinehart & Winston).

Rostow, W. W. (1960), *The Stages of Economic Growth: A Non-Communist Manifesto* (Cambridge, Mass.: Harvard University Press).

Rousseau, J. (1761), *A Discourse upon the Origin and Foundations of Inequality among Mankind* (London: Dodsley).

Sami, E. (1977), 'The social status of primary school teachers: a case study of the Rivers State of Nigeria', unpublished PhD thesis, University of Birmingham, UK).

Samuels, M. A. (1970), *Education in Angola 1878–1914* (New York: Teachers College Press, University of Columbia).

Shaffer, H. G. (1968), 'A critique of the concept of human capital', in M. Blaug (ed.) (1968).

Sheffield, J. (ed.) (1969), *Education, Employment and Rural Development* (Nairobi: East African Publishing House).

Shiman, D. A. (1971), 'Selection for secondary school in Ghana', *West African Journal of Education*, vol. 15, no. 3 (October), pp. 173–7.

Shipman, M. (1975), *Sociology of the School*, 2nd edn (London: Longman).

Shoremi, M., and Mott, F. (1974), *Characteristics and Expectations of University of Lagos Undergraduates* (Lagos: University of Lagos, Human Resources Research Unit).

Sinclair, M. (1976), 'Education, relevance and the community', paper presented to the Seminar on Education and the Community in Africa, University of Edinburgh, UK, June).

Smyke, R. J., and Storer, D. C. (1974), *Nigeria Union of Teachers: An Official History* (Ibadan: Oxford University Press).

Somerset, H. C. A. (1974), 'Who goes to secondary school? Relevance, reliability and equity in secondary school selection', in D. Court and D. P. Ghai (eds), *Education, Society and Development – New Perspectives from Kenya* (Nairobi: Oxford University Press), pp. 149–84.

Suret-Canale, J. (1971), *French Colonialism in Tropical Africa 1900–45* (London: Hurst).

Swindell, K. (1970), 'The provision of secondary education and migration to school in Sierra Leone', *Sierra Leone Geographical Journal*, vol. 14, pp. 10–19.

270 *A Sociology of Education for Africa*

Tanzanian Ministry of National Education (1977), *Regional Distribution of Secondary School Resources* (Dar es Salaam: Government Printer).

Troup, F. (1976), *Forbidden Pastures: Education Under Apartheid* (London: International Defence and Aid Fund for Southern Africa).

Van den Berghe, P. (1973), *Power and Privilege at an African University* (Cambridge, Mass.: Schenkman).

Van den Berghe, P., and Nuttney, C. (1969), 'Some characteristics of University of Ibadan Students', *Nigerian Journal of Social and Economic Studies*, vol. 11, no. 3, pp. 355–76.

Wallace, T., (1974), 'Educational opportunities and the role of family background factors in rural Buganda', *Rural Africana*, no. 25 (Fall), pp. 29–46.

Waller, W. (1961), *The Sociology of Teaching* (New York: Russell & Russell); first ed. 1932 (New York: Wiley).

Watherstone, A. E. G. (1907), 'The northern territories of the Gold Coast', *Journal of the African Society*, vol. 7, pp. 344–73.

Weber, M. (1947), *The Theory of Social and Economic Organisation*, ed. Talcott Parsons (New York: Oxford University Press).

Weiler, H. (ed.) (1964), *Education and Politics in Nigeria* (Freiburg: Rombach).

Wellesley Cole, R. (1960), *Kossoh Town Boy* (Cambridge: Cambridge University Press).

Williams, T. D. (1971), 'Demands for education', in J. Lowe, N. Grant and T. D. Williams, *Education and Nation-Building in the Third World* (Edinburgh: Scottish Academic Press), pp. 26–59.

Young, M. F. D. (ed.) (1971), *Knowledge and Control* (London: Collier Macmillan).

Zolberg, A. (1966), *Creating Political Order: The Party-States of West Africa* (Chicago: Rand McNally).

Zymelman, M. (1971), 'Labour, education and development', in D. Adams (ed.), *Education in National Development* (London: Routledge & Kegan Paul), pp. 118–45.

Index

For Product Safety Concerns and Information please contact our EU
representative GPSR@taylorandfrancis.com
Taylor & Francis Verlag GmbH, Kaufingerstraße 24, 80331 München, Germany